8/06

WITHDRAWN

"I Must Be a Part of This War"

"I Must Be a Part of This War"

A German American's Fight against Hitler and Nazism

Patricia Kollander with John O'Sullivan

Fordham University Press | New York 2005

World War II: The Global, Human, and Ethical Dimension, No. 8
ISSN 1541-0293

Library of Congress Cataloging-in-Publication Data

Kollander, Patricia.
    "I must be a part of this war" : a German American's fight against Hitler and Nazism / Patricia Kollander ; with John O'Sullivan.—1st ed.
        p.   cm.—(World War II—the global, human, and ethical dimension, ISSN 1541-0293 ; 8)
    Includes bibliographical references and index.
    ISBN 0-8232-2528-3 (hbk.)
    1. Korf, K. Frank (Kurt Frank), 1909–2000.   2. World War, 1939–1945—Participation, German American.   3. World War, 1939–1945—Military intelligence—United States.   4. United States. Army—German Americans—Biography.   5. German Americans—Social conditions—20th century.   6. German American soldiers—United States—Biography.   I. O'Sullivan, John, 1939–   II. Title.   III. Series.
    D769.8.F7G48   2005
    940.54'8673'092—dc22

                                                                            2005017142

Printed in the United States of America
07 06 05 5 4 3 2 1
First edition

For my husband,
Bruce B. Fuller

Contents

Acknowledgments

Many people helped bring this project to fruition. Dr. Christopher Keller of Davidson College and Louise French of the U.S. Military History Institute in Carlisle Barracks, Pennsylvania, helped locate valuable information on the ethnic backgrounds of soldiers who served in the U.S. military during World War II. Research assistants at the National Archives in College Park, Maryland, and the Holocaust Memorial Museum in Washington, D.C., were also very helpful. Eileen Simon of the Veterans History Project at the Library of Congress located taped interviews and papers of German-born veterans. I am also indebted to Deborah Lattimore, Diana Burkley, and Michelle Millet, who helped to transcribe taped interviews with K. Frank Korf and his wife, and to Athalia Rodriguez, who typed Korf's memoir draft.

I am particularly indebted to Dr. Harry Kersey, who read a draft of the book and supplied a great deal of insight and valuable advice. I am also grateful to Dr. Alan Berger, who read a draft of the book as well and provided helpful suggestions. A graduate student in the History program at Florida Atlantic University, Charles Riley provided excellent information about the workings of the military.

A one-semester sabbatical from Florida Atlantic University, a research grant from the Florida Atlantic University Foundation, and a release time award from the Dorothy F. Schmidt College of Arts and Letters all provided me with time and resources needed for research and writing.

The anchor of this project was Mrs. Rita Korf, the widow of the subject of this book. Her help, support, and encouragement were invaluable. Last but certainly not least, I would like to thank my husband, Bruce Fuller, and my children, Marcus and Julia, for taking care of each other while I was occupied with this project, and for their infinite patience and support.

Preface

During the summer of 1999 I was called to the office the History Department chair, Professor John O'Sullivan. He had a box of documents on his desk from the World War II period. He explained that they were to be donated to the Special Collections division of our library. The donor, K. Frank Korf, wished us to look them over and assess their value. As John and I examined the documents, we were impressed by their diversity: they included records of an inmate at the concentration camp at Flossenbürg, along with Korf's military records. We wished to know how Korf had collected them. We asked to talk to him about them, and he agreed.

We met K. Frank Korf and his wife, Rita, in their Boca Raton apartment. Korf was in his ninetieth year. He was diminutive and stooped, and he walked slowly and with difficulty. But his memory was remarkably clear, and his wit made the visit very enjoyable. The more John and I talked to Korf, the more fascinated by him we became. With Korf's permission, John and I began to work on a book on Korf's life and accomplishments. Thus began a series of weekly interviews that extended over one year. At the end of nearly every interview, Korf said, "I now have something for you." He would get up, shuffle into his office, and pull out several folders full of documents. The more we interviewed Korf, and the more we examined his documents, the more John and I realized that we had stumbled upon a veritable treasure trove.

But three months into the project, events took an unexpected turn. John was diagnosed with cancer. As he recovered from surgery, I continued interviewing Korf. Shortly after John recovered sufficiently to return to work, Korf was diagnosed with cancer. Neither John nor Frank let his illness disrupt work on the book project. The interview schedule was jiggled to accommodate the various doctors' appointments. John somehow found the time to organize Korf's wartime correspondence. He photocopied dozens of letters and highlighted passages of importance. Korf went through his papers to find more material of interest for the book.

During the summer of 2000, however, the health of both Korf and O'Sullivan began to take a turn for the worse. After John was admitted to the hospital in August, I interviewed Korf for the last time. I found him propped up in a chair in his bedroom, pale and weakened, but his memory was as sharp as ever. On 1 September 2000, John O'Sullivan passed away. Five days later, on the morning of John's funeral, Rita Korf called to inform me that Frank had died. Both men rest at the Boca Raton cemetery.

The death of both these valuable human beings left me to pursue the book on Frank's life alone. I am deeply indebted to them both: to Frank for his memories and to John for his insight and guidance. I am also indebted to Rita Korf, who graciously allowed me to interview her informally about her husband after his death. Frank and Rita intended their papers to raise awareness about the experiences of German Americans during the World War II era; this book, based on the papers, makes clear the importance of this area of study.

Introduction

In August 1942 a German-born U.S. Army private, Kurt Frank Korf, wrote to his mother in Germany:

Now the arms of madness [of Nazism] are stretching across the Atlantic, and they are gripping us with the fingers of those men and boys who were once close to me. They are the ones who are arming the torpedoes that are blasting the ships that supply our food. . . . Maybe they have reservations about what they are doing, but they are doing it anyway. I, however, am committed to fighting against them.

I do know one thing: I must be a part of this war. It is being fought for me and for you. It concerns us both. I hope the army will accept me . . . or I will feel like a coward for the rest of my life.[1]

These words convey something of the essence of a very special man. Korf was born to privilege in Germany. As a young man, Korf was close to his grandfather, a successful publisher who was born a Jew and later converted to Protestantism. With his grandfather's encouragement, young Korf studied law. But the coming of the Nazi regime changed Korf's life forever. Shortly after the Nazis came to power, they issued laws against Jews in the civil service. One of the laws stipulated "non-Aryans,"—that is, people who had one or more Jewish grandparents—were forbidden to take the bar exam. Because his maternal grandfather was a Jew, Korf was therefore denied permission to take the bar exam. The anti-Semitic Nuremberg laws of 1935 further blackened the reputation of Korf's beloved grand-

father, and Korf was disgusted by the fact that he himself was regarded by law as "second grade mixed-breed," or Mischling zweiten
Grades. Korf's work as legal consultant to his family's publishing
concern also ran him afoul of Nazi authorities: his knowledge about
the location of synthetic fuel refineries brought him under suspicion
by German intelligence, and he was interrogated in 1936.

Sensing that his future in Germany was tenuous, Korf decided
to emigrate to the United States in 1937. He came with very little
money and no connections. He worked as an elevator boy until he
became a reporter for an American newspaper published in the German language, the *New Yorker Staatszeitung und Herold*. All the
while, he did what he could to discredit Nazism. He probed levels
of pro-Nazi activity in German-American organizations in the city
and volunteered to inform the FBI about pro-Nazi activity in the
United States.

When the United States entered the Second World War, Korf
was drafted and eventually became a member of Military Intelligence in Patton's Third Army. As a military intelligence officer, Korf
obtained important tactical and strategic information from German
civilians and prisoners of war. He also helped to liberate Flossenbürg concentration camp, and he interrogated the camp leaders. At
the end of hostilities he was charged with finding Nazi war criminals in prisoner-of-war camps. After his discharge from the army,
Korf was employed by the Justice Department, and in 1948 he was
sent back to Germany to investigate the authenticity of the recently
published diaries of Joseph Goebbels, Hitler's infamous minister of
propaganda.

Korf's story is one that is worth telling because he holds a special place in the history of Nazism and World War II. Because he
was a German who became an American soldier, Korf was able to
reflect upon his experiences in a unique way. Most studies on World
War II deal with its military aspects, along with experiences of
American soldiers. Many historians of the latter subject, such as
Paul Fussell and Stephen Ambrose, focus mostly on the experience

of young American men coming of age in battle.[2] But Korf did not fit into these categories. He was not a naturalized American citizen when he was drafted. He was also significantly older than his fellow soldiers. He entered the army at the age of thirty-two, which made him about fourteen years older than 95 percent of the draftees. In addition, soldiers featured in works by Fussell and Ambrose did not have the same agenda as Korf, who wanted to join the army to fight Nazism.

Most studies on Nazism deal with its major perpetrators, its victims, and the history of the resistance movement. Korf's saga, however, does not fit neatly into any of these categories either. Victims of Nazism are typically billed as those who lived under Hitler's regime in Germany—or in areas under control of the German army— for the duration of the war. But although Korf was certainly victimized by Nazi legislation, he left Germany two years before World War II began. Korf was also not a typical member of the resistance movement because he left Germany. But the fact that he continued his opposition to Nazism in the United States as an émigré reporter and member of the U.S. armed forces shows that he resisted Nazism in a unique way.

Korf's story not only lends a special dimension to the historiography of World War II, but it also fills an important gap in the historiography of the experience of German Americans during the war. Most works on the subject do not go beyond the generalization that the vast majority of German Americans opposed Nazism. More recent works have shed light on the plight of thousands of German Americans who were sent to internment camps.[3] None, however, have focused on the experiences of the thousands of German-born men who fought in the war. Over thirty thousand men of German birth served in the U.S. Army during World War II.[4] Half of these men were not citizens of the United States when they entered the armed forces. There is a good chance that most of the noncitizens were recent émigrés who left Germany because of their opposition to the Nazi movement. And though a few German émigré veterans of the U.S. Army have written their memoirs, their works do not attempt to place their experiences in the wider context of the other native-born Germans who fought with them. Nor has any work been done to assess their contributions to the war effort, particularly in Germany.[5]

A prominent feature of this book is the richness of the material on which it is based. Korf carefully preserved all his wartime correspondence, notes, military records, and important documents, all of which contain a wealth of personal observations. The book also features excerpts from interviews with Korf conducted during the year before his death at the age of ninety on 6 September 2000. Korf's memory was exceptionally clear, and he recounted his experiences in great detail. I have corroborated many of Korf's experiences through research in the National Archives, the Library of Congress, the Holocaust Museum Archives, and the U.S. Military History Institute.

Chapter 1 concentrates on Korf's background and upbringing and the Nazi movement's impact on his life. His Jewish background, once a source of pride, became a huge liability after the Nazis came to power in 1933. At first Korf tried to make the best of a bad situation, but then his general disgust with the Nazi movement and his fear that his knowledge about synthetic oil refineries would make him into a traitor compelled him to leave the country. The chapter also shows Korf as witness to several key moments in Nazi history, such as the rigged trial of the man accused of burning down the Reichstag and the book burning in Berlin.

Korf's trials and tribulations in adjusting to life in America highlight Chapter 2. Unable to find a sponsor immediately and low on funds, Korf had to take a menial job as an elevator boy. Soon enough, however, his fortunes began to change: he became a successful newspaper reporter and looked forward to earning a second law degree in the United States. But just as his life was beginning to settle down, he was drafted for service in World War II. The highlights of this chapter include Korf's efforts to combat the influence of the pro-Nazi German American Bund and his intense desire to join the army of the United States to fight the Nazis.

After he was drafted into the army, Korf found himself having to start life all over again for the second time in five years. Chapter 3 details his speedy rise in rank; in the space of a mere year and a half, he rose from the rank of private to fully commissioned intelligence officer. He was shipped overseas in late 1944 and was assigned to desk duties in Paris. Though he could have remained a desk officer in Paris, he was eager to get back to Germany, both to see his mother and to fight the Nazis. He got his wish, and in late 1944 he was transferred to the front.

Korf's experiences fighting the Germans are detailed in chapter 4. In December 1944 Korf found himself in the midst of the Battle of the Bulge interrogating captured German prisoners of war. He also endured a wide and wrenching variety of experiences—from the joy of seeing his mother for the first time in several years to witnessing the horrors of the recently liberated Flossenbürg concentration camp. After the war in Europe ended, Korf was charged with hunting for war criminals. His fascinating experiences with concentration camp directors—and their victims—are highlighted in chapter 5.

Chapter 6 focuses on Korf's exit from the theater of war, his return to America, and his subsequent return to Germany as a member of the Justice Department. Korf was shipped home in 1946 after shattering his leg bone in an accident. During his convalescence, he earned his law degree from Fordham University in New York. Thereafter, he hoped to land a good position working on Wall Street, but he found that his German heritage, which had been such an asset to his military career, now served as an obstacle to success in his postwar career. He ultimately found employment at the Department of Justice in 1948. The department took advantage of his linguistic and legal skills by sending him to Germany, where he determined which Germans were eligible to reclaim property they had held in the United States prior to the war.

Chapter 7 focuses on Korf's most interesting case at the Department of Justice, which involved the diaries of the Nazi propaganda minister, Joseph Goebbels. Korf's work not only unraveled the mystery behind the publication of a portion of the diaries in the United States, but also revealed previously unknown facts about Goebbels. The conclusion assesses Korf's contributions and makes a case for further study of the experiences of German Americans during World War II.

A series of family snapshots and photographs taken by Korf at the end of the war appears in the middle of the book. The latter pictures depart from the usual style of wartime photography. Korf's subjects were not the ruined buildings and weaponry of war; rather, he focused on the impact of the war on both the Germans and Americans who fought it.

The story of Korf's life is a fascinating one. It is highlighted not only by the wealth of his experiences, but also by his witty observations about them. His own words, his personal papers, and his pictures form an unusual and rich chronicle of the war from a German-American perspective, and his story will help fill a gap in the historiography of the period.

1 From Patriot to Outcast: 1909-1937

In November 1907 a very extravagant wedding took place in Berlin. The bride was Margarete Mossner, daughter of the prestigious publisher Curt Mossner, and the groom was Franz Korf, an inspector with the royal postal service. The reception took place in the posh Savoy Hotel, where guests enjoyed a twelve-course meal and were entertained by an orchestra playing melodies of Strauss, Handel and Mendelssohn. A year later, the couple welcomed a daughter, Hildegarde. Their second child was born on 19 November 1909. He was named Kurt Friedrich Franz Korf.

Korf's family background was distinguished on both sides. His father's family traced its roots to the twelfth century, when King Louis VI of France knighted Heinricus Korfus for his role during the Crusades. The king gave the family permission to use the royal symbol, the fleur-de-lis, as the Korf coat of arms. The Korf family remained loyal to the French royal family. When Louis XVI and Queen Marie Antoinette fled Paris during the French Revolution, the queen left under the name of her friend Baroness von Korf, and she was taken to the Bastille under that name. Another branch of the Korf family migrated to Eastern Europe. In the fourteenth century a member of the family became grandmaster of the Order of the Teutonic Knights, which governed Latvia. Some Korfs served in the Russian government as governors of Finland and Warsaw. Another member of the Korf family became a military governor of Alsace and Lorraine during the late nineteenth century.[1]

On his mother's side, Korf was descended from a prosperous family of bankers, the Mossners, who settled in Berlin in the eighteenth century. Their Jewish background did not prevent them from establishing business connections with the Prussian royal family. They also lent the monarchy critical support when it was threatened by the Revolution of 1848. During the revolution, Crown Prince Wilhelm of Prussia found himself in danger of being arrested by revolutionaries after his troops fired on demonstrators. The prince decided to escape the country incognito, and sought out the Mossners for help. The Mossners gave him a generous letter of credit from a London bank and a coach with four horses to get him out of the country. After the revolution was defeated, Wilhelm returned to Prussia and became emperor of Germany in 1871. The emperor expressed his gratitude to the Mossners by officially receiving them at court.[2]

Korf's maternal grandfather, Curt Mossner, played an important part in Kurt's life. As a young man, Curt Mossner defied family tradition and attended a Protestant preparatory school called the Pädagogium Ostrow bei Filehne in Ostrow, East Prussia. A vast majority of the students were sons of major Prussian Junker families; Curt Mossner was the only Jewish student.[3] The fact that he was a member of the "religion of Moses" was indicated on his report card. In 1876, when Curt was sixteen, he traveled to Berlin to visit his father, Julius Mossner, who was depressed over the loss of his fortune in the wake of the Depression of 1873. To make matters worse, Jews were unfairly blamed for the crash. The pressure may have been too much for the elder Mossner. Although he appeared calm during his son's visit, his appearance was deceptive. After putting his son on a train to send him back to school, Julius Mossner donned a formal tuxedo and white gloves, stood in front of a mirror, put pistols against each of his temples, and shot himself to death.[4]

Curt Mossner never revealed his feelings about the tragedy. It is possible that he responded to it by removing himself even further from his Jewish background. He married a Protestant, Käthchen

Lampe, converted to Protestantism, and raised his children in the Protestant faith. Kurt's mother, Margarete, later converted to Catholicism to marry Franz Korf, a Catholic, and their children, Hildegarde and Kurt, were brought up in that faith.[5]

The Korf children were raised wanting for nothing; they lived in a beautiful apartment and enjoyed the privileges of members of the upper class. But tragedy struck the family in 1912, when Franz Korf died. Although Kurt was only two and a half years old at the time, he recalled how his mother came into the nursery, her face red from weeping. She wore a small hat covered by a mourning veil. She told her son to pray for his father, who had gone to heaven. Kurt recalled how he began to cry and could not be comforted. From that time forward, he could never stand the sight of a mourning veil. After the death of his father, young Kurt, along with his mother and sister, Hilde, moved to Berlin, where they lived with two of his mother's brothers. Young Kurt loved the hustle and bustle of the big city, as well as the quiet moments he spent with his mother reading stories. He had no use for fairy tales, since they always seemed to end the same way; he preferred medieval sagas and tales of derring-do.[6]

In the summer of 1914 young Kurt, Hilde, and Margarete Korf toured Belgium, but the trip was cut short by the outbreak of World War I. Four-year-old Kurt remembered the great excitement generated by the beginning of the war; he saw flower-bedecked soldiers happily marching off to war, but he could not understand why many observers were crying. Nor could he understand why the Belgians and French had become the evil enemies. All four of Korf's uncles were drafted into the German army after World War I broke out. Young Kurt grasped the seriousness of what was to come: "It was not called a 'world war' then, but we knew it would be big. It was a dark heavy cloud."[7]

By late 1917 the cloud had descended upon the Korf family. The British blockade of German ports made food and other essentials hard to come by. Young Kurt's feet hurt because only wooden shoes were available; he eventually developed a hammertoe as a result. The family suffered hunger as well; turnips were the only food readily available. The boy recalled that the turnips took on many forms: "We [ate] turnip coffee, turnip marmalade." Meat was a rare treat. By 1917 it was for sale only on special occasions. Kurt's mother, Margarete, and later her maid waited in line for the family Christmas ration of meat, but no meat was to be had because a crowd stormed the store and looted its contents. That Christmas Margarete fried potatoes in black coffee for Christmas dinner. By 1918 the boy heard members of his family saying that Germany was losing the war. He remembered seeing soldiers returning from the front in silence; many of them maimed.

In November 1918 the German High Command signed an armistice with the Allies. Germany's Emperor William II was forced to abdicate, and a new, more liberal government was formed in the city of Weimar. But the new government, the Weimar Republic, was unstable. Under pressure from the Allies, representatives from the government signed the Treaty of Versailles, which blamed Germany for starting the World War and saddled the country with high reparations payments. Many Germans blamed the republican government for caving in to Allied demands and refused to support it. Radical alternatives to republican rule, such as the communist Spartacists, soon enjoyed popularity. The nine-year-old Kurt read the papers and kept up with the news. When the Spartacists attempted to overthrow the new republican government in January 1919, the boy watched in horror as a group of Spartacists tried to seize cars and gasoline housed in the Korf garage, only to be confronted by gunfire from police. In the ensuing melee, a shot was fired into the Korf apartment and the bullet lodged in the corner of the ceiling.

On another occasion during the revolt, Korf's mother had to leave her son to visit her ailing parents. Before they left, Korf's uncle handed his nephew a box built like an egg crate with little cubicles in it. Each cubicle contained a glass ball with a glass handle. Kurt's uncle explained, "If somebody breaks in, just throw one of these, chest high." The boy did not have to use the grenades, but he remained curious about weapons. The following day Korf found a pistol on his uncle's nightstand and jokingly pointed it at a visiting friend, who was terrified. Korf recalled that the frightened man "started dancing" until his uncle relieved the boy of the pistol.[8]

These unsettling incidents persuaded Margarete Korf to move her family to the safety and security of her husband's family's country home in Lippstadt, Westphalia. She told her son that it was now safe for him to play outside; he and his sister no longer had to spend their days cooped up in the house, as had been the case when they lived in Berlin. The boy was jubilant; he was surprised that such a heavenly place could exist after observing the chaos in the German capital.[9]

Though the Weimar Republic defeated the Spartacists, the political and economic situation in Germany remained unstable. The huge reparations payments required by the Treaty of Versailles inhibited postwar economic recovery. Korf later blamed the treaty for Germany's woes. The treaty, he said, "defeated the country economically, also morally. . . . Most of the [means of production] had to be given away. . . . This country was bleeding to death."[10]

When the Weimar government defaulted on reparations payments in 1923, the French and Belgians invaded the Ruhr and compelled the German miners to work for them. The miners refused and embarked on a policy of passive resistance. The Weimar government supported this policy, and printed up massive sums of money to pay the resisters. But this policy of support ultimately resulted in horrendous hyperinflation. In 1914 one dollar had purchased four German marks, but thanks to the hyperinflation of 1923, one dollar now was worth four trillion marks. Currency of this sort had no real value and the middle classes stood on the verge of economic ruin. Korf remembered, "My mother's widow's pension came through the mail, which took two to three days to arrive. By that time, its value had shrunk more than half because of inflation. When it arrived in the afternoon, we had to go out shopping immediately, because the next morning it was worth even less."[11]

Many Germans blamed the Weimar Republic for their economic misery and supported parties that favored dismantling it. One of these parties was the right-wing Nazi party, which plotted to overthrow the Bavarian government. The coup was scheduled to begin in the Munich beer hall, or Bürgerbräukeller, in November 1923.

At that time Korf was taking the cure for his anemia, which had recently become a chronic problem for him, in the mountains near Fischbachau in Upper Bavaria. Trucks containing armaments for the coup made a stop in Fischbachau en route to Munich. When the drivers went into a pub for a beer, Korf and his young friends lifted the tarpaulin in the back of one of the trucks and saw rifles, machine guns, and boxes of ammunition. Shortly thereafter, the woman who owned the general store in Fischbachau went to Munich to buy provisions for her store with her retarded son, who carried the bundles. The errand turned to tragedy when the pair stumbled into the crossfire that ensued when Hitler tried to overthrow the government. The boy was killed, and the Nazis exploited his death by making him an unwitting martyr to the Hitler movement. Reading about the incident, Korf learned an important lesson about how the distortion of truth and the Nazi movement were linked. As Korf later put it, "This feat of propaganda forever was linked in my mind to the Hitler movement."[12]

Though Hitler's coup was defeated, the hyperinflation had nonetheless brought the Weimar Republic to the brink of total collapse. It was saved when British and French statesmen realized that their economies would suffer grievously if the Weimar Republic perished. They worked toward ameliorating some of the harsher aspects of the Versailles Treaty. Reparations payments were put on a sliding scale, which made them less of a drain on the German economy. In addition, the United States began floating loans to Germany. As a result, the republic stabilized.

In 1926 young Korf was dispatched to a Jesuit prep school in Breslau, Silesia (Internat Kurfürst Franz Ludwig). The regimen was very strict; young men spent most of the day in silence except for the recreation time after supper. Accommodations were Spartan: students resided in small, whitewashed rooms containing only a bed, chair, and desk. This atmosphere improved Korf's work habits tremendously. Korf enjoyed sparring intellectually with the Jesuit priests. He remembered, "I found the Jesuits more than a match for my doubts and questions." When Korf challenged philosophical or historical theories, the priests asked him to back up his assertions with proof. Though he learned a great deal in the process, he never out-argued the Jesuits. "A draw," he recalled, "was the best I could get."[13]

The discipline Korf gained from the Jesuits served him well, and he graduated with honors in 1929. His favorite subjects were history and law. He devoured biographies of great men such as Frederick the Great, Napoleon, Bismarck, Schiller, Goethe, and Beethoven. But soon his admiration for great men of politics, poetry, and philosophy gave way to an avid interest in the ways in which states and peoples come to terms with their destinies. What he wanted to learn most of all was how to understand the people, laws, and politics of his own country. The best way to do this, he reasoned, was to become a lawyer.[14]

After his graduation from high school, Korf's grandfather invited him to live with him in his home before the younger man embarked on his university career. At first Korf was hesitant; he did not think that an elderly man of seventy-six and a young man of nineteen could live together harmoniously. But Korf's concerns were unjustified. The two men got on famously. They spent a lot of time discussing the Mossner family. The elder man told his grandson that he had cut his ties with his Jewish background because of his family's opposition to his marriage to a Protestant woman. Though he had converted to Protestantism, religion was not important in his life. He told his grandson, "Friendship is something that grows out of human[ity], not out of a religion. I have to really admire a man to make him my friend."[15] The two also discussed the Nazi movement. Curt Mossner believed that Nazism was growing because ill-trained journalists only echoed Nazi propaganda without getting to the truth about its insidious philosophy. In short, Mossner believed that if he could reform journalism, this profession in turn could prevent political hacks like the Nazis from coming to power. The truth, he believed, "would unravel the Nazis."[16] He was as good as his word and used his influence to expand schools of journalism to train more reporters.

Korf also learned that his grandfather was well known to the leaders of the Weimar Republic. He attended informal meetings with half a dozen of them almost weekly. Attendees at these restaurant gatherings included Hjalmar Schacht, the president of Germany's leading financial institution, the Reichsbank, who later became minister of economics under Hitler. Korf learned that his grandfather was "very well thought of, particularly [for] what he did not print. He knew exactly what was going on, but he was very, very discreet. He opened up channels of communication, which are difficult to open unless you have the confidence of these people."[17]

The more Korf learned about his grandfather, the more he admired him, and the more willing he was to accept his advice. On his grandfather's advice, he selected Freiburg Law School because it was far more liberal than the Heidelberg Law School, considered by many to be far right and pro-Nazi. His grandfather also advised him to join a fraternity to establish social connections for the future. Kurt settled on the exclusive "Ripuaria" fraternity, but he soon regretted this decision. "Snobbery," he recalled, "was the main subject." Korf was instructed how to behave, what to wear and when, whom to see, and how to react. This was bad enough, but when he was told to exit any streetcar that a Jew entered, he resigned from the fraternity. He put the money he would have used to pay fraternity dues to good use by taking a summer course in French at the University of Grenoble.

Shortly after the fraternity fiasco, Korf suffered a crushing blow when his grandfather Curt Mossner died in 1929. Korf remembered, "It was a deep shock for me because he had been my father figure. He had shaped my thinking and I had discussed with him all questions important to me." Curt Mossner was laid to rest after a Protestant service attended by major dignitaries in Berlin.[18]

The year coincided with increasing political instability in Germany. The onset of the Great Depression sent the German economy—which had barely recovered from the hyperinflation of 1923—into a tailspin. The numbers of unemployed grew astronomically. The government was unable to handle the crisis. As a result Germans once again became attracted to radical parties that proposed putting an end to the tottering republic. The Nazis and the communists began to make great gains at the polls.

During this time of political and economic turmoil, Korf spent three semesters taking elective courses at the University of Munich. He particularly enjoyed a course in public speaking taught by Professor Grathewohl. Students were instructed to observe political party rallies. Korf's assignment was to attend a Nazi party rally at the infamous Bürgerbräukeller, the scene of Hitler's abortive putsch of 1923. The speaker at the rally was Adolf Hitler himself. The party leader made an indelible impression on Korf. He remembered:

Hitler . . . slowly started speaking in his guttural staccato voice. He sounded reasonable to an unreasonable conclusion. His voice rose and so did his fists. Foam formed [around] his mouth and he spit [as he talked]. I will never forget my thought at this moment. "Now, I know why these SS men are there. To catch his spit." My neighbors were enthralled. Their fists rose as had Hitler's. They were in a hypnotic spell. I had to control myself not to be affected.[19]

Korf emerged from the speech in a daze. He suspected that Hitler was a madman, and he did not think it possible that he would ever become popular enough to lead the country.

Korf had an even closer encounter with another Nazi leader—the propaganda chief Joseph Goebbels—when the latter spoke to a packed hall of university students in the wake of the Nazi electoral triumph in 1930. Korf described Goebbels as "a spidery little fellow who moved like he was pulled with a string." He "walked quickly, almost jerkily, to the rostrum." Goebbels said, "We are young, we are part of the opposition. And there are these socialist party bureaucrats, fattened at the public trough and sitting in their overstuffed chairs we pay for." Korf was impressed by Goebbels's power of persuasion: "Repulsed at first, the students seemed to become part of an alert and upstanding opposition willing to take the decadent, overgrown socialists out of their offices."

The speech was followed by a question-and-answer session. Korf did not think that the questions were particularly challenging, so, he recalled, he rose and asked Goebbels:

"Mr. Speaker, I understand that you are standing in the opposition. That you are young and lean." There was a little titter. Goebbels sure was lean. He nodded a little impatiently. "And your opposition sits fat and lazy at the trough." He just looked at me. "Well, Mr. Speaker, how do you intend to keep so slim once you yourself sit at the trough?" The titter was now laced with laughter. The anesthetic seemed to wear off. Goebbels waved his hand and suddenly . . . two huge SS men stood in from of me. They did not say a word. The meaning was clear. I got up and followed them, and between them I walked out of the hall.[20]

After having observed Hitler and Goebbels, Korf was forced to agree with Professor Grathewohl's theory on the appeal of demagogues:

A demagogue gets followers by starting slowly; he states facts everybody knows and everybody can agree with in order to gain the confidence of his audience. Then he suddenly shifts his ground, from a premise everybody has accepted to a conclusion for which he has laid no foundation. This is done suddenly and hardly noticed by the audience. Once he has affirmed the new conclusion, he builds his edifice upon it. Once he has unveiled the new edifice his audience can no longer go back. They follow him to wherever he leads them, even to death.[21]

It was difficult for Korf to take Hitler, Goebbels, and the Nazi movement very seriously. But he had no choice but to do just that after Hitler became chancellor of Germany in January 1933. He had dreaded such a thing and had hoped that it would be impossible. Korf decided to get a glimpse of the new chancellor for himself. He went to the Hotel Kaiserhof in Berlin, where Hitler was staying. Crowds were waiting for the new Führer at the main entrance. Korf suspected that Hitler would want to evade the throng and use the side entrance instead. Korf was right. Moments after he arrived at the side entrance, Korf witnessed Hitler's arrival: "Hitler arrived in a Mercedes and jumped out ahead of his bodyguard. He wore his old trench coat and slouch hat." Then something completely unexpected occurred. As Hitler stormed toward the entrance, he mistook a glass door for an open doorway, and smacked right into it. As Hitler reared back from the mishap, he and Korf came to be standing within a few feet of each other. Korf was able to look Hitler straight into his eyes. Korf never forgot what he saw. Hitler's eyes "were the eyes of a madman." Deeply moved by the encounter, Korf told his mother that he might have to leave Germany.[22]

Events of the next few years would strengthen his resolve. Shortly after Hitler came to power, Korf took an evening stroll in Berlin and noticed that the sky was a deep orange. Soon he discovered that the Reichstag was on fire. The following day the newspapers hinted that an arsonist had caused the fire. But the Berliners, remembered Korf, knew better; many suspected that Hermann Göring's men had set the blaze, though this was never proven conclusively. The Nazi leaders accused three communists of starting the fire and used it as a pretext to purge them and all opposition parties from the government.

The falsely accused communists gave their testimony in Berlin. Korf managed to get a ticket for admission to the courtroom. He was seated in the middle of the courtroom and could see the defendants clearly. He remembered the testimony of the prime suspect in the fire, Marinus van der Lubbe:

He was young, of medium height, with a long mane of dark blond hair. His hands were shackled to a leather belt; his head was hanging down and his voice barely audible. He spoke in Dutch and an interpreter tried to catch and interpret his words. His nose was running and the line interpreter finally in disgust asked the court to have the defendant's nose wiped. This was done. I did not have the impression that van der Lubbe really knew that was going on. He looked dazed. It was later claimed that he was doped.[23]

The charges against van der Lubbe were implausible. Korf noted, "How could a little guy (von der Lubbe was barely over five feet tall) climb into the [Reichstag] building with ten large gasoline canisters, empty them, . . . and then climb back into the street? The case was ridiculous . . . and defied the credulity of the spectators." But it did not matter. Korf recalled, "Everyone present knew that here was a sacrificial lamb, a man of little education, cowed and subdued, unable to talk back or defend himself; [he was] the perfect foil for those who had committed the deed."[24] Van der Lubbe was found guilty and executed.

Korf was alarmed at the miscarriage of justice. He was also surprised that his Jewish friends were not more apprehensive about the new anti-Semitic chancellor. They told him that Hitler's theories would be impossible to carry out ("Man kann nicht so heiss essen wie es gekocht wird," which is roughly equivalent to the saying "He'll hang himself if he's given enough rope)." He also contacted Professor Desior, the dean of the Philosophy Department of the University of Berlin. His only comment about Hitler was "Well, we are living in interesting times." He was forced to resign a few months later.[25]

Shortly thereafter the Nazi movement began to touch upon Korf's personal life. In March 1933, less than two months after Hitler came to power, Korf learned from a lawyer friend that the government was to impose new restrictions to admission to the bar beginning in April. Specifically, he learned that the Ministry of Justice would thenceforth deny admission to the bar to candidates who had any Jewish blood. Korf was surprised; he had not thought that the legal profession would be affected so quickly. But he made haste to apply to the bar before the April deadline, despite the fact that he had not yet completed his eight semesters of study. Shortly thereafter Korf received his application, accompanied by the "dreaded" questionnaire, which asked him to disclose religious affiliation of immediate family members.

Korf initially felt he had nothing to worry about, since his paternal grandparents were Catholics and his maternal grandparents Protestants. But he stumbled on the phrase "I hereby declare under oath that there are known to me no facts from which I could conclude that any of the above is not Aryan ancestry." Since Korf's maternal grandfather was born a Jew, he could not declare in the affirmative. Korf was advised to "tamper" with the application, as many other so-called non-Aryans had done. He could either reply that he did not know about his grandfather's religion, or he could have himself "Aryanized."

When Korf learned what "Aryanization" meant, he became more disgusted than ever with Nazism. This process involved making a generous gift to Alfred Rosenberg's Institute for Racial Research, which would confirm that Korf had a truly "Nordic" appearance. In addition, Korf would be required to submit an affidavit stating that his Jewish grandfather had been abroad for at least ten months, so that it would have been impossible for him to have fathered Margarete Korf, née Mossner. In effect, Korf was asked to sign a statement that would make his mother illegitimate. Korf was incensed: "This is the greatest humiliation any man can endure."[26] He had no intention of cooperating. As he put it, "I would not let [the Nazis] drag my grandfather's memory into the mud or my mother's honor. I was proud of my descent."[27]

Korf tried to see if he could get admitted to the bar without filling out the questionnaire. Through his connections, he managed to obtain an interview with the chief justice. Korf remembered, "He was a new man; the other one [had] just resigned 'voluntarily' after he refused to give the Nazi salute." After Korf told his story, the justice replied, "The minister [of justice] does not want any more applications [to the bar] from non-Aryans." He added, "Why do you think there should be an exception for you?" Korf replied, "Your honor, the only argument against my admission is my descent. But that can't be; I'm as good a German as anybody else." He went on to explain how the Korfs had served Prussia for hundreds of years, and how his "non-Aryan" ancestors had distinguished themselves as generals in the imperial army and as members of the press. Korf added, "Is it unjustified that I want to serve my country to the best of my ability?" The justice advised Korf to fill out a new application that stated his case, and he promised to have the minister of justice rule on it personally.[28]

As Korf waited for a decision to be made on his case, he began to reflect on the changes already wrought by the Nazis: "I saw the signs of a new system being unfolded, the structure for a new building of law being laid. But I refused to understand what I saw. I did not realize then that I was truly unfit to play any part in the theater of the 'New Millennium,' upon which the curtain was just being raised. I was young and thought [about] my pride, my family, and the years and the money spent for studying."[29]

The decision, when it came, was disappointing. The letter Korf received from the Ministry of Justice contained only one sentence: "Your application for admission to the State Board of Examination has herewith been denied." The signature on the document was illegible. The document made it impossible for Korf ever to be admitted to the bar and practice the law in court.[30]

Korf did not want this incident to stand in his way of becoming a lawyer, and he was determined somehow to bypass the restrictions imposed by the Ministry of Justice. His solution was to work toward a doctorate in jurisprudence. With his doctorate Korf could become a legal counsel and represent Mossner publications in its business dealings. Normally, this doctorate was automatically awarded after one passed the bar, and to get it without the bar exam was far more difficult. This solution was far from perfect; he still had to deal with a nagging fear that even if he did complete his doctoral dissertation, it stood the chance of being rejected because of new changes implemented by the government. As he put it: "This year was one of the worst of my life. Everything crumbled. It seemed hopeless to work on a project [without knowing whether], if completed, it would be accepted."[31]

Nonetheless, Korf pressed on. He researched his doctoral dissertation at the Law Library of the University of Berlin. After leaving the library late one evening, he saw a huge fire kept alive by large, wooden beams. There was a stand jutting out over the flames and Joseph Goebbels was on it. He held a book in his hand and there were stacks of books to his right and left. He tossed books by Thomas and Heinrich Mann and other Jewish writers into the flames, which were stoked by SS guards. Korf was appalled. He observed, "Goebbels's face and figure seemed to dance in the flames; in the heat his features contorted into a grimace, his head seemed to expand, and suddenly I saw him—Mephistopheles himself."[32]

As he worked to complete his doctoral degree, Korf became more and more alarmed at the rising tide of anti-Semitism. His acquaintances at Freiburg openly conspired against a Jewish fellow who had submitted his dissertation and applied for graduation. They proposed to confront him publicly and have him thrown out of the university. Korf decided to warn the intended victim discreetly of what was going to happen, but the young man refused to allow Korf to tell him what to do, and he was ultimately banned from the university. Disgusted by the incident and the fact that none of the professors defended the victim, Korf distanced himself from the university as much as possible. He even declined to run after he was nominated for president of the student body.

After taking a battery of very difficult exams, Korf finally became a Doctor of Laws. He earned the degree summa cum laude. After graduation Korf became a legal counsel at Mossner publications and compiled data for its financial publications. Thanks to this work, Korf became very familiar with German import and export figures as well as the financial setup of major German industries.[33]

Although Korf managed to bypass government restrictions, receive his law degree, and obtain a position at the Mossner publishing house, the rising tide of anti-Semitism upset him more with each passing day. He began to feel like a guest in his own country.[34] The Nazi program against the Jews was institutionalized by the Reichstag's passage of the Nuremberg laws in September 1935. The laws included the Reich Citizenship Law and the Law to Protect the German Blood and the German Honor. The first stated that "a citizen of the Reich is only that person who is of German or kindred blood and who through conduct shows that he is both desirous and fit to serve faithfully the German people and the Reich." What this meant was that full citizens of the Reich not only had to be full-blooded Germans, but also had to be members of the Nazi party. The laws effectively severed all Jews from official life in Germany. They were not even allowed to show the German flag.

The second regulation affected Korf directly. It made Germans who were not "full-blooded" into "mixed breeds," or "Mischlinge." According to the laws, a "mixed-breed" was "an individual of mixed Jewish blood descended from one or two grand-parents who were racially full Jews." The "mixed breed" category was further broken down into first-degree (half Jews) and second-degree (quarter Jews) mixed breeds. The former were to be treated as Jews and absorbed by them, whereas the latter would be allowed to marry only non-

Jews, not each other. But the quarter Jews were not home free. Though they were permitted to serve in the armed forces, they could not be commissioned and were not allowed access to most of the party organizations.[35]

The laws discriminated against most of the German aristocracy, since it had freely intermarried with wealthy Jewish families during the nineteenth century. As Korf put it, "In one fell swoop German society was decapitated. Germany lost its important physicists, writers, philosophers; it lost its culture. The rank and file of the Nazis did not care. They had never known culture anyway and would not feel the loss of it."[36] Korf remembered a popular joke from that time: "Seek to exchange my Jewish grandmother for a sailboat in good condition."[37] Korf said that there were no takers. Over time, the laws did more than simply discriminate against half Jews like Korf's mother or against quarter Jews like Korf himself. The historian James F. Tent notes: "Germany's Mischlinge led abnormal lives, lives that were profoundly altered by National Socialist persecution. The longer Hitler's regime lasted, the more harshly Germany's citizens of Jewish-Christian ancestry [were] treated. It is no exaggeration to say that, like their fully Jewish relatives before them, they became a hunted people."[38]

The passage of the laws had a direct impact on the Mossner publishing concern, which had been devoted to publishing newspapers and financial books. Since the laws decreed that non-Aryans were barred from publishing newspapers, the Mossners had to give up the newspaper business and concentrate on financial book publishing and the financial wire service.

What Korf resented most about the laws was the way in which they criminalized his grandfather. Curt Mossner had been a patriot who was proud of his country and his family's contributions to its history. He had had an opportunity to benefit from the hyperinflation when the government asked him to stop printing books and financial newspapers and devote his whole printing plant to printing money. Mossner had been assured that he would make a fortune. But he refused. "I will not make money out of this tragedy" was his answer. He was one of the founders of the Organization of the German Press (Reichsverband der deutschen Presse) and furthered the establishment of faculties for journalism at the Universities of Berlin, Munich, and Heidelberg. He worked tirelessly to improve the working conditions and the quality of the German press. He had believed that better education and quality journalism could defeat National Socialism.[39]

But the Nazis had triumphed and did their best to destroy Mossner's accomplishments. After Hitler came to power in 1933, Nazi storm troopers (the Sturmabteilung, or SA) carried the bronze bust of Mossner on a bier across the street to the lake on the grounds of the Berlin Zoo. Shouting insults and waving torches, they hacked the bust to pieces and threw them into the lake.[40]

Korf was grateful that his grandfather did not live to see how the Nazis had desecrated his accomplishments. But now he had to contemplate how he himself was going to live with the laws. Korf was horrified by the laws and their impact: "You suddenly discover in 1935 that you are not a German at the same level with anybody else. [This] is so incredible, coming from a family which goes back almost a thousand years!"[41] He was stunned that Hitler, "this Austrian housepainter, could classify me as a 'bastard of the second degree.'" The laws compelled Korf to rediscover his own true identity: "If I by decree could be declared a second-class citizen, what was true and real for me? What was in me that was beyond the touch of the Nazis? I discovered that the only real worth was in myself and that I had to prove it."[42]

Korf began to realize that leaving Germany was preferable to staying in a country where he was regarded as a second-class citizen. More important, he came to realize that his Mischling status would eventually force him to face two unacceptable alternatives. First, his status did not exempt him from the draft. If the Nazis waged a war of aggression, as he suspected they would, Korf would be forced to fight alongside them. As it turned out, over one hundred thousand

Mischlinge ended up serving in Hitler's army during World War II. On the other hand, his Mischling status made him vulnerable to persecution as a non-Aryan. Since neither of these alternatives was acceptable, Korf considered going underground to resist Nazism, but he sensed that given the strength of the Nazi terror network, resistance would be extremely difficult at best, and at worst put his family—especially his more full-blooded Jewish relatives—at greater risk. Weighing his options, he came to the decision to leave Germany. He was committed to fighting the Nazis from the outside if the opportunity became available to him.[43]

So, while Korf continued to work dutifully for the Mossner publishing company, he discreetly began to make preparations to leave Germany. He started by selecting a country to serve as his haven from the Nazis. He started a private archive on the economic development and strength of the countries around the globe. It soon became clear to him that the United States of America had the strongest economy, even though it was just coming out of the Depression.

He then researched the extent to which Germany's neighbors were capable of fighting the Nazis, since he was certain that they were going to war. In March 1936 he took a Mediterranean cruise and was outside the port of Casablanca when the news came that Hitler had remilitarized the Rhineland. Though this move violated the Versailles Treaty of 1919 and the Locarno Pact of 1925, the French and the British, the principal guarantors of the treaties, did nothing. The coup served only to increase the popularity of the Hitler regime. Korf recalled being ambivalent about the event. Thanks to his work, he had insight into the state of German industry, and he knew that Germany was not prepared for war in the event that the French and British opposed the remilitarization. But he hoped that the coup would be followed by stern warnings from the British and French that no more aggression would be tolerated. None were issued.[44]

The Nazis gave Korf the final push to leave the country when his activities in the financial publishing business became suspect. In 1936 he was asked to go to the Counterespionage Headquarters of the German High Command (Spionage-Abwehr Kommando der Wehrmacht) to speak to a group of officers. Korf had no clue why they needed to talk to him. They opened the interview by stating, "We understand that you are going to publish a book on synthetic oil."

Korf nodded in the affirmative. As a member of his family's publishing company, he had been working on that book for some time. He knew that Germany was building a huge synthetic oil and petroleum industry in its northern region. He was acquainted with one of the leading scientists in the field, a Professor Bergius, and sometimes went out with his daughter. Each of the newly constructed plants had received a questionnaire from Korf (along the lines of Moody's) asking recipients to report on location, capacity, capitalization, and so on. "Do you have the figures on location and capacity?" the senior officer wanted to know. "To the extent that my questionnaire was answered, yes," replied Korf.

One of the interrogators barked, "Do you know that you are coming close to treason if you publish that?" Korf replied that since the German army was limited to one hundred thousand men under the Treaty of Versailles, it would have no use for an innovative and immense synthetic oil industry. The interrogators exchanged glances, and Korf knew that the opposite was probably true. Korf then tried to take the edge off the conversation by offering to submit page proofs of the book before publication. He added, "You just strike out what you think has military significance. I am no soldier and no judge of military secrets." That was not enough for the interrogators, who said, "No, we will hold you personally responsible for any misstep."[45] The conversation was closed.

A near misstep occurred shortly thereafter. An official from Brannabor, an automobile manufacturing company, informed Korf that he had just gotten an order from the German government for fifty million marks for "medium-sized cars." Korf duly gave that information over the wires. The next day somebody from the Ministry of Propaganda yelled at him over the phone: "Are you crazy to reveal the information about Brannabor?" "Why?" Korf asked. "Everybody knows that 'medium-sized cars' is the code designation for medium-sized tanks," snapped the official.[46]

These incidents convinced Korf that he had to leave soon, as he believed he stood a good chance of being arrested for knowing too much about Germany's rearmament plans. As he put it, "The ground was growing hot under my feet." When he told his mother that he would leave soon, she cried but added, "You are doing the right thing." Korf also discussed his situation with a friend of his, Henry Marx, who had been recently released from the concentration camp Oranienburg near Berlin. His crime: distributing a speech that was unflattering to Hitler at the bank where he worked. They went for a walk since they feared that their phones were tapped. Korf told Marx that he was leaving Germany. Marx said that he had the same intention since he knew with his concentration camp record it was only a matter of time until he was arrested again.[47]

Korf wasted no time. He applied for a tourist visa to "visit" the United States on business for Mossner publications. He also needed permission from the army to leave the country because he was eligible for the draft. Korf also learned that the army would no longer supply exit visas for potential draftees after 1 February 1937. Fortunately, Korf had little trouble securing the necessary papers from the army. "The officials at the local army headquarters were quite amiable," he recalled. In December 1936 Korf was granted ninety days' leave of absence to the United States. He booked passage on a ship leaving in late January 1937.[48]

An encounter with the former finance minister von Dernburg on New Year's Eve 1936 erased Korf's lingering doubts about his departure. When Korf asked him whether the Nazis would collapse under their own weight, von Dernburg replied, "No, never. People are just fooling themselves. The Nazis will never let go until they are defeated . . . in a disastrous war. Only blood will wash them away." Korf never forgot these words.[49]

January went by fast. Korf did not change his routine in any way. He deposited money in the bank to make it look as if he had no intention of emigrating. He sold a few things privately to raise the money for his passage. He wrote letters to DuPont, General Motors, and other large American firms that he intended to visit them to get information for Mossner publications. This would legitimize his journey in the eyes of the government. Korf needed connections in the United States in order to find work. His sister seemed to have a strong lead. For some time Hilde had been managing the Berlin properties of her friend Julie Vogelstein. A wealthy woman who had a minority interest in American Metals Climax Company, Vogelstein had emigrated to New York after the Nazis came to power. Hilde wrote that her brother would be visiting soon. Julie wrote back and asked that Korf bring a suitcase full of her personal effects with him. Hilde packed the suitcase. Korf never asked what was in it, but it took up most of his baggage allowance.

On 25 January 1937 a large contingent of Korf's family went to the Anhalter Bahnhof to see him off on his "visit" to the United States. Except for his mother and sister, none of the family members knew that Korf had no intention of returning to Germany until the Nazis were gone. Many years later, when relatives reproached him about this, he replied by telling them that he had no choice but to leave quietly. Had he told them he was leaving, word could have gotten out that he was not planning to come back. In this case, Nazi authorities might have prevented him from leaving.[50]

Korf was nervous about crossing the German border at Aachen, not only because of his fear that his intention to leave would be discovered, but also because he was transporting Julie Vogelstein's luggage. If it was discovered that he was transporting her property, he could be subject to the death penalty for protecting it. Since Korf did not know what was in the suitcase, he had no idea what he was protecting in the first place. Fortunately, no questions were asked, and he proceeded to Paris, where he met Henry Marx. Together they boarded the SS *Paris* in Le Havre.

As the coast of France slipped out of sight, Korf stood alone at the stern of the ship. The sky was gray and so was his mood as he began to question whether he could cut his ties to Germany and start life all over again in a new country at the age of twenty-seven. He resolved that he would be able to do this only if he totally divorced himself from Germany and concentrated completely on becoming an American. Korf knew that becoming an American would possibly entail fighting against Nazi Germany. Given what he and his family had endured under the Nazi regime, this was something he was fully prepared to do.

2 How to Become an American: 1937–1942

On 3 February 1937, a cool and sunny day, the SS *Paris* arrived in New York Harbor. Korf nervously waited in line to enter the country. Finally his turn came. When the immigration inspector asked him the purpose of his trip, Korf replied that he was on a business trip and presented his letters of invitation from DuPont and General Motors. This did not impress the inspector, who asked if anyone was meeting Korf. He replied in the negative, and was ordered to stand in a corner. There he waited for about an hour. By that time the crowds had thinned out.

Korf did not know that being met by an American was a condition for entry into the country, and he was understandably fearful that he would be shipped back to Germany. His friend Henry Marx had already been met by his uncle, and the two had left for the latter's home in Little Rock, Arkansas. There was no one to help Korf.

Suddenly he saw a young man with whom he had played table tennis on deck accompanied by the American uncle who had met him. As they walked past him, Korf quickly whispered to the uncle, "Please say that you're here to meet me." The uncle asked Korf for his name. Korf told him, but he was terrified since he was fairly certain that the inspector had overheard the exchange. But after the inspector spoke briefly to the uncle and shook his hand, he told Korf he was free to go. Korf was dumbfounded. He asked the uncle why the inspector had let Korf go when he knew that he and the uncle had just met. The uncle explained that he had given the inspector a handshake practiced only by Freemasons. Since the uncle was a fellow Mason, the inspector inferred that he was telling the truth about Korf.[1]

When Korf stepped onto American soil in 1937, there were 1.6 million people of German extraction living in the United States. Approximately 600,000 of this number had immigrated since the end of the First World War.[2] Of this number a little over half were still German citizens.[3] As was true of all immigrants, Korf's first concern was getting a job. After taking a small room in a hotel in the West Thirties, he assessed his financial situation. His funds were meager indeed. He had been allowed to take only $120 out of Germany. He had left tips for first-class service on the SS *Paris* in the amount of $50. The expenses of arrival had left him with a grand total of $60. He needed sponsorship and employment as soon as possible. He wasted no time in seeking out his only contact in the United States, his sister's friend Julie Vogelstein. Korf called Julie Vogelstein at the Plaza Hotel. Her brother Theodore answered the phone and explained that his sister was out of town. Theodore agreed to meet with Korf at the Plaza for lunch. Over lunch Vogelstein asked Korf what he intended to do in the United States. Korf replied that he wished to work. When Vogelstein asked what kind of work, Korf replied that he would be willing to do any kind, including menial jobs. Vogelstein huffily replied, "Dr. Korf, in *our* circles we don't do that kind of work."

Korf had forgotten what a snob Vogelstein was. He had been a lecturer at the University of Frankfurt but never made professor; he became a success only when he inherited his brother's money. Vogelstein continued, "Unfortunately, I am in no position to help you. I am flying to London tomorrow." Then he added lightly, "You can send my sister's suitcase either to me here at the Plaza or to my sister at the Pierre [Hotel]." Korf left the Plaza without a job and obliged to shoulder the cost of transporting the suitcase to the Pierre Hotel, which came to $20, leaving him with less than $40.[4]

After the Vogelstein fiasco, Korf checked more names and addresses that he had been given in Berlin and decided to contact Father Joseph Ostermann, head of the Catholic refugee committee, located at Leo House on West Twenty-third Street. Father Ostermann was very cordial, and he agreed to support Korf until he would be able to lawfully immigrate. Without an immigration visa, Korf was not legally allowed to work, but Ostermann promised to keep Korf's head above water. Korf replied that he did not want charity; he wanted to work. When the priest asked Korf what he was willing to do, Korf said that he would do anything. Ostermann offered Korf a job as an elevator boy at the Leo House. Korf accepted the job at $6.50 per week plus tips, room, and board. He requested the graveyard shift from 4 P.M. to midnight so that he could search for a better job during the daytime.[5]

As befitted his new station as elevator boy, Korf's accommodations were far from luxurious. His room was located in the old part of the hotel that was no longer usable for guests. His room consisted of a bed, metal chair, and washstand. The first night he woke up in the middle of the night after dreaming that he had stepped into a hornet's nest. He turned on the lights and found that his legs were covered with bedbugs. In the morning he asked the handyman to get rid of them. His reply was "You will get used to that." Korf persisted, and the handyman eventually took care of the problem.

The quality of Korf's meals barely surpassed that of his accommodations. He was permitted to eat from the hotel refrigerator when his shift ended, but the nun who ran the kitchen thought that the new elevator boy ate too much; on one occasion she locked all the food compartments except the one that contained milk. More often she would scrape the burned bottom of the huge pots for his dinner. When Korf complained about this, she replied, "The day will come when you will pray to the lord to have food as good as this."[6]

Korf accepted the poor accommodations and meager food rations with good grace and remained determined to get ahead. He resolved to become an American citizen by the end of 1942. To do this, he knew that he had to embrace American language, politics, and culture. He first tackled the hurdle of language. Though he had studied English for seven years in Germany, he had never had the opportunity to speak it. To become fluent, he enrolled in a free government-sponsored English course for immigrants. When Korf arrived at the class he found forty students who came from a wide variety of backgrounds and educational levels. He failed to see how he was going to become fluent as quickly as he wanted to. After class, he told the teacher that the class would not help him. If anything, it would only convert his German-accented English into Polish-accented English. He asked her to tutor him privately. She responded that she was unable to give him individual attention. Korf asked about the minimum size for a class. When she said six students constituted a class, he asked, "If I sign the worksheet with six names per lesson, will you teach me English?" She nodded. The ensuing lessons were difficult for teacher and pupil, but Korf made progress.

As the days and weeks passed, Korf lived something of a double life. During the daytime he was Dr. Korf, the editor of financial publications, who was looking for a job. At night he was referred to as "hey you" the elevator boy. Both roles were frustrating. The latter existence squandered his talents, education, and intellect. The former yielded no positive results. His daily visits to publishing companies brought him into contact with many important people but resulted in no job offers. Publishers of financial magazines had no use for Korf, since the threat of war had put a stop to their plans to extend their European exposure. Nonfinancial publishers such as McGraw-Hill and even *Women's Wear Daily* told Korf that he lacked experience.[7]

For the time being, Korf was therefore left with no choice but to make the best of his job as an elevator boy. Keeping his dignity in this job was not always easy. One of Korf's first passengers was a young, tall, and husky seminarian who proceeded to kick Korf in his buttocks without saying a word. Instead of retaliating right away, Korf responded to the attack by calmly asking him which floor he wanted. While the seminarian studied Korf's relaxed response, Korf held the elevator wheel firmly, braced his right leg, and kicked the seminarian back with such force "that he flew through the cab to the back wall." The seminarian, now humbled, asked Korf about his kicking technique, which he had learned in school long before. The two eventually became friends, and the seminarian passed the word throughout the hotel that Korf was not a person to be trifled with.[8]

Other clergymen made a powerful impression on Korf. The first was a French Canadian priest who was in his late fifties. He seldom spoke and his hands were always bandaged. One night Korf casually asked after his health. The priest replied, "'You know, I have leprosy.' He removed what there was of his left hand from the right and showed me a stump, without hand or wrist, but grotesquely shaped." Korf was startled by the sight, but kept his feelings hidden. When the elevator reached the priest's floor, Korf opened the door courteously and said, "I hope you are getting better, Father." He told a coworker about what he had seen, and the coworker responded with a cry and fled into the night, abandoning his switchboard responsibilities. Korf now had two jobs.[9]

Korf had a much more lighthearted experience with Archbishop Rummel of New Orleans. Korf described him as a true "prince of the Church": he was a tall man who emanated dignity and strength. He stayed at the hotel once a month and Korf carried his brown leather suitcase. Korf remembered, "It was heavy and the sound of the bottles in it convinced me that he was not drinking Coca-Cola." One afternoon the archbishop stormed into the elevator, visibly upset. "What floor, Your Eminence?" asked Korf. "Go to hell," was the answer. Korf quickly replied, "I am sorry, Your Eminence. I never stop there." The archbishop was amused. He later commented to Father Ostermann that he had a very funny elevator boy.[10]

One day a young couple who had signed in as husband and wife entered Korf's elevator. The woman timidly asked the man in German, "Do you think they noticed that we are not married?" She added, "Be careful what you say, he [Korf] might understand German." The man snorted, "That fellow, he looks too stupid to understand German." Korf couldn't resist responding to the exchange. Keeping his back to the couple, he said in perfect German, "You can never tell." To keep the affair silent, Korf earned the best tip of his career, one dollar. He later quipped, "I am certain it [the tip] was in appreciation of my linguistic talents."[11]

Though he managed to make the best of a bad situation, Korf could not help feeling depressed about his situation at times. He remembered: "I had no relatives, no friends who could take care of me, only a few dollars and no protection against the scourge of the ages. But I carried on mechanically."[12]

Thanks to Korf's tenacity, his situation began to improve. He saved every penny he could. He would get "five cents per suitcase . . . twenty-five cents was tops." Soon he had enough money to hire an attorney from Moses, Borromeo and Haas to facilitate his immigration. The attorney informed Korf that he would have to go to Canada or Cuba and reenter the United States—this time with the proper documents that would lead to permanent residency.[13]

By the summer of 1937 his papers had gone to Canada. He needed only one more affidavit of support. He asked a former family employee—who owed him a favor—to write it. The employee had worked for a Mossner subsidiary company called Inter-Rayonne, which was located in Brussels. The Mossners had helped the employee, a Jewish communist, escape the Nazis. Korf now asked him to write a letter to the Immigration and Naturalization Service stating that Korf was on his payroll and that he would not become a public burden. But the former employee refused to submit the necessary affidavit. Korf now had to exercise the second and far more expensive option—reentry through Cuba. This time he secured affidavits from Professor Mankiewitz of City College, who was distantly related to a friend of the family, and a teacher by the name of Perlmutter. The road to Havana was clear.[14]

Korf traveled from New York to Miami on the Greyhound bus line. The thirty-six-hour ride was brightened by the companionship of a young acquaintance named Ann. When she asked him why the driver had to make a full stop at every railroad crossing, Korf decided to play on her youth and naïveté. He replied, "He will get shot if he does not. You see the little man sitting just behind him? Well, he has a pistol in his pocket and will shoot him if he does not stop." That put an end to Ann's queries.

Korf described the trip from New York to Jacksonville as being "like a trip through an endless tunnel. . . . In Jacksonville daylight suddenly came." By the time that Korf reached Miami, he was nearly "frozen" into the sitting position: "I could hardly look over the hotel counter when I registered." Soon thereafter, Korf and Ann took a plane to Havana. Since Ann knew a supreme court judge in Cuba, she and Korf were treated as VIPs during their stay. He thoroughly enjoyed Havana's "brilliant days and hot steamy nights." Better yet, it took authorities only a week to process Korf's papers.[15]

Back in New York, Korf was confronted once again with the problem of finding work, since his stint as an elevator boy was up. Korf's friend Henry Marx soon came to his rescue. Marx had tired of his life with his uncle in Arkansas and returned to New York, where he found a job at the *New Yorker Staatszeitung und Herold*, an American newspaper written in German. It was owned by Victor Ridder, a first-generation German American. In 1938 the newspaper had a circulation of about eighty thousand readers; most were second- and third-generation Germans.

Marx informed his friend that the paper had an opening. Korf went to see the city editor, Ludwig Oberndorf, for an interview. Oberndorf instructed Korf to check out several local bars frequented by German Americans and return by midnight to write up his experiences. Korf did exactly as he was told. Several bar patrons bought him drinks, but Korf managed to keep his mind focused on the job at hand. Exactly at midnight he stepped out of the elevator, and Oberndorf yelled, "You're hired!" Korf replied, "But I haven't written a line." Oberndorf explained, "Whoever can go through all these dives and still come in on his own steam on time is a damn good reporter!" In his first few days on the job, Korf repeated the scenario of his first night. He recalled, "I did not realize at the time that reporting entails about 90 percent drinking and 10 percent connections. Because in order to get a story, you [had] to drink with them. I had made a 'connection' with the bartender that I would get a ginger ale instead of a real drink. Otherwise, in the beginning it entailed six [or] seven drinks."[16]

Politically, the newspaper was neutral. When an acquaintance of Korf's later charged that the paper was pro-Nazi, Korf was quick to deny it. "We see ourselves as completely un-Nazi," he wrote. He added, "[We] have repeatedly pointed out that the *Staats[zeitung]* is an American newspaper written in German. It is not a newspaper for the [Third] Reich Germans, and the paper has been outlawed over [in Germany] for quite some time."[17]

Korf's first assignment was to cover activities of German American organizations in Hudson County, New Jersey, a narrow stretch of rocky land west of New York City, stretching from Bayonne in the south past Union City in the north, almost up to Teaneck. The county's German-American residents had emigrated in the 1920s after the hyperinflation had wrecked the German economy. As a recent immigrant, Korf soon found that he was different from the German Americans he was assigned to cover. They were from the poorer and less-educated classes and held jobs similar to those they had left in Germany. According to Korf, "They had kept their songs, language, Bratwurst, smoked eel, and leather pants and voted Republican." The recent immigrants, on the other hand, were "much more sophisticated, and they read things which were not necessarily written in German, in English, and they had much wider interests. Because these groups were like oil and water, and I tiptoed between them."[18]

Korf's position at the newspaper improved because of the negligence of a colleague. One night Nazi sympathizers staged a fight and made big headlines in New York City's "Germantown"—the Yorkville section in Manhattan's East Eighties. But Korf's Manhattan colleague stayed home, thinking that nothing would happen. He was fired, and Korf got his desirable Manhattan beat.[19]

The new position opened all kinds of opportunities. Korf was given a press card shaped like a police shield, which was issued with a new color every month by the New York Police Department. Once he placed the card in his hatband, he could go virtually everywhere. He was able to attend the opening of the World's Fair in Flushing and was a member of the press corps interviewing President Franklin D. Roosevelt, who presided over the opening. Korf remembered FDR "sitting in the back seat of his car and answering the reporters' questions with a broad smile." Korf was stunned by the ease with which FDR dealt with the press: "He knew everybody's birthday, how their kids were, and how the pregnancy of a reporter's wife was progressing." Suddenly, a diminutive man tugged at Korf's jacket. It was New York Mayor Fiorello La Guardia. Korf was struck by the mayor's appearance. "He looked like a mushroom with his dark broad-rimmed western hat, which loomed over his stout figure," Korf remembered.[20]

Korf saw FDR again at the entrance to the hallway where he was about to speak. "Aides lifted him out of the car, gripped him under the arms, and dragged his body up a ramp that had been built especially for him to a lectern. The president pushed himself up, locked his braces, and there he stood, a giant." The president was introduced to the crowd by his wife, Eleanor. FDR opened his speech by saying, "You all know my wife, Eleanor. You probably know her better than you know me." The audience laughed. Observing the audience, Korf felt that FDR had a grip on it that he had rarely felt from anyone else: "You felt that here [in FDR] was the whole width and breadth of the United States. He embodied it like no one before or since."

Korf also had the opportunity to observe the British royal family close up. He was shocked to learn how badly King George VI stuttered; he could barely get his sentences out. As a reporter, Korf could learn about things that were rarely mentioned in the newspapers; nothing had prepared him for FDR's helplessness or the British king's speech impediment. Korf cites omission of these weaknesses as examples of "selective reporting."[21]

Korf's job also brought him into contact with famous Germans and Austrians who were fleeing the Nazi terror. He attended the first press conference of the famous German author Thomas Mann. Mann's daughter tried to interpret for her father, but when she faltered, Korf stepped in and helped him communicate with the other reporters. Mann took Korf aside after the conference to thank him personally.

Korf also attended a press conference with the von Trapps, the family of singers who had recently escaped Austria after it had been absorbed by Nazi Germany. The von Trapps wished to discuss their U.S. debut concert at Town Hall, but the reporters wished to hear only about their escape from Austria. They were also interested in hearing the story of the mother in the family, Maria, who had been a nun prior to her marriage to the family patriarch, Georg von Trapp. Korf wrote an article about the von Trapps to publicize their concert and attended it as well. Though the concert played to a sellout crowd, it was a failure because the von Trapps performed music on rare old instruments, which, as Korf said, "just do not play in New York." Maria von Trapp called Korf after the concert to thank him for his article. She added that the family had spent the last of their money renting the hall, and they were grateful that Korf's article had helped to fill it. Fortunately, the von Trapps took the reviews of their concert to heart and revamped their act. They jettisoned the old instruments and relied on old folk songs. This proved to be the key to their success. Their act became popular, and their story later inspired the popular Broadway play and Oscar-winning movie *The Sound of Music.*[22]

Other refugees from Austria included members of the Habsburg family, the royal family of the moribund Austrian Empire. Korf attended a press conference with Archduke Otto, the heir to the nonexistent Habsburg throne. Korf was impressed by the archduke's intelligence and dignified carriage and by the fact that he did not boast the famous Habsburg receding upper lip. His brothers Karl Ludwig and Felix were more like what Korf expected: they had weak chins, thinning hair, and high foreheads. Their sister, the Archduchess Adelheid, wore a simple black dress and rather old-fashioned black cotton stockings. When Korf met her many years later, he commented on those stockings. Blushing, the archduchess replied, "We came directly from the ship, and I did not have the chance to buy new ones."[23]

As Korf's life in the United States began to settle down, his sister, Hildegarde Korf, began a series of adventures that would lead her to her brother's new country. She was a woman of many talents. She received a bachelor's degree in philosophy from the University of Berlin, and she had taken courses at the Journalism Institute at the university. She was in charge of publicity for the first talking movie produced in Germany, *Three Hearts in Three-Quarters Time*.[24] She also began to develop a strong interest in science. In the mid-1930s she studied metallurgy at the Technical Institute in Berlin, and she did spectral analysis for the Zeiss chemical works in Dresden.[25]

In addition to these eclectic activities, Hilde also managed the Berlin properties of her Jewish friend Julie Vogelstein, and in so doing had struck up a friendship with Julie's attorney, Curt Kallmann. By 1939 Kallmann, a Jew, could no longer practice law, and he wanted to leave Germany. He had a visa for the United States and planned to leave, but Germany's declaration of war in the fall of 1939 disrupted his plans. One evening Kallmann called Hilde in a panic: he had learned that the German secret police, or Gestapo, were coming to arrest him before he could leave the country.

Thinking quickly on her feet, Hilde helped Kallmann escape. She sent a physician friend and his nurse to Kallmann's house. Hilde then reserved a compartment on a train bound for neutral Sweden. In the meantime, the physician and nurse sedated Kallmann, put him on a stretcher, and had him transported to the railway station. En route to Sweden, the physician and nurse announced that they had to go back to Germany. Kallmann, however, had suffered a nervous collapse; he could not enter the country alone. Hilde agreed to escort Kallmann to the American consulate in Stockholm. Upon their arrival, Hilde informed the consul that she was discharging herself of responsibility for Kallmann. But the consul replied that the ailing Kallmann would not be permitted to enter the United States unless he had someone to take care of him. The consul offered to include Hilde on Kallmann's visa to enter the United States—if she married him.

At this point Hilde was not without options. The Zeiss chemical works company contacted her in Sweden and offered to continue her employment. She was assured that she would not be prosecuted for helping Kallmann escape, and that her status as a second-grade Mischling would not be counted against her. But Hilde, like her brother, had become disgusted with the state of affairs in Germany and wished to emigrate. She agreed to marry Kallmann and accompany him to the United States. The trip was arduous: since war had broken out in Europe, the Kallmanns had to journey via the Trans-Siberian railway to Vladivostok. They then traveled to Japan, and from Japan they sailed to California.[26]

Once the Kallmanns had landed in Los Angeles, Hilde told her new husband that their marriage of convenience was over. But now Kallmann threatened to commit suicide unless his wife stayed. Hilde felt that she had little choice but to stay on. She was not in love with Kallmann, and she was bored. Korf recalled, "She was thinking of something [to do]; she thought to herself, 'What can I do where I don't have to think about him [Kallmann] and still not leave him?' So the thought came to her [to study] pure physics." She went to UCLA, where she received a B.A. and an M.A. in physics in 1945 and 1947, respectively. In 1955 she went on to become the first woman to obtain a Ph.D. in physics from that institution. Later Korf joked with his sister, "How is it that you are a famous woman physicist? You were lousy in school [back in Germany]." Hilde quipped, "Don't tell anybody!"[27]

With Hilde safely in the United States, Korf was eager for his mother to emigrate as well. But the hurdles to emigration were greater than had been the case when Korf left Germany. In addition, Margarete was not eager to leave her family and friends behind. When the war broke out in Europe in 1939, there was nothing Korf could do to get her out of Germany. He later deeply regretted not having pulled her out earlier. In 1942 he wrote to her: "Dearest mother, believe me, I did everything in my power to bring you here. . . . I knew that I wouldn't be able to live with myself if I hadn't tried to do this. It's hard to put my feelings into words, but Hilde knows how hard I tried and how much I wanted you here."[28] He sent this and many other letters to her via the Red Cross, but because of the precarious nature of wartime correspondence, he had no way of knowing whether she received them.

Margarete Korf's predicament inspired her son to do what he could to fight the growth of Nazism. Korf used his experience as an investigative reporter to expose the nefarious influence of one of the most noted pro-Nazi organizations in America, the Deutsche-Amerikanische Volksbund, more popularly known as the Bund. It was led by Fritz Julius Kuhn, who emigrated from his native Germany to the United States in 1924. Though most members of the organization were recent German immigrants or Americans of German descent, a good number were American defectors from various right-wing organizations. The Bund preached the desirability of all Germans of the world uniting in support of the Nazi cause.[29]

Korf's assignment was to study the extent of the Bund's influence in New York's German community. He attended meetings of German American gymnastic societies (Turnvereine) wooed by the

Bund. Korf's presence as a reporter was not welcome at meetings of the Turnverein of Union City. One night he was thrown out after he was accused of being a spy. One member warned, "Don't come back here if you know what is good for you." One evening he encountered many members of this group as he was walking home. They saw Korf. Undaunted, he walked straight through the group.[30]

Though the Nazi government initially supported the Bund, its existence constituted something of an embarrassment by the end of the 1930s. By that time Hitler was anxious not to arouse the ire of the United States as he pursued his aggressive foreign policy in Central and Eastern Europe. The Bund, however, was committed to stirring up trouble in the United States. It railed against the policies of President Franklin Roosevelt in general and communism, the CIO, Jewish influences, and boycotts against Germany in particular. In February 1938 the Nazi government tried to loosen its ties with the organization: it issued an order forbidding German nationals to join it. The German ambassador to the United States, Hans Heinrich Dieckhoff, informed U.S. Secretary of State Cordell Hull of this decision, and a statement to this effect appeared in U.S. newspapers in early March.[31]

Korf was instructed by his editor to discern the Bund's response to Dieckhoff's statement. He took a copy of the Associated Press report on the ambassador's statement with him to Bund headquarters on Eighty-fifth Street, in Yorkville. He knew the door was well guarded and operated by remote control. But when Korf pushed it, it opened. He went upstairs into the main room and gave the AP report to Kuhn's deputy, Klapproth, who thought that Korf was "one of the boys."

Klapproth immediately called a meeting, which included Kuhn. Klapproth handed Kuhn the report. Korf remembered that Kuhn nodded and said, "Yes, I know about it. The ambassador called me from Washington and said that he had to do it to pacify the press. That's for the outside. Inside, nothing changes." Kuhn then turned to Korf and said, "Who are you?" Korf replied, "I am a reporter."

Everyone was speechless. Kuhn finally spoke up and said, "You won't print this if you know what is good for you." Korf laughed and said, "Why do you think I'm here?" Korf ignored the threats and simply walked out of the building and wrote the story.[32]

What Korf did not know, however, was that Kuhn was lying when he dismissed the Nazi government's rejection of the Bund as a ruse. In reality, Kuhn was so panicked by the order that he went to Germany to have it reversed. His efforts were in vain. Worse still for Kuhn, the Nazi government exploited his absence from the United States by ordering its consuls in major cities to advise German nationals to withdraw from the Bund.[33] When Kuhn returned from Germany, he boasted about having met with Hitler, though no meeting took place. The boast, however, made both the Federal Bureau of Investigation (FBI) and the House Un-American Activities Committee (HUAC), chaired by Martin Dies, step up their respective investigations of Bund activities.[34]

Though the membership numbers of the Bund declined after the edict against German nationals, the government continued to regard it as a threat, especially after Hitler's victories over Austria and Czechoslovakia in 1938. Instead of lying low, Kuhn raised suspicions of a Nazi threat in the United States by staging a huge Bund rally in Madison Square Garden in February 1939. Twenty thousand people filled the Garden. A huge picture of George Washington, flanked by Bund symbols, decorated the main stage. Though the rally was ostensibly pro-American, speakers castigated Jewish influence, denounced President Roosevelt, and called for a united fascist front.[35]

Kuhn hoped that the rally would strengthen the Bund. Instead, it contributed to its eventual demise. After many newspaper reports of the rally alleged that the Bund was part of a German spy network, U.S. government officials became convinced that the Bund constituted a Nazi threat to the United States and had to be dismantled. The decision was made to go after Kuhn, in the hope that once he was eliminated, the whole organization would falter. Ironically,

Kuhn's rally also soured authorities in the Nazi government. The German consul in New York reported to Berlin that the rally had "tarnished Germany's image in the United States and had done great damage to the isolationist cause."[36]

But dismantling the Bund would not be easy. Kuhn and most of his major henchmen were American citizens and had ostensibly done nothing worse than demonstrate their rights to free speech and assembly. While government officials considered their next move, Mayor Fiorello La Guardia decided to act. A vehement anti-Nazi, La Guardia charged his district attorney, Thomas E. Dewey, to dig up something against Kuhn. Dewey found what he needed by searching through the Bund's books and tax records. The records indicated that Kuhn had embezzled close to fifteen thousand dollars of funds raised from the rally. He was indicted in June 1939 and released on bail. His trial was scheduled for December. In the meantime, Dewey and government agencies continued to accumulate more evidence against Kuhn.

Through a strange twist of fate, Korf became part of the FBI investigation against Kuhn. As he was walking home shortly after the outbreak of World War II in Europe, he found himself behind a man whose gait and burly figure looked familiar: it was Fritz Kuhn. He soon discovered that he and Kuhn lived in the same building. The next morning Korf casually asked his landlady the name of the gentleman on the second floor. She replied, "That is Fred Karsten, a chemist from Detroit. He works for Ford."[37] Korf later learned that "Fred Karsten," or Fritz Kuhn, was actually on an unpaid leave of absence from the Ford Motor Company.[38]

With this information, Korf went to the FBI. Agents were surprised to hear what Korf had to tell them. They had no idea that Kuhn had a second apartment in the West Eighties; they had had him under surveillance in Queens, where he lived with his wife and children. The agency asked Korf to keep tabs on Kuhn's comings and goings. Korf commented that this would cost him a lot of sleep, and he asked an agent why the FBI could not do this. The agent replied, "Well, this is a residential area, and if we put a post there, it would stick out like a sore thumb." Grudgingly, Korf agreed and observed Kuhn for six weeks, and he was able to establish a pattern of Kuhn's activities. As he had predicted, Korf lost a lot of sleep.[39]

After Korf submitted the surveillance report, FBI Special Agent Starr asked him to get into Kuhn's apartment to examine his documents. Once again, he demurred. He asked Starr, "Why don't you do it? After all, it's your business." Starr replied, "We cannot get a search warrant because we do not have probable cause." He added, "If you could get into his room and get a look at his papers, you would do the country a great favor." Korf later commented, "Funny—I, the new immigrant, became a [spy] for the FBI."[40]

Korf first needed to gain access to Kuhn's apartment. He found a board where spare keys to all the building's apartments hung. He took Kuhn's spare key and had it copied, and put the spare back. Once he had access to Kuhn's apartment, he knew that he could not do what the FBI requested without help. He needed a lookout, a car, a driver, and a reliable copy shop. He confided his mission to his *Staatszeitung* editor, Oberndorf, who hugely enjoyed the prospect of one of his reporters spying on Kuhn. Oberndorf agreed to have his reporter son Ludwig serve as lookout man and driver. He found a nearby Photostat shop and made a deal with the owner to keep the shop open late in the evening. Korf studied the newspapers to learn where Kuhn was scheduled to speak. One day he discovered that Kuhn was to give a speech at Camp Siegfried on Long Island, located seventy miles from New York. The trip would take at least three hours.

He went to Kuhn's apartment and opened the door with the key he had had made. He went through Kuhn's luggage and found several folders. He grabbed the folders and slipped out of the room. His palms were sweaty, and he realized that housebreaking was not going to become his life's ambition. Ludwig Oberndorf met him, and the two went to the copy shop to duplicate the documents. It took a long time to do so, but the men were able to return the documents just before Kuhn's return.

The contents of the files exceeded the FBI's expectations. They included thirty pages of correspondence between the Bund and the Institute for Foreign Affairs in Stuttgart, which was routed through the second secretary of the German consulate general in New York.[41] The documents contained the names and addresses of all the most influential Nazi sympathizers in the United States, along with their replacements in the event that they were arrested. Korf also uncovered payment vouchers made through the New York consulate liaison man (this was apparently unknown to the consul general), and a full account of the assets and liabilities of the organization.

Special Agent Starr was more than happy with Korf's work and offered to refund his expenses, but Korf refused. As far as he was concerned, uncovering incriminating evidence against Kuhn was payment enough. Starr also offered Korf and Ludwig Oberndorf jobs with the FBI. Oberndorf accepted and worked for the FBI as a translator.[42] Korf, however, was not interested. The Kuhn affair had soured him on cloak-and-dagger work; he preferred employment that was aboveboard. As he told his wife many years later, "I want to be able to put my cards on the table and know what's cooking."[43]

Printed sources on the history of the Bund and FBI records do not mention Korf's contribution. However, his story is plausible, given the cloak-and-dagger character of FBI operations involving anti-American organizations at that time. These operations were made possible by a close alliance that developed between President Roosevelt and FBI Director J. Edgar Hoover. After he came to office in 1933, Roosevelt made it clear that the United States would not get entangled in European affairs. A sizable majority of Americans agreed with him. Privately, however, he was intensely concerned about the growth of fascism and communism abroad and at home. He therefore asked Hoover to keep a close eye on the activities of Nazi organizations in the United States.[44]

The growth of fascism in Germany, Italy, and Spain by 1936 made the president more anxious; he wanted pro-fascist organizations in the country kept under even closer scrutiny. Hoover was given the green light to conduct detailed investigations of pro-Nazi organizations, including the German-American Bund. Some of these investigations included wiretapping. Although wiretapping was theoretically illegal, Hoover justified it as a means to ensure security of the country against the influence of its enemies. Korf's seizure of documents from Kuhn's apartment was just as illegal as the wiretapping, but it was also viewed as justifiable, given the directives of the FBI at that time.[45]

By 1939 the FBI had also begun to compile lists of potentially dangerous German legal resident aliens. According to the historian Timothy Holian, "By creating these lists, the government implicitly indicated those residents they felt posed the most serious security risks to the United States, as well as the individuals they planned to arrest first in the event of hostilities."[46] There is little doubt that Korf's findings added significantly to the lists of those the government planned to arrest when war broke out.

Because the FBI knew the precise location of the Nazi sympathizers in the country, it was quickly able to "collect them in one fell swoop," as Korf later put it. By 9 December 1941, only two days after the attack on Pearl Harbor, the FBI had taken 620 German aliens into custody; 47 of this number came from the state of New York. In other words, Korf could take at least partial credit for the fact that the FBI did not have to waste any time trying to locate Nazis after war was declared.[47]

By December 1939 the cards were stacked against the Bund. Though investigations had concluded that it commanded the loyalty of far fewer members than it claimed, it was nonetheless seen as "a subversive, conspiratorial and un-American threat to the United States."[48] This conclusion tipped the scales against Kuhn. In December 1939 he was found guilty of embezzling Bund funds and sentenced to a two- to five-year jail term in Sing Sing. Released in 1943, he was subsequently stripped of his American citizenship and held for extradition on Ellis Island. He returned to his native Germany in 1946 and died five years later.[49]

Korf had another chance to leak valuable information in 1940 when he covered the press conference of Hitler's envoy Duke Carl Eduard of Saxe-Coburg-Gotha, who was a grandson of Queen Victoria and related to the British royal family.[50] The official purpose of the duke's visit was to promote the interests of the German Red Cross. Unofficially, he intended to show the Americans that the German aggression in Europe was justifiable. He staged a large press conference at the Waldorf-Astoria on 18 March. Although the duke was educated at Oxford and spoke excellent English, he had the first secretary of the German embassy, Tannenberg, serve as his interpreter.

Reporters from the *New York Times* and *Herald Tribune* had a lot of questions for the duke, who was evasive in his answers. Finally, Korf got his chance. "Is it correct that you are a general in the SA, the Brown Shirts?" Korf asked. The interpreter shrugged off the question and replied, "The duke is here on a humanitarian mission, not a political crusade; let us focus on questions dealing with the German Red Cross."

Korf pressed on, "Is it true that the German Red Cross does not deliver any packages to the Jews in Poland, even if they are sent by Americans?" This time the duke replied, in German, "Unfortunately, yes." But Tannenberg whispered to the duke in German, "We can never admit to that. I'll take care of the question." He turned to Korf and said, "These are details with which the duke is unfamiliar." Korf said, "All right, let us be a bit more general. What is the German Red Cross doing to help the Jews in Poland who are in need?" In German the duke muttered, "I cannot think of anything." But Tannenberg said, "The German Red Cross does not know of any discrimination."[51]

After the conference, reporters from the *Times* and *Herald Tribune* caught up with Korf in the lobby of the hotel and asked him to translate the comments made in German, and Korf agreed. Both papers carried prominently placed stories the next morning with translations of the full text of the duke's comments, which totally discredited his mission. Korf's disclosures had consequences: for days after the press conference he was followed wherever he went. When Korf informed the FBI about this, an agent told Korf that a Gestapo agent was probably trailing him. He added that the FBI could do nothing to the agent unless he violated U.S. laws.

The Gestapo not only trailed Korf, but they also periodically visited his mother. As a half-Jewish Mischling she was subject to scrutiny simply because of her background. The fact that her son had left Germany on a tourist visa but had never returned also made her a subject of interest.[52] Several times agents visited her to inquire what had become of her son. When Margarete Korf visited Hilde in Sweden before her daughter's departure for the United States, she came up with a code to inform her children that the Gestapo had questioned her. In her letters to her son, the phrase "I must tell you that" indicated that whatever followed was a request made by the Gestapo, not by her. At one point Korf's mother wrote to her son that she wished him to join the Kyffhaüser Bund, a cover organization for the Nazi party in the United States. Thanks to the code she developed, her son knew that the request was utter nonsense.[53]

Incidents such as these only intensified Korf's desire to become an American. To become better acquainted with the political culture of his adopted country, in 1939 he enrolled in courses in government at New York University, in Washington Square. He was stunned to find that radical politics was as common at U.S. institutions of higher learning as in Germany. The hot topic of the day was the Spanish Civil War. Students were entreated to fight for the Loyalist "democrats" in Spain against the fascism of Francisco Franco. When Korf talked to the students he was amazed at their ignorance of European affairs but impressed by their idealism.

Radical politics at NYU did not deter Korf from his mission to become an American. By 1939 Korf could say with confidence that he had made significant progress. His coursework at NYU gave him insight into the American political system, and his fluency in the English language had improved markedly. He even passed a prerequisite course for future teachers of English in preparation for the Board of Regents exams.

Now feeling settled in the United States, Korf wished to revive his dream of practicing law. He had his records evaluated by New York University and soon discovered that his German law degree did not automatically entitle him to practice in the United States. Despite the fact that he held a doctorate of laws in Germany, Korf still had to complete a battery of courses in an American law school and pass the bar exam. He canvassed the law schools in the area to see which one could accommodate the needs of a student with a full-time job. Fordham University was an easy choice; the school not only was close to his office, but also offered night classes. The atmosphere at Fordham was different from what he had encountered at NYU. As he put it, "You could feel the vibrations of hard work and concentration. There was no talk of politics. There was no time for it." Korf did well at Fordham. He was on the dean's list for two years. He was asked to edit the *Fordham Law Journal*, but turned the job down because of time constraints.[54]

Korf became friendly with one of his professors, Dean Wilkinson, whom he met regularly after church every Sunday for a walk. One day he asked Korf, "What do you think of our law school?" Korf replied, "Your school is good, your exams not. Your exams are not worthy of adults. You should have no true-or-false questions. That is just guesswork. The law seldom is yes or no." When Wilkinson asked Korf what his alternative to the existing system would be, Korf suggested that essay exams would be preferable. "Nobody can learn the answers by rote," he told Wilkinson, and added, "You have to think. After all, thinking is what you teach." Wilkinson pondered what Korf said, and replied, "You are right, but I cannot afford to change the examination system. I would lose 60 percent of my students."[55]

While Korf pursued his legal career, he also tried to serve his adopted country. After President Roosevelt signed the Selective Training and Service Act of 1940, thereby creating the country's first peacetime draft, Korf volunteered his services as an interpreter. He was duly appointed a member of the Volunteer Registration Committee of the Selective Service Administration for New York City in October 1940. He was also required to register for the draft. The Selective Service Act of 1940 required male aliens who wished to become U.S. citizens to register for service. This made Korf and others like him "declarant aliens"; under this proviso, they were subsequently classified the same way as citizens of the United States.[56]

But at the same time his adopted country was beginning to regard citizens of Germany such as Korf with suspicion. In August 1940 Congress passed an act requiring noncitizens to be registered and fingerprinted at their local post offices. In the event of war, the government would be able to use the list to identify noncitizens who came from enemy countries. These people, in turn, would be classified as "enemy aliens." In the summer of 1941 officials from the War Department and Justice Department agreed that in the event of war, the Federal Bureau of Investigation would investigate enemy aliens. War and Justice appear to have been unaware of the fact that the FBI had had aliens under scrutiny for some time. In any event, the three agencies agreed that aliens deemed to be security risks would be either on parole or interned in detention camps for the duration of the war.[57]

Between law school and work, Korf managed to squeeze in a semblance of a social life. One evening, when he was covering a charity affair for the paper, he renewed his acquaintance with Rita Baunach. The daughter of German-born immigrants, Rita was a secretary at an insurance company where Korf held a policy. The two had met at the insurance office before the charity affair. Rita remembered him, but Korf did not remember her. Rita was roped into selling chances at the affair, a task she did not relish, and wandered by the press area, where Korf was seated. Though Korf did not recognize her, he asked her, "Don't I know you?" and was surprised when she responded in the affirmative. When he found out that Rita was selling chances, he gallantly offered to sell them for her. Korf was a good salesman; within five minutes he sold five books of chances. When he finished, Rita politely thanked him and returned to her family. A few days later, he called her for a date.

Their relationship began to develop as the United States was drawn into World War II after the Japanese bombed Pearl Harbor. Korf called Rita the day it happened. He was particularly upset that a female friend had dismissed the significance of the event, and he trusted that Rita felt different. She did. The relationship blossomed, and the two began to date exclusively. Rita's parents were not immediately enthusiastic about the match. They had divorced themselves from their German heritage and did not even speak German at home to Rita and her younger brother, Alfons. After Rita introduced Korf to her parents, they lamented, "Why couldn't you have brought a nice American boy home?" In time, however, they grew to like Korf very much.[58]

Though Korf was not the "nice American boy" that Rita's parents had hoped for, he felt that he had done his best to become one. By 1942 Korf had conquered the barriers posed by a foreign language and foreign ways and had made a decent life for himself, with help from virtually no one. But as he told his mother, his successes had come at a price:

Naturally, I am proud of the fact that I was able to pull myself up by my own bootstraps, and that I have achieved everything that I have with no outside help. But I should have taken better care of myself through it all; as it is, this has taken years off of my life. . . . I've been here for over five years. It seems more like ten; years of struggle should count twice as much, and those years show on me. I've set one goal after another for myself, and I have worked on each slowly and carefully. You know that I'm not stubborn but modest and reasonable. It's hard to make long-range plans. It's best to take things one day at a time.[59]

It was indeed difficult for Korf to make long-range plans, since the entry of the United States in the war was to change his life once again. After Japan and its allies, Germany and Italy, declared war on the United States, Japanese, Germans, and Italians residing in the United States who had not acquired U.S. citizenship became classified as "enemy aliens."

Approximately 315,000 German citizens living in the United States came under this classification. Enemy aliens were put into a separate category from naturalized citizens. They were not allowed to vote or hold public office. They were also ineligible to receive licenses to practice medicine and law. They could not travel more than five miles away from their homes during the day, and could not stray beyond a mile of their residences after dark. They were also subject to FBI probes to determine whether they represented a threat to the United States; those believed to be a threat were sent to internment camps generally located in the southern and southwestern sections of the country.[60]

Recent refugees from Hitler and Nazism were not immune to this classification. One of them, Gottfried Bermann Fischer, argued to his fellow émigré Thomas Mann that a distinction needed to be made between refugees from Hitler and the so-called enemy aliens. He wrote, "The undifferentiated registering of all German emigrants as 'Enemy Aliens' signifies a heavy moral blow to the emigrants, who had expected everything except the misperception and disregard of their principles and beliefs." Mann replied, "You can well imagine that the enemy alien matter has also kept me continually occupied and depressed." He added that he and other recent émigrés had already sent an open letter to President Roosevelt requesting that the president make an official distinction between "the potential enemies of American democracy on the one hand, and the victims and sworn foes of totalitarian evil on the other."[61]

At first the classification of enemy alien did not bother Korf. Because he was a member of the press, he was exempt from the travel restrictions of enemy aliens, and he went about his work as a reporter as before. But his sense of security did not last long. In March 1942 the FBI searched his apartment. Korf was dismayed that his work for the FBI on the Kuhn case did not protect him from that agency's investigation of enemy aliens such as himself. As he reported to Hilde, "Unfortunately I was not at home. The [agents] put everything back in its place."[62]

Obviously put off by the intrusion, Korf went to the FBI to inquire why his apartment had been searched. He wrote to Hilde: "The [FBI] agent apologized profusely but said that he had to follow this procedure with all foreigners like us. But I still made my case, and added that you live in Los Angeles, that your husband was of Jewish heritage, and that you helped him escape G[ermany]. Our conversation got much friendlier. . . . By the way, [they] went through your letters; naturally they found nothing of interest in them." This exchange made it clear that Korf had nothing to fear from the FBI. Other German émigrés and recently naturalized German Americans were not as lucky. A friend of Rita's brother was one of approximately eleven thousand German Americans taken to internment camps during the war. According to the historian Arnold Krammer, "Most were peaceful people with no greater disloyalty to the United States than a chance remark or a complaint of a disgruntled neighbor."[63]

Korf was drafted in the spring of 1942. Though he was eager to serve, a few things had to be ironed out before he could. Although Korf had duly registered for the draft as a "declarant alien," the Selective Service Act stipulated that *enemy* aliens could not be inducted unless they were deemed acceptable to the armed forces.[64] Therefore, Korf had to petition to join, and in October 1942 he received a "Notice of Alien's Acceptability" form, clearing him to serve. Korf also had to get around the issue of his hammertoe, which made him nominally eligible for a 4-F classification. He succeeded and was deemed fit for "limited service" in the army. Many years later his wife commented about Korf's willingness to fight: "I think he went into the army with the full knowledge that he would probably have to fight. He gave up his 4-F standing. . . . He could have stayed here, [he] would not have to do anything. But he didn't feel that was right. He said, 'I'm a part of this country now and if they want me to fight that's what I'll do.' And that's what he did." In November 1942 he finally received his notice to report for induction into the U.S. Army.[65]

The notice, though long awaited, came at a bad time. He had only one more semester of law school remaining, and he knew that a prolonged absence would make completion of his law studies difficult. His career as a reporter was beginning to take off as well. He was increasingly called upon to cover events attended by VIPs such as the chief of staff, General George Marshall, and members of FDR's cabinet. He had worked for years to achieve a comfortable existence, only to have to leave it.

But Korf was not bitter about leaving, because his need to fight the Nazis surpassed other considerations. He made his feelings quite clear in a letter he wrote to his mother after he was drafted. The purpose of the letter was to explain his reasons for joining the army. He asked her to recall that he had left Germany because he had felt that there was little he could do to combat Nazism in his country: "When I came here, I said to myself, I have no control over what is going on over there [in Germany]. I would only be able to change things if I had stayed on and fought [the Hitler regime] as a revolutionary. Regrettably I was not suited for this."[66]

But despite the difficulties Korf endured in his mission to become an American, he loved his new country and was very eager to prevent the spread of Nazism in the United States: "The only thing that matters now is my new country. I will do what I can from here to ensure that the tragedy [of Nazism] does not repeat itself." Though he did not give his mother details about his work for the FBI and his writings about the evils of Nazism in the press, he did tell her that he had fought the menace in his new country. "I have tried to fight [Nazism]," he wrote. He added, "I believe that I have educated many [about its evils]. How I have done this isn't important, but I have tried to keep the evil [of Nazism] at bay."[67]

But more had to be done. Korf sensed from his dealings with the Bund and from his interview with the duke of Saxe-Coburg-Gotha that Nazism posed a real threat to his new country. Korf was willing to take the next step by going into the army: "I do know one thing: I must be a part of this war," he wrote his mother. "It is being fought for me and for you. It concerns us both. . . . I must be a part of this, or I will feel like a coward for the rest of my life." He feared that, given time, Nazism could spread across the Atlantic, and he wanted to fight this:

Now the arms of madness are stretching across the Atlantic, and they are gripping us with the fingers of those men and boys who were once close to me. They are the ones who are arming the torpedoes that are blasting ships that supply our food. They are the ones who are planting mines. They are the ones who are inciting the Japanese against us. Maybe they have reservations about what they are doing, but they are doing it anyway. I am wholeheartedly committed to doing something about this; I have no reservations whatsoever.[68]

Korf's hatred of Nazism overshadowed the idea that he might have to kill some of the people with whom he grew up. He confronted this issue in a letter he wrote to his mother shortly before he left home: "'Would you shoot your own countrymen?' I've been asked. I have answered, 'Yes.' This question cannot be evaded, and no compromises can be made about it. It doesn't matter where one stands when one is in a war, because one must kill—indirectly or directly—those with whom one grew up. Am I right to shoot those who went to school with me, [the same] boys who were close to me and married the girls I used to date? Yes."[69]

He did not approach the task without a sense of bitterness; had there been no Hitler, Korf would not have been in this position. He reproached his former countrymen for allowing Nazism to triumph:

Why did they tolerate what has happened? Why did they shrug their shoulders and say, "Let the chips fall where they may"? Why did people betray everything that they were taught to value? Why did teachers who taught me humanity and liberalism also show the new masters how to tighten their hold on power? These men and boys were raised just like I was. We thought the same thoughts. But they went astray all the while knowing that they were doing the wrong thing.[70]

Korf, however, did admit that as a non-Aryan, he was more disadvantaged than many of his former boyhood friends who did not fall under that classification:

I know that I don't have the right to be so judgmental; I shouldn't demand that they do what I did. They could always reproach me by saying, "Yes, dear boy, you were a non-Aryan, after all. That means that you had no chance for advancement. That helped you make up your mind, didn't it?" . . . How can I deny this? I am no hero, but I was not forced to leave, like others were. No one put a gun to my chest. I could have stayed, just as other NON-ARYANS like myself have chosen to do. That gives me the right to say, "You [who stayed behind] made yourselves guilty [for what is happening to you now]."

Armed with this logic, Korf was more than ready to fight. "I have analyzed and agonized over events [in Germany]. I've tried to reconcile myself to the way things are over there and I've tried to be as objective and non-judgmental about [events] as possible. Slowly it dawned on me that I was right. Slowly, my intellect confirmed what my emotions knew to be true. I am absolutely convinced that this has nothing to do with my heritage, and that I would feel the same way even if I was not [a German]."[71]

Many recent German émigrés to the United States felt the same way. Joachim von Elbe, who left Germany 1934, was almost forty years old when his adopted country went to war. His age made him eligible to opt out of military service, but he had no intention of excusing himself. In his memoir Elbe wrote that he felt threatened by Hitler's declaration of war on the United States: "To fight Hitler," Elbe concluded, "was a matter of self-defense. . . . It was either him or me."[72] Hans Schmitt, who emigrated to the United States in 1938 at the age of sixteen, was also eager to fight:

December 7, 1941 . . . the time of passive suffering was over. Now I could do something. The next day, I hastened to the recruiting office. . . . Soon my turn came, but not to enlist. The non-commissioned officer who spoke to me was civil but firm I was an enemy alien and could not volunteer. I must wait until my draft number was called. Crestfallen, I went back to my typewriter. . . . For the time being, I would have to continue to help decorate the elegant homes of Chicago's North Shore and leave the epic struggle against evil to those of more fortunate birth.[73]

Kurt Gabel, who left Nazi Germany at the age of fifteen in 1938, wrote, "Unlike a great many men . . . I was delighted with my induction order."[74] Ulrich Heinicke also left Germany as a teen, but he was at first opposed to fighting and considered becoming a conscientious objector. But he later relented:

I struggled within myself and finally decided to register 1-A as a "good American" even though I was an enemy alien. I had more reason than most to know the danger imposed on the world by Hitler, and to recognize the values we had in America and how important it was to save them. Once I made the decision to go, I was prepared to do whatever necessary, to give up whatever I must, in order to carry out the mission of the United States in World War II.[75]

The notice Korf received in November 1942 ordered him to report to the Reception Center at Fort Dix in New Jersey for basic training. He was now part of a force that had grown astronomically since Pearl Harbor: in 1940 there were 1.65 million men in arms; that number had soared to 8.3 million men by 1943. Of this number approximately 300,000 were born outside the United States.[75] Eventually, Korf would become one of the 5 million of who would see action overseas.

Korf's departure for the theater of war was commemorated by the *Staatszeitung*, which published an article entitled "U.S. Fighters of German Background," which featured a picture of Korf wearing a hat with a press pass in the hatband and smoking a pipe.[76] A mere five and a half years after Korf had started life all over again as a lowly elevator boy, he was going to do the same thing as a member of the lowest rank in the Army of the United States of America.

3 A German in the U.S. Army: 1943-1944

On a chilly November morning in 1942 Korf packed a small suitcase and reported to Pennsylvania Station. He soon found himself in a crowd of men as the names of future soldiers were yelled out and tickets distributed to them. Finally, Korf boarded the train and it slowly steamed out into the misty day. The men disembarked at Fort Dix, New Jersey, where there was more yelling and more confusion.

Korf hardly had the chance to put down his suitcase when the command came for all men to fall out. Korf had no idea what the order to "fall out" meant. He guessed that it meant that they had to go outside. The men formed a line and were marched off to the supply depot to be outfitted with uniforms. Finding one for Korf was not easy. He was only five feet seven inches tall and had a slight build. "I was the wrong size for the army," he later recalled. The shoes he was given were three sizes too big, and when his army overcoat was tossed to him Korf's knees buckled: "It was the biggest, heaviest thing I had ever seen and felt." Korf's experience was not at all uncommon. The historian Lee Kennett recounts an inductee's reception of his uniform: "The sergeant asked if everyone had a lovely fit. . . . Those who did not were to take three steps forward. Then the sergeant said if something could be buttoned it was not too tight. If it stayed with you when you stepped forward, it was not too loose."[1] Despite the ill-fitting attire, Korf felt that he was part of the army now: "I changed my civilian exterior to my army exterior."

A stout private addressed the new recruits. He finished his remarks with the command "Look at me, act like me." Korf found it amazing how quickly and drastically his life had changed. Just a few days before, he had chatted with the army chief of staff, General George Marshall, at a luncheon. But now he was "a tiny cog in a huge machine" who had to salute a private.

He took the changes in his life in stride. Many years later he summed up his feelings on the subject:

You always remain the same being but your world and your surroundings change. Was I less [of a person] when I was an elevator boy than when I was a student? Was I less [of a person] when I was a soldier than when I was a newspaper reporter? No. As long as you know your own worth, you are the same person no matter in what position you are placed. Your belief in yourself and the use of your capabilities and your stubbornness will carry you back to the position where you can do the most good for your country and the people whose world you touch.[2]

Korf's bunkmate did not make the transition to army life so easily. During his first evening in the army, he tried to hang himself with his belt. Korf described the suicide attempt as "very clumsy." He saved the man before it was too late and admonished him: "Goddamn it, you never had it so good. You get three meals a day, and [your] thinking is done for you."[3] The man calmed down.

Korf was relieved as well; he felt that the army would give him a welcome break from the life he had been leading before he was drafted. He had been working fourteen to sixteen hours a day at his job and studying law at the same time. He studied during meals, on the subway, and at every possible moment. He described his job and school responsibilities as "a crushing burden, but I could handle both." Now he had only one job. In the beginning army life did not tax Korf's energy. He did not have to worry about making choices; he simply did as he was told. Like the other recruits, he kept busy waiting in lines for equipment and shots and viewing informational films. He was amused to discover that the GIs dubbed a film on the hazards of illicit intercourse and the threat of syphilis "I will never f——k again." Korf found that the food was nice and warm, but was amazed that "perfectly fine and fresh ingredients could be turned into such inedible slop."⁴

Korf felt energized by his new life. As he wrote to his sister, "I feel like I am awakening from a long slumber. You know that I always wanted to do something, and it looks like I have a chance to."⁵ But the question of what Korf would actually do was not so easy to answer. He soon discovered that he was ineligible for duty as a foot soldier because of his hammertoe, which made him incapable of prolonged walking. The condition was the direct result of his inability to obtain properly fitted shoes after World War I. He thought it ironic that the Allied blockade of goods coming into Germany during World War I had resulted in a condition limiting his ability to fight for the Allies later on.

Korf was transferred to Fort Bragg, North Carolina, for field artillery basic training. His first day, however, had nothing to do with field training. Instead, he was sent to the kitchen for a full seventeen hours of kitchen patrol, or KP, duty. He spent much of his time scrubbing floors. The work was grueling: "With a coarse brush and yellow soap you were supposed to bring out the beauty of what was underneath this grimy surface. The flesh on my hands became spongier by the hour. They finally turned gray and it looked like the flesh was going to fall off."⁶ But he did not complain. He wrote to Rita, "Yesterday had the KP from 4:30 AM until 9 PM without a minute's rest. A very good exercise. Everything is OK and I hope I will get ahead."⁷

At age thirty-four, Korf was at least a dozen years older than the average American soldier. Physically, the age difference did not matter. As he wrote to Rita, "The training is not always easy. But I can do it as the other fellows do it too." Psychologically, however, the age difference did set him apart from the other men. The younger men, he told Rita, were seeking him out for advice: "They start coming to me with their problems and there are many."[8] Friends were hard to come by, because of the transient nature of army life. He observed, "Friendships in the army are pretty preemptory; they have to break up quickly; fellows are transferred here and there. They meet easily and part lightly. A postal card is about the most you ever hear from them again." He added, "Nobody talks about the war, because the war is present and looks over the shoulder."[9]

What is interesting about Korf's experience to this point is that he was able to blend into life in the U.S. Army despite the fact that he was an enemy alien who spoke with a slight German accent to boot. Not all men of non-American heritage were allowed to do the same; Japanese Americans and African Americans were segregated from the others. In the case of the Japanese Americans, the judge advocate general of the army justified the policy for security reasons; he feared that "disloyal elements" among them would have "unlimited opportunities to commit sabotage, espionage and other acts of treachery."[10] Evidently the same was not feared where the German Americans were concerned. The exclusion of the German Americans from this policy of segregation is all the more mysterious when one considers the fact that Austrians, Norwegians, and Greeks were also segregated, for reasons that are unknown.[11]

Soon enough, Korf settled into the routine of army life. He told Rita it had certain benefits; he had lost a few pounds. "My belly is gone," he wrote, and added, "and I feel much healthier than in a long time." He described his day-to-day activities: "First call at 6:30 AM. . . . Breakfast at 6:45, then bunk cleaning, street policing, etc. From 8 to 12 drill. After lunch, drill, military movies or lectures until 5 PM. At 5:30, retreat. After that supper and mail call, which keeps you busy until 7 PM. By that time you are very tired and just have time to clean your rifle, shoes, shave etc, when the lights go out at 9 PM."[12]

The leisurely pace ended a few weeks later. As he told Rita, "We had an overnight hike with [a] 50 pound pack, rifle, helmet, etc.

Slept in little tents on the ground." He decided to spend a brief furlough in a hotel, where he could "sleep in a broad and soft bed, take a real bath, and take it as easy as possible."[13]

Though Korf felt energized by the routine of KP and drill, he had no intention of spending his military engaged in mundane, repetitive tasks. He wanted to become an officer and fight overseas.[14] Other draftees did not feel the same. He recalled, "Many others definitely preferred to stick around a safe berth. 'Overseas' was a horrible word to them, full of death and misery."[15]

Korf's ticket out of mundane work may well have been an article about him that appeared in the 20 January 1943 edition of the *Fort Bragg Post*. The piece, entitled "Advanced Student of Many Subjects Takes a New Course in Third Regiment," showcased Korf's talents in business, languages, and the law and described him as a man who was eager to do "his bit towards winning the war."[16]

In many ways it seems strange that, at a time when the army was planning its invasion of Nazi-occupied Europe, a man with Korf's superior education and linguistic skills should have been left to advertise his way into higher ranks. It has to be remembered, however, that the top priority of the armed forces was to fill the demand for manpower, which increased geometrically after Pearl Harbor. While local draft boards did a good job of filling this demand, the system had its drawbacks. According to the military historian Lee Kennett, "The system had one disadvantage in that the government could not reach into the pool and pick up individuals it might have special need of."[17]

The article in the *Fort Bragg Post* worked as Korf had hoped it would. Within a month of its publication, Korf was ordered to leave Fort Bragg to undertake a "secret and special" mission. He was told nothing about his destination or duties. He soon found himself on a train with three reporters from the *New York Times*, the *Herald Tribune*, and the *Newark Ledger*. Since their orders were "secret and special," the reporters believed that they had been selected to cover the Allied invasion of North Africa.

After a seemingly endless southwesterly journey, the men were ordered to disembark in New Orleans. When they boarded an army truck, Korf asked the driver where they were headed. The driver replied "NOSA." The men soon discovered that NOSA stood for the New Orleans Staging Area. Korf thought the name to be very "theatrical . . . like war is a performance. To the military it is. The term 'Theater of Operations' testified to the concept of war as a performance."[18]

The men were driven to a supply house and met by a sergeant, whose greeting shattered their illusion of going to North Africa: "There you are, youse guys. I asked for reporters. They can type. I had to be sure to get guys who can type requisitions." Clearly, the men were destined for mundane deskwork. Korf later recalled his chagrined response, as well as that of his colleagues: "You could hear the hot air leaving our ego balloons."[19] Korf tried to be philosophical about the recent twists and turns that his life had taken. As he told Rita, "It is really impossible to tell in the Army what the next day might bring. All my plans [have] turned out differently. So, the only solution is to take things as they are and to try to make the best of it."[20]

Korf was assigned to company headquarters. The captain, complimenting Korf on his education and background, asked him to assume the duties of the acting first sergeant and accept a verbal promotion to private, first class (PFC). Korf accepted: "It seemed like a very tempting offer for somebody as green as I was." But he soon regretted his decision because a verbal promotion meant little.[21] In March 1943 Korf told Rita that his workload had increased, but his rank had not: "I have not yet found the opportunity to talk to the Capt[ain], who honors me with more and more work, but has not [given me] the stripes yet."[22] But Korf was persistent. As he told Rita, "My [rank of] PFC does not fill me with awe, and I have already taken steps to add a few more stripes to it."[23]

When the next offer for a promotion came, Korf tried to benefit from his previous experience. When the first lieutenant at headquarters was about to ship out, he called Korf and offered him his job. Korf agreed to take the job on three conditions: immediate promotion to buck private, promotion to staff sergeant within thirty days, and a swivel chair. The first condition was immediately granted, but he had little luck with the other two: he never got the swivel chair; Korf was told that only officers could have such equipment. And thanks to a freeze on promotions, Korf's promotion to staff sergeant was put on hold for several months.[24]

In the meantime, Korf busied himself in his new job, which involved looking after the needs of the enlisted men. He was supported by a very competent civilian secretary and some noncommissioned officers.[25] Korf found himself in a position to help not only himself but also other fellow Germans serving in the army. One day he discovered that thirteen unnaturalized Germans in his company were about to be shipped to Europe. Korf immediately warned his commandant that the since his men were still German citizens, they could be shot by the Germans as traitors. The commandant asked Korf for his solution to the problem. "Naturalize them," Korf replied. The commandant agreed, and Korf contacted a judge at the Federal District Court in New Orleans. A few days later Korf marched his men into the courtroom. "They raised the right hand and were sworn in. I marched out fourteen American citizens, including myself."[26] On 17 April 1943 he proudly wrote to Rita, "I got the final papers . . . a week ago; I am an old citizen already, practically [off the] Mayflower."[27]

This incident was a welcome respite from a job at NOSA that Korf found to be increasingly routine and uninspiring. After some research, he discovered that his position was superfluous. He therefore proposed to his superiors that the army would be better served if his position was dissolved and his men were allowed to perform more useful duties. Korf himself wished to apply to Officer Candidate School (OCS). His proposal was accepted by his superior officers.[28] Korf felt that his legal skills would be put to optimal use at the Judge Advocate General Officer Candidate School in Washington, D.C.

While Korf was waiting to hear on the status of his application to OCS, he considered a major change in his personal life—marriage to Rita Baunach. He and Rita had corresponded religiously during his training, and he had visited her twice in New York. He wrote to Rita that he was lonely when he was not on duty; he attended concerts by himself. In his letters to Rita he made it clear that other women he had met at army dances did not measure up to her. Though he had found that many were pretty, they were "very young, too young. I enjoy dancing, but not talking to them. [They're] green like grass." Clearly, his relationship with Rita filled a void in his life, and he was now ready to move further. In July he wrote to Rita:

The situation is this: you miss me and I miss you. Twice a year to see each other is not very much, and it looks to me like we not only miss, but also need each other. . . . Of course, there is the uncertainty [concerning] how long it might take until I am called for OCS. Things are moving slowly, sometimes fast. But I do not think that this fact should stop us. If we had [the rest of] this summer together, it would be a great gift, and we should try to make us worthy of it. . . . Let me know what you think of all this. . . . We want to work together; I need your help and your advice just as much as you might rely on mine.

Since Korf's pay as buck private was low, the two decided to put off further talk about marriage until his promotion to staff sergeant came through. In mid-July no promotion seemed likely in the near future. As Korf told Rita: "'When' is most uncertain. The ratings are still frozen; they might be opened any day or hour, or it might take longer. . . . I am tired of playing . . . PFC. 'How long' it may last is just as uncertain and depends upon the call to OCS or other unforeseen events in the Army."[29] As the days slipped by, Korf became understandably impatient. He wrote to Rita: "All in all, I am rather disgusted. Nothing turns out; I seem to be treading on the spot. I am empty, dissatisfied, waiting, waiting."[30]

In late July Korf finally received a promotion to the rank of sergeant-technician fourth grade, but the raise in salary was still not sufficient to get married. Korf explained to Rita: "I am working very hard to get the Staff [position] as soon as possible; time is racing and I would like to have you down here as soon as possible. But $78.00 [a month] is not enough."[31]

Korf also doubted whether he would ever be able to become an officer. He had no problem meeting entrance requirements for OCS. The sergeant administering the tests was impressed by the fact that Korf's scores improved with each subsequent test. Korf replied, "Well, I am slowly getting the hang of it."[32] To Korf's chagrin, however, there were no spaces open for him at the Judge Advocate General Officer Candidate School. The only branch of the OCS accepting candidates was Transportation OCS, providentially located in New Orleans at Camp Plauche. Graduates would be given commissions in the Transportation Corps, the branch of the army that was in charge of delivering supplies to the soldiers at the front. After he was accepted, Korf had to wait once again until a spot would be open for him. The longer he waited, the worse his prospects appeared. As he wrote to Rita:

The whole OCS seems to be more or less a mirage. I was before the board again yesterday for Transportation [OCS] and told them frankly that my experience in that field mainly consists in having traveled myself. They were very thorough and pretty tough, but gave me again the best rating out of 15 boys. Going to OCS is another thing again and I think I can lean back and let things happen. If they don't I certainly did my best and the Army has its loss. But I am not going to feel sorry, and life as a non-com[missioned officer] may be more pleasant and easier in many respects.[33]

While he mulled over his fate in the OCS, Korf's promotion to staff sergeant finally came through in late August 1943. He called

Rita in New York and said, "How about getting married? I am entitled to thirty-six dollars a month increase in family allowance pay."
Rita said, "Yes." Korf was delighted to have someone with whom he
could share his life. He had been lonely ever since his arrival in the
United States. Hilde lived in far-off Los Angeles, and he had had
only sporadic contact with his mother through the Red Cross since
the beginning of the war. Rita, said Korf, "was the only firm element
in my life, which was sliding with ever increasing speed into battle.
There never was a question of her loyalty and devotion, and her
love."[34] The wedding was to take place on 21 September 1943 in
New Orleans.

Rita wished her future husband to give her a preview of what
her life as an army wife would be like. He replied:

You see, the whole Army world is much different from the world of our
middle classes; it comes much nearer to the bohemian world or that of the
early settlers in their covered wagons, or the wandering gypsi[e]s. If you
even stay somewhere, you must be set to move at a moment's notice; you
can never forecast the future [even] for a week; you must be ready to pack
your bundle. You cannot grow roots and you must have great stability in
yourself, where there is not stability from the outside.[35]

He also shared some interesting observations about the nature of a
soldier's life:

The days are slowly moving forwards, nobody knows where they are moving to, but everybody hopes towards the end of the war. There seems to be
something purposeless about our existence; we are there, but we know that
we can be replaced at [a] moment's notice. It is some kind of isolated existence; hardly any connection with the outside world. . . . We are soldiers
and our uniform is as much a part of ourselves as our skin. We talk shop
in a language that no outsider understands and we move in thoughts which
are strange to outsiders. The bridges to the other world are burned and

many of us worry how they ever can be rebuil[t]. It will not be easy and some will never be able to do it.[36]

Because of their jobs in war factories, Rita's brother and father were unable to make the trip to New Orleans for the wedding. Rita and her mother were due to arrive during the afternoon of 18 September. That morning Korf went to Chaplain McCarthy and informed him of his wish to get married in three days. The chaplain replied that this could be done, as long as the banns had been posted. Korf did not know what the banns were, and was dismayed when the chaplain informed him that once posted, they would have to appear for six weeks before the wedding could take place. The only way around this, said the chaplain, was to obtain a dispensation from the local archbishop. When Korf discovered that the archbishop was none other than Archbishop Rummel, whom he had known during his days as an elevator boy in New York, he felt a glimmer of hope.[37]

He called the chancellery and asked whether the archbishop would possibly grant an audience to "Kurt Korf, the elevator boy from the Leo House in New York." An hour later he was informed that he could see the archbishop the next afternoon. Rummel immediately recognized Korf and was willing to grant the dispensation. He balked, however, when he discovered that the wedding was to take place so soon; the chancellery was closing for the weekend and no one was around to write out the necessary documents. But seeing the dismay on Korf's face, he relented and filled out the documents, shook Korf's hand, congratulated him, and wished him luck. Chaplain McCarthy was amazed at this turn of events. When he asked how difficult it was to obtain the dispensation, Korf sniffed, "Piece of cake."[38]

Korf met his bride and her mother in front of the hotel in the afternoon of 21 September. Rita wore a cream-colored suit and looked "lovely" in the eyes of the groom. But Korf was dismayed that she had no flowers. His future mother-in-law reminded him that it was his responsibility to get them. Korf strode over to the flowerbeds in front of the hotel and fashioned an impromptu corsage. He recalled, "They did not look princely, but Rita was very calm and just put them on. She balanced out the shockers of life with great composure."[39]

The wedding ceremony took place in the small chapel at Camp Hanrahan and was attended by Rita's mother, Korf's commanding officer, his secretary, and a few sergeants. The chaplain launched into the ceremony. Its text was familiar to everyone except Korf, who had never heard it in English before. He followed the ceremony intently until the chaplain uttered the phrase "And I pledge unto you my troth." Not knowing what the phrase meant, Korf asked, "What?" The chaplain gave Korf a withering look, but he refused to answer his question, which, Korf thought, "was fully justified." The chaplain started the ceremony all over again. This time, it went off without a hitch.[40]

As Korf and his new wife left the church, his sergeant handed him a document that entitled the groom to take leave for his honeymoon, and he gently reminded him that he had neglected to put in for it. That evening the wedding party and a few friends dined at Arnaud's restaurant in New Orleans. Rita later affectionately looked back at her wedding and wrote to her husband that it was "exciting and solemn and funny and I wouldn't exchange it for the biggest 'fanciest' wedding, for anything in the world."[41] The next day the couple embarked upon a three-day honeymoon weekend at the Edgewater Gulf Hotel in Biloxi, Mississippi. As they drove over the marshlands toward the coast, Korf recalled repeatedly hearing Bing Crosby's song "Paper Moon" over the radio. "We were so young," he recalled, and "heading into an uncertain future."[42]

After his return Korf was called into his commandant's office. The latter sternly asked Korf if he was "willing to volunteer for extra-hazardous duty behind enemy lines." Korf was stunned by the request and by the fact that it came from the Office of Strategic Services (the precursor to today's Central Intelligence Agency). Korf replied that he had been married for only a week and wished to discuss the matter with his wife. "You cannot do that," said the commandant. "You have to give me your answer right here and now."

Korf asked for more details about the mission, but they could tell him only that it was "very important for the war effort." Korf finally agreed, and he was immediately whisked off to a physician who was to determine his fitness for the mission. After learning that Korf was well under six feet in height, weighed only 130 pounds, and wore a size seven shoe, the physician pronounced him unfit for the mission. He explained that a man of Korf's dimensions parachuting from an airplane and carrying a fifty-pound pack would end his jump with shattered feet. He concluded, "You would be no good to anyone." The commandant and his adjutant looked distressed, but Korf was relieved. He later learned that had he qualified, he would have been dropped behind the lines in the mountains of Nazi-occupied Yugoslavia to join the communist partisans in their fight against Hitler.[43]

Two months after his marriage, Korf was finally granted permission to enter Transportation OCS at Camp Plauche. The course of instruction consisted of a very vigorous four-month training program. Korf's day consisted of six hours of classroom instruction, two hours of outdoor drills, and evening study periods. Because Korf was required to live at OCS, Rita went back to New York to stay with her parents. His free time was so limited that he could write to his wife only once a week.[44] In his first letter to her after their separation, Korf discussed the rigors of his training: "It is 7:30 PM now and since 5:30 AM there was no chance even to sit down." He also wrote of his happiness in his marriage: "After many years, I know again that I belong somewhere; we both are not alone in this world any more."[45]

Korf found it ironic that an eighteenth-century German—the Prussian general von Steuben, who had fought for King Frederick the Great—influenced the curriculum of the OCS. Von Steuben had passed his drill book on to West Point, and it served as the bible of the U.S. Army. His motto was "Kadavergehorsam," or "obedience until death."[46] When his commandant, Lieutenant Colonel Stephen Ackerman, asked Korf what he thought of the training methods at OCS. Korf replied, "Sir, it is interesting for me who has fought the Prussian spirit all his life, to now have to adopt it to fight it." Korf believed that Ackerman understood what he meant.[47]

Korf experienced little difficulty mastering the academic portion of his training; his average in his course work was over 90 percent. Outside academics, however, he found the training pace "merciless; everything was done on the double." He confided to Rita: "It is not wholly hard, and physically I am hardening again, I guess. But the pressure is turned on, one inspection after the other, one exam after the other, perpetually on parade."[48] A month into his training, he observed:

Sometimes, I feel an inner revolt against this constant pressure, being on the run 16 hours a day, driven faster and faster. You know that I do not mind driving myself, but that I resist being driven [to the point] that my "freedom of action" [is taken away]. You are so tired that [you] can hardly stand—but the show must go on. It is one of those human tragedies that you only can fight for freedom by giving it up. . . . There is a whip over us, teachers, candidates; a cruel one and without pity, the urgency of the war; we are running on the double, we can hardly catch up with ourselves, as a matter of fact, we cannot.[49]

By early 1944 the pressure was bearing down on Korf quite a bit. Though he kept his academic average above 90 percent, he faltered in the drill portion of his training. In January he reported to Rita, "The day was not a good one—I made out badly in Drill. [This was] the first time that I really fell down on a job and I have no excuse for myself."[50] Two weeks later he was called before the board of the school, which consisted of his colonel, the colonel's deputy, the tactical officer, and others arranged according to rank. Korf was warned that his performance in drill needed to improve if he was going to graduate. The experience jarred Korf; "The whole thing left a little sour taste in my mouth," he wrote. But he vowed to continue.

The pressure, however, began to intensify once again as several of Korf's classmates washed out of the OCS training program. "Our class lost 5 fellows this week; the board was [hard at] work, " he wrote to his wife. He added, "That does not mean [that] everybody has to go before the board; only if there are special reasons. Three [candidates] flunked exams, [others exhibited] physical deficiency, and other things."[51]

Korf began to feel that his position in OCS was not too secure. Not only did he have difficulties with the drill, but he also found that he had little in common with the other candidates. Korf's class consisted of fifty men, grouped into five squads of ten each. Most of the men were ten years younger and thought differently from him on several issues.[52] A night exercise along Lake Pontchartrain made these differences clear. The candidates were instructed to proceed to a set of coordinates. When Korf's group arrived, they discovered that the coordinates were located in the middle of the lake. When Korf waded into the water, he concluded that the exercise was fruitless and said, "There is no sense in drowning us. I am going back." His fellow candidates disagreed and kept heading into the lake. When Korf arrived onshore, the officer leading the exercise spluttered, "I gave the wrong coordinates. Where are the men?" Korf pointed toward the lake and said, "They are already swimming."

On another occasion candidates were instructed to cross a deep gulch. Korf found a tree trunk that bridged the chasm and shimmied his way across. Ignoring the tree trunk, the other men went into the gulch and got wet and slimy in the process. When Korf asked them why they did not take his route, they replied, "Nobody told us to use the tree trunk." Korf retorted, "Well, nobody told us not to."[53]

In this and in many other ways Korf began to stand apart from his classmates. Korf soon saw that the most popular men were those who did not stand out for any particular reason. Korf did, however, because he was foreign-born, intellectual, and lacking a strong command voice. Since he could do nothing about the first two, he concentrated on correcting the last. He practiced increasing the volume of his voice nightly.[54]

Through all his difficulties at OCS, Korf had one great consolation: his new wife. He remembered: "Rita was great source of strength and comfort. She did what she could to revive my shaken self-confidence."[55] Her daily letters to him made his difficult training endurable. He told her how much they meant to him: "I open the letter right away, then the w[h]istle blows and sometimes I don't even have a chance to read it until [the] next day. But I glance at the words, at . . . the signature and I carry it as a piece of yourself. You really help me."[56]

Korf exhibited another fault at OCS: he did not know how to play baseball. When he was once forced to participate in a game, his inadequacies were painfully obvious. He remembered, "I must have looked ridiculous." Shortly after this embarrassing incident, Korf was called before the OCS board. He recalled, "It looked like a court-martial." The purpose of the gathering was to inform Korf that he had washed out of OCS for "failing to exhibit leadership qualities."[57]

When Korf was asked if he wished to say anything in his defense, he remembered thinking about how he had come to OCS wishing to help the war effort. He remembered how he had been willing to share his expertise on the German synthetic oil industry with the army. Yet despite all the assets he brought to OCS, he felt that he was being rejected because he did not know how to play baseball. He wanted to say, "Gentlemen, I came here to help win the war and not to play baseball." But instead, standing "ramrod straight," he said, "I have no statement." He saluted, made an about-face, and exited the room.[58]

Korf was bitter about his failure at OCS. He felt that he had been dismissed because he was German.[59] He was also dismayed when he discovered that other men who had gone before the board for dismissal were reinstated thanks to connections with congressmen or other influential individuals.[60] Apparently, he acquired tangible proof of this, and he was tempted to go forward with it so that he could get reinstated. But then he had second thoughts. As he wrote to his wife:

You will remember that I had the feeling the squad rating was not quite fair. Today I have very definite proof that it was not and that some boys saved their own precious little hides by sacrificing mine. But the question is: what would it help me to uncover it, considering the fact that it would uncover quite some dirt? . . . There is one thing I can do: work to get back on my own merits. Maybe it was a mistake that I always thought I could stand on my own merits, even if the conditions and the combinations were against me. I will keep on trying, and trying the clean way.[61]

Colonel Ackerman, Korf's superior at OCS , supported Korf's commitment to do things the "clean" way. He encouraged Korf to apply for admission to the next OCS class. Since the new class would not begin for several months, Korf was left idle, and he asked Ackerman to give him something to do. Ackerman offered Korf a job teaching a course on inland waterways. When Korf insisted that he knew nothing about the subject, Ackerman shrugged and replied, "Nobody else does, either." Though Korf did the best he could, he struggled with the course because he taught officers who had no respect for an instructor who was an enlisted man. Korf remembered that he had only one prayer: "Dear Lord, please freeze the European rivers when we come, so we do not have to use the inland waterways."[62]

Korf's career as an instructor was cut short after a recruiter from Military Intelligence Training Headquarters at Camp Ritchie, Maryland, came to Camp Plauche looking for new men. Ackerman immediately suggested Korf. The potential candidate, however, was initially skeptical about leaving OCS because he had only two weeks to go until he was reinstated as a candidate. The recruiter then hinted to Korf that he could receive a commission upon arrival at Camp Ritchie. He added that his new assignment would enable him to save lives. The offer was too good to refuse, and Korf, now joined by his wife, left for Camp Ritchie, a former National Guard installation situated on the shores of a picturesque lake in the Blue Ridge Mountains.[63]

The men who came to Camp Ritchie were trained to become battle specialists, photo interpreters, and interrogators of prisoners of war. Korf was one of nineteen thousand men who trained there during the course of the war.[64] Camp Ritchie was the brainchild of the army's Washington-based strategic intelligence organization, the G-2. This organization, which had over two thousand members, was "responsible for political-economic information . . . and detailed combat information for the current situation in each theater. . . . The operating arm of the G-2 was the Military Intelligence Service (MIS) [which] relieved the G-2 of controlling the field intelligence units. The MIS organized and trained the teams of interrogators, interpreters and other intelligence specialists that helped at every level from division to field army."[65]

The rosy picture painted by the Ritchie recruiter changed soon after Korf's arrival. Not only did Korf fail to receive the commission, but he also learned that he faced uphill competition to get one at all. There were eighty-two candidates, but only two commissions were available.[66] The quality of the candidates was higher than had been the case at Camp Plauche; on the whole, they were better educated. Some were members of the most prominent families in the country. The heir of the Armour meatpacking company was in Korf's class, along with the nephew of the U.S. ambassador to Italy.[67]

Korf found life very interesting at Ritchie. Parts of the camp were created to look like a German army camp, replete with German-looking buildings and soldiers wearing German uniforms and singing German songs. The student body was quite diverse. Candidates included Jewish refugees, sons of Germans and Italians, and men who had majored in foreign languages in college. They were taught several subjects, including map reading, the fundamentals of Morse telegraphy, and the organization of American and British armies. The most important part of training was intensive study of the German army. Candidates learned about its organization, military terms, and military maps and weaponry. Most important, they learned how to interrogate German prisoners of war.[68] Korf was trained to extract phony military secrets from phony prisoners of war and soon found that he had a flair for the job. While a full colonel was observing him, Korf extracted not only the military "secrets" but also the soldier's birthplace in Pennsylvania and his father's occupation. Evidently, Korf did his job too well; the colonel broke off the interrogation by yelling, "Stop, stop, enough!"[69]

Korf found the physical requirements of intelligence school more demanding. A typical night field-training exercise involved pairs of candidates being dropped off at unfamiliar locations and finding their way to specified coordinates. Those who failed to find them had to make their way back to camp in the dark.[70] Korf's final exam was a twenty-four-hour solo assignment to find a hidden tent. When he found the tent, he was given another assignment requiring him to traverse brush, rivers, and mountains. After the exercise, Korf was exhausted: "I lay down flat on a wooden board between two saw horses and fell asleep. I never fell."[71]

When it was all over, Korf had the highest score in his class and received one of the two available commissions. He was commissioned as a second lieutenant in the infantry for service in military intelligence. He was eager to don the epaulets that were insignias of his new rank, but he discovered, much to his chagrin, that none were available for purchase at the camp. Upon hearing of her husband's dilemma, Rita enlisted her landlady, who was also a seamstress, to fashion epaulets for Korf. Rita soon discovered why epaulets were referred to as "shave tails": the landlady made the epaulets from the tails of the regulation shirt for enlisted men.[72]

Korf and his wife were overjoyed by the epaulets and the higher rank that they signified. It was a great victory for him and it took the sting out of his negative evaluation from OCS in Louisiana. As he explained to his sister, Hilde, "It seems an irony of fate that I am now wearing the crossed rifles of the Infantry, after the Transportation Corps did not think my drill good enough for a commission."[73]

Having secured his commission, Korf knew that it would not be long before he was shipped to Europe; military intelligence units had suffered terrible losses at the invasion of Africa and in southern Italy, and replacements were urgently needed. Allied forces were also closing in on Germany, and men with Korf's linguistic abilities were desperately needed at the front. This explains why Korf was not required to supplement his combat training at Camp Sharpe in Pennsylvania, as his predecessors had done. But incomplete training had its drawbacks; officers in the European theater voiced concern about the "lack of basic military training" among members of their military intelligence specialist teams.[74] Nevertheless, Korf felt ready to go: "After military training of the body, the mind was focused upon the task ahead."[75] When asked if he wished to waive his class C standing (which classified him for limited service) so that he could go into combat, Korf had no problem doing so. As he recalled, "I felt very strongly that I should go into combat, because these boys— they came from Pennsylvania and South Dakota—they didn't even know what a Nazi was. They had no idea what they were fighting for, and they were going to get killed for it, too. I felt I had a much higher obligation."[76]

Soon enough Korf received notification that he was being shipped overseas. Before his departure, Korf made sure that his mother would be taken care of in the event he did not return. He also wrote to her about how his life had changed since he had gone into the army two years earlier. Thanks to his marriage, he was no longer lonely, but he missed his mother very much:

Just as before I miss the same person to whom I owe so much—you. Rita and I have often talked about the time when the three of us could live together after this awful war, and we hope that this dream will soon become a reality. [But] if something happens to alter this picture, it is my wish that you leave war-torn Europe and come to live in freedom and peace in our country. . . . I know that Rita will do everything in her power to take care of you. . . . My promotion to officer has not changed my views at all, but I do hope that the promotion will give me the opportunity to better serve my country.[77]

Rita packed up their apartment in Maryland and said good-bye to her husband at Blue Ridge Summit.

In preparation for departure, Korf and his men stripped themselves of any identification and were forbidden to make phone calls; there were to be no more connections with the outside world. Korf described what it felt like for him to give up his identity: "It is strange to leave like a ghost and go nowhere; [we are] blotted out [but] still know that we live in the hearts of people more real than our actual existence."[78]

Rita learned from a friend that Korf's troop train was scheduled to depart at 6 AM, and she and her friend stood near the tracks as it left, and she caught one final glimpse of her husband.[79] Korf later reflected on the fact that their last days together before he left had been difficult:

Maybe it was the shadow of coming events, a certain subdued nervousness—which made the days not quite as bright as they should have been. This should have taught us how wrong it is to let future things run the present—even if no good can be derived from it. It should have shown us that only one thing counts: our love for each other. . . . Everything else is small and has to be treated accordingly. And then, we will never leave up to the next days anything, which might stand between us, as small as it might be; we will never rest without each other but in full harmony. And the everyday life and anxieties never will have the power to overshad[ow] our feelings.[80]

Korf's next stop was Camp Kilmer, on the New Jersey side of the Hudson. There he met the men who would become members of his team. They included Sergeant Hermann L. Kurz., Private Stefan G. Koref, Technical Sergeant Herbert Kaufman, and Private Walter J. Koll. Koref was Austrian, the others German. One night they got the command to "fall out" and were marched to the Brooklyn docks. The area was in complete darkness because of wartime blackout conditions. Inside a huge enclosure on the pier the soldiers spotted a ship.

They walked up the gangway in dead silence. Korf heard only "the shuffling of feet; there was no other sound." Suddenly, a soldier shouted, "Is this trip really necessary?" That comment, remembered Korf, broke the ice. Though it had been used as a slogan to inspire Americans to conserve fuel, it seemed more accurately to depict the feelings of the soldiers as they ascended the gangplank in the dark night. They wondered whether the sacrifice of their lives was necessary, and how many of them would come back.[81]

The ship that ferried Korf and his men across the Atlantic in late October 1944 was a relatively small troop transport that could carry up to twelve hundred men. The twelve officers were housed in a small cabin; the rest of the men occupied huge, cavernous spaces and slept in bunks eight layers high. There were only two meals a day for enlisted men; officers were supplied with additional sandwiches. The officers knew that many of their men went hungry, so they hoarded sandwiches for them—until the cook decreed that each officer would receive no more than three. During the initial part of the voyage, the men had to do battle with boredom because there was nothing to do on board except wait in lengthy lines for meals. Korf remembered, "Eating and waiting took most [of] the day."[82] Another veteran recalled, "We had been given a small pamphlet, *What to Do Aboard the Transport*, to acquaint us with the things which were worth knowing on a sea voyage. There were no duties to perform except throwing garbage into the sea or attending brief instruction sessions."[83]

The boredom of the men was ended by an unwelcome distraction: rough seas. Korf, whose quarters were close to the bow of the ship, remembered, "Each time the bow lifted out of the water, it came down with a boom, which ran out into a shudder. It felt like the ship was bursting apart." This was not an exaggeration. The officers knew that many transport ships such as theirs, which had been built in haste, had broken apart. Such disasters, Korf recalled, had not been publicized for security reasons.[84]

The officers worked in four-hour shifts looking after their men, most of whom suffered intensely from seasickness. The officers took many of them up to the sick bay, but they were dismissed with the remark "Everybody is seasick. Get the hell out of here." The men were dragged back to their bunks.[85]

Korf described the rigors of the trip in his letters to his wife: "We have a pretty rough sea; my typewriter is dancing on the table and I am dancing with it. So far, I was not seasick, but it might still come. It was a grandiose and ghastly spectacle to watch the waves; they came like mountains, broke into white foam and behind us was only a strip of light green and blue, over which quickly the gray curtain of rain close[d]."[86] He also considered the impact that their separation would have on their relationship: "The days are going by and every new one carries me away from you a little farther. But all of this does not seem bad if we understand each other and are able to bridge the space with our thoughts and feelings."[87]

The ship sailed in a convoy at a speed of about seven knots. On a rare clear day, Korf was able to see "a huge armada, spread out to the horizon." Initially pursuing a southerly route via the Azores, the ship reached England after a ten-day journey. The men disembarked at the port of Birmingham on a Sunday evening. At first the dockworkers slated to help unload the ship were nowhere in sight. The commandant was irate; he also feared that the men and supplies would be vulnerable to an air raid. He shouted, "Goddammit, we are unloading ourselves. We are not going to wait until the Krauts [Germans] get us like sitting ducks." Fortunately, the dockworkers appeared a short time later. With the ship unloaded, the men finally were able to leave it. Flashlights with slits over the bulbs enabled the men to navigate their way through streets kept in complete darkness because of the blackout.[88]

Conditions in England were far from pleasant. The weather was miserable, "cold, wet humidity penetrated everything." Korf never forgot one soldier's remark about the weather: "Let Hitler come over here, catch pneumonia and die. The war will be over. Come to think about it, the rest of them deserve this weather too."[89]

Korf had grown accustomed to wartime restrictions in the United States, but England was a different matter altogether. Frequent air raids had inflicted heavy damage on the country and goods were far more severely rationed than in the States. Korf remained singularly impressed by the "stiff upper lip" exhibited by the British in the face of the hardships they had to endure, and by their kindness to the Americans. When Korf's washerwoman returned his laundry, she gave him an egg. Korf asked, "How many eggs do you get per week?" "One," she replied. Korf said, "And you want to give me that egg?" She insisted: "Yes, you Americans help us, and we are grateful." When Korf saw a play in London, a sign next to the stage flashed an air raid alarm and warned the theatergoers to seek shelter, but no one moved. On another occasion, he passed by an elaborate home. Though its roof had been destroyed by an air raid, the house was lit and dinner guests were enjoying a formal dinner. In short, though London was a disaster area, "nobody seemed to mind."[90]

When Korf was granted a brief leave to visit friends, he found the windows of their home blown out and replaced by tarpaper. In the middle of the night he was tossed from his bed by the force of a shattering explosion. His hostess calmly reported the next morning that the explosion was the result of a V-2 rocket hit. When he went to survey the damage, he found a deep hole where a home for the elderly had once been. Fifty people had died. He soon learned that it was impossible to detect an incoming V-2 attack because of the swiftness of the rocket. Its predecessor, the V-1, could be seen and heard. When its engine stopped, it would come down. This gave potential victims the time to seek shelter. With the V-2, such was not the case.[91]

Korf toured Coventry and Bath, where he saw more war damage. In Bath he was amused by the way that British managed to combine their wartime privations with a sense of finesse. He attended a banquet hosted by the lord mayor and the city government. The place settings consisted of beautiful old china and wrought silver. "Huge trays with silver covers were brought in, the covers [were] lifted. Spam. But it had style." Korf also met Sir Anthony Eden, Churchill's heir apparent, while on a viewing stand at a parade. They shook hands and exchanged pleasantries. When Korf observed him closely, he concluded that even top government officials were subject to rationing and privations. Though Eden's suit was smartly tailored, it was so worn that the fabric shone.[92]

One evening Korf and some friends were invited to a party by a British duchess. She was a gracious hostess, but her grasp of American idioms was rather faulty. When the men spoke about the inevitability of shipping out to Germany she said, "That is TS, as you Yanks say." Korf asked politely, "Do you know what TS stands for?" She brightly replied, "Oh yes, that has been explained to me; it means 'terribly sorry.'"[93]

Korf's duties in England took a far more serious turn when he was called to headquarters to translate a German document. When he examined it he knew it had been written in the military language of the German High Command. After several hours, Korf produced a translation. The next morning headquarters informed him that he had been selected to be one of three men whose jobs involved translating German High Command documents that had been seized at Normandy. Korf's commandant added, "It is of utmost urgency to have them translated as quickly as possible. General Eisenhower is personally interested in this matter." Korf asked why he, a low-ranking officer, had been selected for the job. His commandant replied that they had tried every other German expert in England, and only three had the qualifications to do the job. Korf was one of them.[94]

The task was formidable. Because the documents were written in what Korf referred to as "a strange patois; nouns followed by nouns, without any verbs," progress was slow. Though he worked twelve-hour days, Korf could never translate more than four pages in a day. But the importance of the task became obvious. The documents not only showed the position of German troops in Normandy, but also divulged their fallback positions in the event of invasion. After translating the documents, Korf noted, "I had the feeling that I knew Normandy better than my home in New York."[95]

Korf's intelligence briefings in England also brought news of horrors occurring in German concentration camps. He had certainly known that such camps existed as far back as 1933, when his friend Henry Marx had been released from Oranienburg. But this was the first time that Korf learned about atrocities being committed against the Jews in the camps. Although Korf was hearing about this for the first time in late 1944, the army had been aware of these atrocities for several months. According to the historian Joseph Benderesky, military intelligence had been aware of widespread massacres of Jews in Latvia, Lithuania, and Hungary since the spring of 1944.[96]

At the end of November 1944 Korf received orders to ship out to France. As the officer in charge of his military intelligence combat team, Korf was given supervision over several noncommissioned officers (NCOs), two jeeps, and a trailer. They drove in formation through the cold and dreary landscape of central England into the mining country of Wales, and eventually arrived at Weymouth, a small port on the south coast. Red Cross girls distributed doughnuts and coffee for free. "After all," one of them said, "you are going into combat." The men drove right on to an LST (landing ship, tank)[97] and waited—and waited. When Korf asked why they were not moving, a senior officer replied, "There is a storm in the channel and the Jerries [Germans] are dropping magnetic bombs. We have to wait."[98]

They waited for a week. Korf recalled that the cramped life aboard the small vessel was "oppressive." The GIs staved off boredom by going into town and getting into fights with the locals. After that they were ordered to stay on board. Suddenly, after six days, the quality of the food on board drastically improved, and the men feasted on steaks with all the trimmings. The men were delighted, but the skipper was angry. He barked, "You force us to use the good food which we reserve for the trip back after we have dropped you people off. This is a waste of good stuff and you bastards are going to bite the dust anyway." Korf replied sarcastically, "Thanks," and enjoyed his meal.[99]

In his letters to his wife Korf said nothing about the boring wait and the meal with ominous connotations. He looked forward to being finally able to make use of his months of training and hard work: "I am not at my previous address any more. As a matter of fact, even England is behind us and before us are all the anticipations of our work, of sweat and cold and a lot of other things. But we are [in] excellent spirits and as well-equipped as possible."[100]

Events soon showed that Korf was not as well equipped as he claimed. When the LST finally departed for France, it traveled in a convoy and was protected by an antiaircraft battalion moored to the top, with four men to each unit. Suddenly German planes appeared overhead, but not a single antiaircraft gun on board fired. Stunned, Korf asked the battalion commander, "Why don't you fire?" He replied, "Are you nuts? Look at this tub. It is so old that if we fire, the vibrations will shake loose all the nuts and bolts and we'll go down like a stone." Korf recalled, "The reality of war was upon us."[101]

The convoy was approaching the coast of France when a white wall of water suddenly rose on the starboard side of a nearby transport. It had hit a magnetic mine. Korf and his men watched as the surviving men were picked up by another LST and it proceeded on its prescribed route. Amazingly, the vessel that had been hit did not go down.[102]

The men breathed a sigh of relief as the LST neared its destination. Korf found himself staring at the French coast. Coincidentally, the port of entry to France was Le Havre, the same place from which he had left Europe seven years earlier. He had turned his back on his homeland; now he had returned to liberate it. The first stop for Korf and his men was Reims. As they went up the Seine and Marne Rivers toward Reims, Korf observed that the left bank of the river was piled high with any kind of military equipment that could not float. In escaping the U.S. invasion, the Germans had left the equipment behind so that they could cross the Seine. Korf found Reims "a city of rubble with a gray pallor hanging over it. . . . Wooden construction walls were everywhere." The men unchained the bow of the LST and drove their jeeps onto the sandy riverbed and headed for Paris.[103]

Korf's orders were to report to the headquarters of the military intelligence service at Le Vesinet, a suburb of Paris, but no directions were provided. As he and his men drove into the city, Korf spied a sign that read "HQ, MIS" with an arrow below it. Korf thought it ironic that the army had gone to the trouble to dispatch him and his men with all the paraphernalia of secrecy: they had no identification, no numbers on the jeeps or their bumpers. They were to possess no hint of their previous existence. Yet the army in its wisdom placed very obvious signs pointing to the direction of their headquarters.[104]

Other indications of lax security measures soon became apparent. When Korf and his men were waiting for their instructions at military intelligence headquarters the next day, an attractive Frenchwoman came in to inquire after an American lieutenant. When Korf replied that he was not there, the young woman remarked that he must have shipped out with his outfit. She knew the name of the outfit, though it was supposed to be secret. The signs to MIS and the indiscretion of its lieutenant made it obvious to Korf that security at MIS stood in need of improvement. Korf described the situation as "careless"; American soldiers "had heard the phrase, 'a slip of the lip will sink a ship' [but] it apparently did not stick." He suspected that security was slipping because everyone believed that victory was close at hand.[105]

He described his feelings about being back in Europe to his wife: "It is so strange to see, after so many years, the coast of France again, see French faces, the same ones and still so changed. Lots of other things have changed and the traces of things gone by are still marked. It takes a little while to get the range but slowly the picture will unfold."[106]

Korf also reflected on his feelings about being away from home and the uncertainties of his future: "What will happen to me personally is still entirely in the dark, but I probably will learn it pretty soon. . . . Home seems so far away; it gets dim[mer] and dimmer; only the beautiful things stick out and we do a lot of dreaming about it. On the other hand, we worry more about home than about ourselves—maybe because that is about the only influence we really have [or] maybe because our fate is . . . entirely in God's and the Army's hands."[107] Given the unanticipated twists and turns that Korf had experienced after his emigration from Germany, he knew that to plan for anything, especially under his current circumstances, would be futile.

Korf described the mood in Paris in November 1944 as "uneasy." Although the Germans were gone, reminders of their presence were still very much in evidence. Their machine-gun bunkers remained. Many buildings were in ruins, and the rubble had not yet been removed. The Parisians, Korf recalled, did not exhibit the mood of a joyfully liberated people. He wrote to his wife, "The people have suffered awfully much, and it is still evident."[108]

Since Korf spoke French fluently, he was in a good position to assess the attitude of the French toward their American liberators. He found them less kindly disposed toward the Americans than the

British were. The French thought of the Americans as conquerors, not liberators. He suspected this attitude was due to the fact that the Americans had bombed France extensively during the opening phases of their invasion, and that the French "resented the terrible loses in life and property which our air force had inflicted upon them in taking France." The liberation had also resulted in critical shortages. One man told Korf, "Before you came, we had enough food and coal, now there is not enough to go around." Liberation also put an end to the profits made by many Frenchmen who had collaborated with the Germans.[109] One Frenchman quipped: "Every Frenchmen who earned more than twenty thousand dollars during the occupation ought to be shot, because there was no other way to make that much money than to work with the Germans."[110]

The Americans, according to Korf, tried to accommodate the French as much as possible. American soldiers paid subway and tram fees, whereas the Germans had paid nothing.[111] They bought goods and services from the French at highly inflated prices. Korf and a friend, Herbert Klotz (later an undersecretary of commerce under President John F. Kennedy) went to the Lido one evening, and his ticket cost him a whole month's salary. American soldiers were paid in "valueless francs" instead of dollars.[112]

One of Korf's duties was to determine whether all German soldiers had left the city. They had not. He and his men found a number of them holed up in their apartments and with their French girlfriends. They claimed that they just wanted to forget about the war. He also discovered that the women who had fraternized with German soldiers had easily switched their loyalties to the American soldiers.[113]

Korf's work in Paris brought him into contact with prominent people. He wrote to Rita: "I have been invited [to visit] many French families of the better classes up to the high aristocracy, but they all have suffered quite a bit. Their hospitality is amazing, and once in a while they eat very well, but the [day-to-day state of affairs] is pretty sad."[114]

One of his fellow officers offered to take him along to meet Pablo Picasso. Korf initially balked. As intelligence officers with top security clearance, it did not "look good" for them to be meeting the artist, who was also a well-known communist. But Korf went anyway and took a can of lard—a rare and precious commodity in postwar Paris—as a gift. When Picasso asked Korf if there was anything that he could give him in return, he declined. In retrospect, he wished he had asked the artist for "a sketch, a drawing, a line, anything. . . . But I declined, which is something I will always regret."[115]

On Christmas Eve 1944 Korf dined with French friends he had met long before his departure from Germany. It was extremely cold upon his return to his barracks at Le Vesinet. Korf did everything he could to get warm: "I slipped into my comforter roll, which Rita had turned into a bedding roll by sewing a zipper on two sides, leaving only the top open to crawl into the bag. It did not help. I turned on the electric heater. The fuse blew. I put in the strongest fuse I could find. The lights went out all over Le Vesinet." Later that night, he recalled, the Germans started an air raid, "to spice up the festivities."[116] The next day Korf learned that the raid was part of a mission to eliminate General Dwight D. Eisenhower, supreme commander of Allied forces in Europe: one bomb had squarely hit Eisenhower's private car. Fortunately, Eisenhower was somewhere else. But Korf remained impressed that German intelligence had come so close to pinpointing the general's location.[117]

Rita's frequent letters and packages provided a welcome distraction from the cold and the air raids. He remembered that she "sent beautiful packages full of things hard to get on both sides of the Atlantic." On one occasion Korf was jubilant when several arrived at once. He recalled, "There were enough packages to fill a whole postal bag. The bag was so big I could not get it into the small observation plane I used at the time. . . . There was so much love and caring in those letters and packages."[118]

Korf encouraged his wife to make her letters to him as personal as possible. As he explained: "If our letters are not close and personal and actually give something of ourselves, the whole paper is wasted. Only what is reborn every day will live and we have it much harder to recreate than a lot of other people who see each other every day and can thrash things out."[119] But although Korf wanted his wife to be as open as she possibly could be about her feelings in her letters, there was little he could tell her about what he was actually doing. "My letters mostly were short and, true to my profession, said very little," he recalled.[120]

Rita's correspondence momentarily distracted Korf from his growing concern with his mother's welfare. He had not heard from her for quite some time. He guessed that she had left bomb-ridden Berlin for her husband's family home in Lippstadt, which was behind the front lines. He guessed that she nonetheless needed his help; the only way he could do this was to go to the front.

The way to the front became clear when Korf was summoned to the Supreme Headquarters of the Allied Expeditionary Force (known as SHAEF), which was located in a Paris hotel close to the Arc de Triomphe.[121] He was escorted to a lavishly furnished room and was surprised to see a bust of Hitler on the mantelpiece. Before he could reflect on this anomaly, the colonel got straight to business and began asking Korf questions about his German background. He asked Korf, "You were born in Germany? "Yes," Korf replied. The colonel continued, "Do you have a mother still living in Germany?" Korf replied in the affirmative and also assured the colonel that he had top security clearance.

The colonel then told Korf that if he wanted to go to the front, he had to change his name to something that sounded "more American" than the name Kurt Friedrich Franz Korf, which sounded "too German." If captured under his birth name, the colonel warned, Korf would be shot as a traitor. Taken aback, Korf replied, "Sir, to be shot is one of the risks of war." Korf remembered that the colonel grinned slightly in response, but continued to insist on the name change. Finally, the two men came up with a compromise: instead of changing his name completely, Korf agreed to abbreviate his first name to K, omit his second name, Friedrich, and Americanize his third name, Franz, to Frank. Thenceforth he would be known as K. Frank Korf.[122]

Many years later Korf wondered whether the exchange with the colonel had been in reality a test of his loyalty to the United States and its army. But Korf's experience was not unique—other soldiers of Korf's ilk had changed their names for fear of being shot as traitors if captured.[123] Regardless of the reason for the name change, Korf felt bound by the compromise he had reached with the colonel and kept the name K. Frank Korf for the rest of his life and introduced himself as "Frank" instead of "Kurt."

Shortly after Korf's interview with the colonel, he finally received the chance to do what he had wanted to do for some time—go to the front. He was directly assigned to HQ ETOUSA (Headquarters of the European Theater of Operations of the United States of America). In late December he was ordered to report for duty as an interpreter for military intelligence to Intelligence Mobile Unit 32, stationed in Namur, Belgium. The unit was assigned to obtain information from prisoners of war that pertained to long-range intelligence. The timing of Korf's transfer could not have been more auspicious, for Namur at the time was in the midst of the largest battle fought on the western front during World War II, the Battle of the Bulge.

4   Into the Abyss: 1944–1945

The Battle of the Bulge began on 16 December 1944, when the German army staged a surprise attack against the weakest section of the American front, which stretched for fifty miles between Monschau, Germany, and Echternach, Luxembourg. The focal point of the German offensive was the town of Bastogne, a major road junction. The battle raged for three weeks, and casualties were heavy on both sides, but in the end U.S. forces prevailed.[1] Korf remembered: "Bastogne held, and that was vital. The Germans never crossed the Meuse River; they were stalled there because they literally ran out of gas. I saw a tank abandoned in the field. But right behind Namur we had one of the largest gas depots. Had the Germans known about it, we would have had little resistance to offer and it could have prolonged the war quite a bit."[2] By the time of Korf's arrival shortly after Christmas, the battle was still in full swing. In this situation, everything had to be done in haste. He recalled: "There was no time to organize teams, equip and send them out. Specialists were needed immediately."

As Korf journeyed to the front lines, he felt confident about his intelligence team, which included four enlisted men (Sergeant Kurz, Technical Sergeant Kaufman, and Privates Koll and Koref); all had trained at Camp Ritchie. Two of them were Jewish; he did not know about the religious background of the others. As far as Korf was concerned, it made no difference. He and his men became a close-knit group. The enlisted men appreciated how Korf had attended to their needs during the harrowing crossing to England. All of them, by Korf's lights, "proved to be of great value to the war effort."[3]

As Korf traveled past abandoned farmlands in the vicinity of Namur, army trucks made stops to collect stacks of "Jerry cans"— five-gallon gasoline cases that had been dropped by a supply unit known as the "Red Ball Express," which got credit for refueling the army during the battle. Korf later learned that many members of the unit made a fortune selling gasoline on the black market in Paris. One man was rumored to have made so much money that he bought a brothel in Paris.

The trip to Namur was treacherous, because the Battle of the Bulge had expanded to the Meuse River north of Namur, and because most bridges over the river had been blown up to stop the advance of the Allied forces. In Namur, Korf and his men were put up in roofless houses and in a former prisoner-of-war enclosure. There was some grumbling among officers and intelligence specialists who had never suspected that they would come so close to actual combat. They were frequently heard to say that this was not their job. A postwar official evaluation of military intelligence service specialist teams bears this out: "The biggest single criticism of MIS personnel is their seemingly ingrained idea . . . that they are of a different mold than the average soldier, should be treated as such, be given unusual privileges, and allowed to be their own bosses."[4] Korf recalled that several of them were permitted to return to Paris without threat of a court-martial. Thanks to the departure of such men, Korf and his men were on duty most of the time at Namur. There was little opportunity for recreation. He saw a couple of movies in French with Flemish subtitles. The nightly spectacle consisted of watching German V-1 rockets flying overhead, headed for Antwerp and southern England.[5]

Korf was fascinated by the way the French and Belgians viewed the American soldiers. He reported to his wife: "Kids cling to your shirttail insisting upon 'gum,' the only English word they know.

They are convinced, and so are their parents and grandparents—
that Americans are some of the strangest people on earth, loaded
with chewing gum and money who jitterbug all night."[6]

Although the Battle of the Bulge was finally won by 7 January
1945, the war was far from over. Korf's job was to obtain information from German prisoners of war that would help to advance the
Allied assault on Germany. Korf remembered his day-to-day activities clearly: "Every morning we received from SHAEF a list of intelligence targets, arranged in the order of priority. Each officer had a
German POW non-commissioned officer handling the administration." Korf had no problems whatsoever dealing with the German
prisoners of war. He recalled, "They were good, they knew the business and they could be trusted, even though they were prisoners of
war. They returned to their enclosure at night."[7] Korf's men were
given lists of names of the latest arrivals among the POWs who
were high-ranking officers and their occupations. They were interrogated by military intelligence officers whose civilian occupations
most closely matched their own.

The work was not easy, but Korf seemed to enjoy the challenges
it presented for him. He remembered: "I always felt in interrogations that I had to get to the bottom of the brain of the other guy
and understand what he did. Once I was on a path with him I could
get the information. To get there was not easy"[8] In the first months
of 1945 his top priority was to acquire information from prisoners
about sources of fuel for the Allied advance into Germany. His job
was made easier when he found a familiar name on the list of recently captured prisoners of war: Wilhelm Graf von Magnis. He not
only was a gas officer with the 20th Panzer Division, but had also
been Korf's roommate and friend many years before at the Jesuit
boarding school in Breslau. Their reunion was unsettling at first;
Magnis was taken aback by seeing his old friend in an American
uniform, and Korf was surprised by Willie's gaunt and unkempt
appearance.[9]

After a few awkward moments, the two men reestablished their rapport. They chatted casually about Magnis's family, and Magnis mentioned that the Russians had seized many of his family's properties in East Prussia. Then Korf asked him how he became a gas officer. His prisoner replied that his uncle was commanding general of the 20th Division and had made his nephew a gas officer because the job was not particularly demanding. Korf then got to the point. "Do you have any gas?" Magnis replied, "Hell, no. Do you think they would have made me gas officer if they had any gas? If I did, I could kill most of the division by mistake." Korf persisted, "Are you sure you don't know anything about gas?" Magnis replied that Korf had to remember how poorly he had performed in his chemistry classes. Korf then recalled that Magnis had never scored higher than a D in the subject.

Korf believed Magnis. He immediately reported to his superiors at SHAEF that Magnis's 20th Panzer Division had no gas. He personally vouched for his old friend's statement on the subject. He also did his former chum a favor: "I marked him for transport to the United States. He would be safe there and he had earned it in my book."[10]

While some German soldiers gave him more trouble than others, none regarded Korf as a traitor. As he put it: "The strange thing is that during my whole time in Germany nobody ever treated me as a traitor. The fact was that the people had been . . . demoralized . . . [and] were so sick of this war; they wanted to get it over with and most of them had hoped the Americans would come. Which was mixed in a little bit with a feeling that the Russians might get there [first]. . . . The Germans . . . accepted us and they accepted us gladly because they knew everybody else was worse."[11] Korf's view of the Germans was not hostile, either. As he put it, "I was not there to destroy them. I was there to help the war and any kind of revenge would have been out of the question."[12]

One German prisoner did not even make a distinction between American and German officers. "An officer was an officer, period."

When Korf asked his German non-comm whether there was anything he could do to reward him for his hard work, the non-comm,
clicking his heels, replied, "Sir, I would appreciate it if you would
promote me to Feldwebel [master sergeant]." At first Korf thought
that the man was kidding. He wondered how an American officer
could possibly promote a German to a higher rank in the German
army. But the expression on the German man's face suggested otherwise. Korf felt that he had nothing to lose by making the man
happy. He asked the man for his Soldbuch, or army passport, and
wrote in his promotion. The next day the man reported to work
with the new stripes indicating his elevated rank.[13]

Such lighthearted episodes could not distract Korf from the devastation he had witnessed since going to the front. In February 1945
he wrote to his wife:

I wish you could *see* Europe, now. Not in years when all the terrible
wounds are healed, but now when they are bleeding, and when people
mourn their tortured relatives, wives their imprisoned husbands—away
for 5 years and longer—when homes are still in shambles, and the rain and
snow blow into the unheated, glass-less rooms, when hands are swollen
from rheuma[tism] and teeth are cracking from lack of vitamins. If you
could see people who still tremble when the [air raid] bell rings, over 7
months after they are liberated, if you could *hear* these terrible night-
mares—you would bless us all for being over here.[14]

The letter made quite an impression on Rita, who replied: "Your
description of the conditions was so vivid [that] I could feel the
tortures, the starvation, the bitter cold that those poor people have
felt. Most likely you are right when you say that we should bless
you all for being there and helping."[15]

On one occasion Korf was able to help a mentally unstable soldier. One day a member of his team, Koref, complained that a fellow
soldier quite literally stank because he refused to wash or bathe.
Korf replied, "Koref, you know what to do when a man stinks—

wash him!" Koref and others obliged by throwing the fully uni-
formed man into the shower and scrubbing him with yellow lime
soap. This, however, did not solve the problem. Korf talked to the
man and discovered that he did not wash because he did not want
to go to the front. Korf found a solution to the problem by having
the troublesome soldier transferred back to headquarters in Le Vesinet, where he became a shower orderly. When Korf went back to
Le Vesinet after the war he found "the happiest and cleanest shower
orderly" he had ever seen.[16]

Korf discovered that insubordination was not limited to U.S. ser-
vicemen. He interrogated a German officer who disobeyed orders to
blow up the Ludendorff Bridge over the Rhine River at Remagen in
March 1945. The officer explained that the bridge had been mined
at all four corners with heavy loads of explosives. He then sent his
men to a railroad tunnel to shelter them from the blast. He began
making his way toward the tunnel and dropped to all fours as he
heard American artillery near the bridge.

But as he crawled away the officer began to think of his home
on the other side of the bridge, which was in enemy hands. He
realized that if the bridge was destroyed, he might never see his
family again. He therefore made a snap decision to stop the destruction of the bridge. He crawled to each demolition pile and used the
edge of his military shovel to cut the wires to the explosives. After
watching the Americans cross the bridge, he went back to his men
in the tunnel and was captured there. His capture saved his life,
because Hitler court-martialed and executed four other officers who
had failed to destroy the bridge.[17] The seizure of the bridge helped
establish the first Allied bridgehead across the Rhine, which in effect hastened the Allied advance toward Berlin.

What Korf learned from the officer constituted but one of many
theories concerning what happened at Remagen. In the 1950s Ken
Hechler interviewed Korf for his book *The Bridge at Remagen*.
Hechler did not incorporate Korf's account. Instead, Hechler concluded that the "rumbling vibrations of American tank fire" disabled

the firing mechanism of the bombs. This forced the Germans to set off a backup device, which damaged but failed to blow up the bridge.[18] The prominent World War II historian Stephen Ambrose, on the other hand, holds that "the wire leading to the Germans' demolitions had been cut by a stray bullet."[19]

Though the events surrounding the capture of the bridge remain in dispute, the fact remains that the seizure of the bridge constituted a great victory for the Allies. Eisenhower recalled the news as "one of my happy moments in the war." Approximately eight thousand U.S. troops crossed the bridge before it collapsed on 17 March 1945, killing twenty-seven American soldiers.[20]

As Korf's unit pushed farther eastward toward Germany, his first priority was to get information about his mother, who he suspected was residing on a family estate in nearby Lippstadt.. One day he interrogated a German officer by the name of LeMaitre, who happened to be from Lippstadt. Korf asked him what had become of the town. Korf learned that his uncle's home had been destroyed, but that his grandmother's house was still intact. Korf dispatched LeMaitre to a POW camp in the States. He also sent LeMaitre's wife an anonymous note telling her that her husband was safe.[21]

But although the American advance eastward progressed toward Lippstadt, Korf and his men remained behind the front lines. This was not what Korf wanted. He could not get to his mother if he remained behind the lines handling long-range intelligence. A transfer to combat intelligence, Korf reasoned, would put him closer to the front and his mother. To get the transfer, Korf had to report first to the headquarters of the 97th Infantry Division of the Third Army at Camp Lucky Strike in northern France. Headquarters proceeded to "attach" Korf and his men to the G-2 Section of the 97th Division of the Third Army for combat. What this meant was that while Korf's duties would now be performed for the 97th Division, his chain of command still went through his original assignment with HQ ETOUSA. The army had made a practice of attaching units during the heat of battle as they were needed, rather than subjecting them to the lengthy and cumbersome process of transfer.[22]

On 23 March 1945 Korf was put in charge of MII (Military Intelligence Interpreter) Combat Intelligence Team 537-G (G stood for Germany) with the 97th Infantry Division. The team's primary mission was to obtain intelligence from German citizens. This appointment came with a promotion to the rank of captain. He was told that the promotion would be delivered in the field.[23]

The 97th Infantry Division was commanded by Brigadier General Milton B. Halsey (a nephew of Admiral William Halsey, hero of the Pacific Theater of Operations). General Halsey asked Korf when he reported for duty, "Lieutenant, what is your mission?" Korf replied, "Sir, I have not the faintest idea, but I will do my best." Halsey laughed. Korf attended the general's first meeting with his staff, which included his assistant chief of staff, Lieutenant Colonel Fitzpatrick, and his deputy and the OIC (officer in charge) of the various intelligence teams. The assignment of the division was to press into Germany. Halsey said to Korf, "You are with the forward element." At that moment, Korf recalled, he felt "an icy chill going down my spine." He knew that his combat intelligence team would reconnoiter with the army advance into Germany. Korf was to remain on the general's staff with Koref. Halsey then added that the other three men on Korf's team would be attached to each of the three regiments. Korf would accompany each man with his respective regiment when it went into combat.[24]

The trip back into Germany was unsettling. Nothing seemed familiar. "I had been in that countryside before, but now I had no idea where I was," Korf recalled. The area was completely deserted; only ruins remained. He finally saw a large sign that read, "You are now entering Germany through the courtesy of the First Infantry Division." He also saw remnants of the Maginot Line and passed the historic city of Aachen (Aix-la-Chapelle), where Emperor Charlemagne had been crowned in the year 800. Korf remembered, "The city burned like one torch."[25]

He wrote to his wife about his uneasiness in being back in his homeland: "It might sound funny, but it is the truth: I am inside Germany now. Things happened very fast and slowly. I am trying to account for them myself. . . . I am glad to be in this, as we hope, last big cleanup."[26] He did not wax nostalgic about the country of his birth at all. As he wrote to Rita: "I am already well in Germany—it is indeed an interesting trip, very interesting. . . . But then I would like to get home as quickly as possible. . . . I want to be together with you in the good old States, a country where you can breathe in peace and where there is peace in the hearts."[27]

Their next stop was München Gladbach (Mönchengladbach since 1950), located on the left bank of the Rhine opposite Düsseldorf. Korf drove up to the riverbank to get a view of the situation. He then heard a loud whooshing sound and instinctively hit the dirt. He soon realized that he was in the path of an eighty-eight-millimeter gun, "the most accurate and deadly that the Germans had. It could drill a neat hole through a stack of books, and could be moved easily and we could be folded easily."

General Halsey's deputy, Major Ramsey, called a meeting and asked Korf and his men what they knew about the defenses around Düsseldorf. They did not know much; they had drawn heavy artillery fire and assumed that the defenses were adequate. Aerial photos showed numerous eighty-eight-millimeter batteries and troops in and around the city. It was only later that Korf learned that the locations revealed on the photos were part of an elaborate ruse: "We learned that the Germans had only about half of the artillery pieces shown on the photo cover. They had cut tree trunks the size of artillery pieces and moved them around at night. The troop movements were done with empty trucks."

To get a closer look, Ramsey elected to send two patrol boats across the river at night. Conditions were favorable for crossing the river because there was no moon and light cloud cover. Korf wished to go along, but Ramsey refused: "We would have no replacements for you. We cannot get new intelligence people after all the losses we have had." Ramsey was right. Not one man returned from the mission. This incident made it clear to Halsey that an attack across the river was too risky, and he moved his troops south. They traveled past Koblenz and the now partially submerged bridge at Remagen and made it to Siegburg, northeast of Bonn. Though they encountered some resistance, they got into town safely.

Korf picked one of the best homes in the town as his headquarters. Despite his opulent surroundings, he and his men could not sleep because the Germans bombed the town all night. The next day Korf got down to business and began to elicit information from the locals. It was not difficult to get them to cooperate. He threw one woman an envelope with Nescafé coffee. Delighted, she waved him over. She said, "You see that house? It was a brewery and the owner has left the town. But he has a large cache of wine, liquor and champagne in the cellar. It is walled up now." When Korf investigated, the brewery was in ruins, but the cellar was intact. Korf was prevented from investigating further by the outbreak of enemy fire. He and his men withdrew from Siegburg, but Korf made a mental note of the location of the liquor cellar.[28]

A few days later, the army retook Siegburg. Korf went to the cellar with a set of tools. Once he broke down a wall, he gained entry to a spacious storage facility filled with an excellent collection of German and French liqueurs and wines. The next problem he had to confront was how to distribute the booty "without raising any hackles." Korf decided to do it by rank. First, cases of Champagne were sent to the provost marshal and to the commanding general. Then each of Korf's men filled trailers with whatever they wanted. Korf took several bottles for himself and sent the rest to the G-2 with the recommendation that each man in the division be given a bottle. He later learned that his instructions had duly been carried out: "The stuff did not get stuck with the officers." Thanks to Korf, Siegburg became a place that the division would not soon forget.

Many months later, when Korf was interrogating German POWs, he ran across the man who had owned the liquor hoard. He was a high-ranking member of the Nazi party and a desk officer. Korf resented him because he had "never smelled gunpowder," and he was smug to boot. Put off by the prisoner's attitude, Korf barked, "Wipe off that smile. We found your cache of liquor and drank it." That, said Korf, soured the prisoner's mood considerably.[29]

In Siegburg Korf had his first opportunity to observe the interaction between the German population and American troops. Though Korf had little difficulty dealing with German prisoners of war, the civilians had been led by propaganda to believe that all Americans were "gangsters" bent on harming Germans. Korf sensed this mutual hostility when he attended Easter services at a local church in April 1945. As he reported to his wife:

Inside [the church] the people stared at me, and I had plenty of room for myself. The folks were all dolled up for Easter. They look much healthier and better-fed tha[n] the people in France, Belgium and Holland. . . . Their spirit does not seem to be broken, even if they are plenty scared. The whole relationship between population and soldiers is so much different from other countries; the kids do not come up to you, the folks look straight ahead, as we do. Some will tell you they are disappointed because they have been waiting for us all the time. Hell, why did we have to fight for this place then?[30]

Despite this uneasiness, Korf had little difficulty getting information out of the Germans.[31] An evaluation of military intelligence specialist teams written just after the war corroborates this. The report noted: "Information from German civilians was . . . reliable, according to a great many G-2s. Though initially reticent, the average German, when pressed, would divulge information that generally proved precise and accurate."[32]

Some Germans were easier to talk to than others. Germans who held positions of authority were usually members of the Nazi party.

Korf saw that some tried to hide their identities; they "tried to blend into the woodwork and become as inconspicuous as possible." Others, he recalled, "tried to cooperate to get brownie points"; they did not hesitate to "rat" on their former comrades in arms.

In Siegburg, Korf also encountered members of the pro-Nazi "Werewolf" movement, which committed acts of sabotage against the Allies as a last line of defense against the invasion. When they were apprehended, nails and wire were found in their pockets. When Korf interrogated them, he found that they were only sixteen years old, looked like Hitler youths, and were scared. They had all sorts of explanations for the contents of their pockets, but finally they divulged the truth. They had participated in a "fitness course" given by party members and had volunteered for the "Werewolf movement." They had been given instructions on how to sabotage U.S. phone lines. Their catalogue of sabotage possibilities was endless and the means were simple.[33]

Korf now had to decide what to do with the young men. Under the terms of the Geneva Convention, they could have been shot as franc-tireurs, or civilians committing acts of war. But Korf shrank from doing this. Instead, he instructed his sergeant to find the parents of the young men. After they arrived Korf apprised them of what their sons had done. Korf added: "You are guilty, more so than your boys. You knew what they were doing or should have known."[34]

After chastising the parents, Korf had them sign an agreement promising that the boys would be punished and confined to their homes. Korf warned the parents that if the boys were ever caught again, they would be treated as prisoners of war. Korf was gratified that he could save these boys from a far worse fate. He had heard reports that some Nazi youth leaders had thrown youths in front of their own German troops, expecting to stem the American advance. Tragically, the Americans did not realize that the "troops" were mostly boys and had mowed them down. In disgust, Korf observed: "The Nazis deliberately sacrificed their children in their desperation to hold up our advance. Only cowards have their children fight a war."[35]

Korf's duties included establishing contact with the anti-Nazi underground. He interviewed a man who said he was from the ANTIFA, or antifascist group. The ANTIFA was a new name for an old organization, the communists. The man had valuable documents, including maps of minefields and information about the location of German gun emplacements in areas where the Americans were planning their next attack. The advance knowledge that the ANTIFA member supplied helped to spare many American lives.

Although many lives were saved, Korf almost lost his own when he was ordered to give a general a tour of the front. The general had come to Germany directly from the Pentagon. He now wanted to see what battlefield action was like and asked for a ride along the battlefront. Korf was not particularly happy to drop everything to give a tour to a man who "had commanded from a safe distance." Korf was assigned to drive the jeep, and the G-2 accompanied them. Soon enough the general got what he wanted when their jeep came under sniper fire. Korf recalled that one bullet "zipped right through the front and rear seat of the jeep." The general ordered Korf to stop driving, but Korf ignored him and drove away as quickly as possible. When they reached safety, the general was irate that Korf had disobeyed him. His face, Korf recalled, "was beet-red with anger." Korf said, "Sir, haven't you ever heard small arms fire close up?" The general did not reply.[36] Korf could well have been reprimanded for disobeying a superior officer. Though he was not, it is likely that the episode may have cost Korf promotion to a higher rank down the line.

On another occasion, the "army way" caused Korf to surrender to his own army. One evening Korf met his men in a farmhouse on the right bank of the Rhine River to discuss their mission. They spoke in German. Korf espied an American GI crouching near a window listening to their conversation. He disappeared. Shortly thereafter, four jeeps suddenly drove up to the farmhouse. Several men jumped out with their weapons trained on Korf and his men. A captain entered and demanded that Korf and his party surrender. When Korf asked why, the captain did not reply and proceeded to herd him and his men into the jeeps.

Korf knew quite well why he was being detained. He had heard of a special German army group named after their leader, Waffen SS Officer Otto Skorzeny. His commando group was composed of English-speaking Germans who posed as American GIs. The Skorzeny men caused a lot of trouble during the Battle of the Bulge when they slipped behind enemy lines, cut communications wires, changed road signs, and wired false information to U.S. troops.[37] Because Korf and his men were spotted wearing American uniforms and speaking German, they were mistaken for Skorzeny men.

The captain asked Korf for his orders. Korf replied that they were secret and that he was not permitted to show them to him. The captain's response was to aim his .45-caliber weapon at Korf. They drove away in Korf's jeep at a high speed. Inside the jeep trailer was his cache of liquor seized from Siegburg. Korf asked, "Captain, do me a favor and drive a little more slowly? I have wine in the trailer and the bottles are liable to break." The captain did not reply. To Korf's chagrin, he heard a bottle break.

The group drove up to a castle that served as army headquarters. The captain had radioed ahead that he had captured an "enemy" unit. As Korf entered the castle grounds, he saw that the troops were prepared to confront the enemy: "The guards stood at attention . . . [and] the colonel was standing majestically at the top of a long flight of outdoor stairs, surrounded by his staff." Korf got out of the jeep and asked the captain to allow his men to remain in their jeeps. "I did not want him to be more embarrassed than necessary." After Korf saluted the colonel, he asked to speak to him and the captain alone. He then pulled out his orders, marked "secret," and showed them to the colonel. After reading them, the colonel's face reddened, and he said, "Captain, how could you make such mistake and think that they are spies in our uniform? These are our own intelligence people."

The captain cringed. Korf, however, defended the captain. "I think the captain did his duty. We have had cases where Skorzeny men have tried to infiltrate, and caution is better than negligence." The only thing that upset Korf about the incident was that some of his captured liquor was gone. He mildly chastised the captain for driving so fast: "You broke so many bottles; there was no hurry to get here."[38] The captain could only nod in agreement.

As Korf and his men made their way north toward Düsseldorf, they liberated POW Camp Hoffnungsthal. They found close to 800 prisoners, 177 of whom were Americans captured during the Battle of the Bulge. Though Americans had been generally treated well at German POW camps, Hoffnungsthal marked an exception to the rule. Korf was prepared for the fact that wartime shortages could account for the poor condition of the inmates. But what he saw went beyond shortages. He described conditions as "gruesome." He learned that prisoners had been wantonly abused. An American pilot who had shattered both legs parachuting from his plane was forced to walk to the camp and denied medical treatment. They also found thirty-three cases of dysentery. The prisoners were evacuated immediately.

The next batch of German prisoners yielded important information about the German secret police, or Gestapo. On 15 April 1945 Korf interrogated a man named Hans Zensus, who worked as a chauffeur for the Cologne branch of the Gestapo. Zensus led Korf and his men to a place where the remnants of the Gestapo Cologne were hiding out. Korf and his men raided the hideout, with backup from the CIC (Counterintelligence Corps).[39] More than a dozen Gestapo agents were captured.

In the process of sorting out the prisoners after the raid, the regular Gestapo were separated from the SD, or Sicherheitsdienst, men. The latter were "professional murderers licensed to kill anywhere, at any time." The interrogations of the captured men went on into the night. Korf gained an indelible impression of the Gestapo and how it worked:

The picture that emerged was that of an incredibly finely honed machine that had only one goal: to get rid of all opposition, even if this meant getting rid of one of their own men. Any means that ensured success were permitted from poison to shooting in the street. No one was allowed to escape. The people I dealt with in the house were all professionals, hardened professionals. Concentration camps were [but] one of the means [used by the Gestapo to keep the people in line].[40]

One of the prisoners was a striking young woman who claimed that she had been kidnapped and tortured by the Gestapo. Korf was skeptical. He asked, "How badly were you beaten? Show us your marks." The woman replied that she was beaten with wet towels, which did not leave marks. Korf thought that the story sounded fishy. Korf let her go, but he later learned that she had been the interpreter for the head of the Gestapo in Paris. When Korf and his men went to arrest her, she was found in bed with a CIC man who had apparently believed in her innocence. A search of the bedroom yielded boxes of captured weapons. Korf allowed her to get dressed before she was handcuffed and taken away.[41]

Korf also obtained crucial information that helped the U.S. Army capture the city of Düsseldorf. Korf's talks with Dr. A. Widerhofen and Alois Odenthal, who led the "Freies Deutschland" (Free Germany) resistance movement, yielded information about the city defenses and provided directions for safe entry into the city for U.S. troops. A few days later, on 17 April 1945, American troops went into Düsseldorf, and Korf was part of the first assault wave. He rode into the city in a jeep directly behind the first three tanks to enter the city. Thanks to Korf's information, the assault battalion was able to avoid tank traps and the entry was accomplished without loss of American lives.[42]

When he asked a woman for directions to police headquarters in German, she replied that if Korf hadn't been wearing an American uniform, she would have sworn that he was born in Düsseldorf. She was right, for Korf was born only a few miles away from the city. Korf thought, "What a way to meet again!"[43]

Korf was among the first to enter the police headquarters. As the Germans ran out of the building into its courtyard with hands raised in surrender, Korf ordered: "Police to the right, Gestapo on the left. Leave your weapons in the middle." They obeyed. One policeman strode toward Korf and volunteered to give him the keys to the main safe of the department. Korf ordered him to stand still. He then ran upstairs into the office of the police commissioner. He passed by a large conference room with a long table. At the end of the table he saw a life-size painting of Hitler. All Korf's anger toward the man who dishonored his family and ruined his homeland welled up inside him. Perhaps recalling the fact that the first thing that had impressed Korf about Hitler was that the latter had the "eyes of a madman," Korf shot both eyes out of the portrait.[44]

Immediately thereafter the phone rang in the commissioner's office. Korf answered it. He was informed by a breathless man that the Ammis (Americans) were coming. Korf couldn't resist asking, "Where are they?" "They're already in the suburbs." Korf asked, "And where are you?" The man on the other end realized what was going on. He laughed briefly and said, "I guess they are already there." Korf replied, "You are right," as the line went dead.[45]

When he returned to the courtyard, Korf found "everything in flux"; only the man who told Korf he had keys to the department safe was standing in the middle of the courtyard, "stock-still." When Korf asked what he was doing, he replied, "You told me to stay where I was." Korf now asked him to lead the way to the safe. It was housed in a small room on the second floor. The man slept in the room on a small cot. "He pulled out the cot and took three pieces of metal out of his pocket. He folded the three pieces into each other. They fit like a puzzle. He then turned the wheel and finally used the key, which by now had become rather long."

The man began to open the safe, but Korf told him that he did not want to go in without witnesses. He found a colonel, and they entered the vault, which was filled to capacity with valuables from other public buildings in the city that had been bombed out. Korf observed the bags and boxes in the room. He then ordered the policeman to lock the safe. Korf put the key into his left breast pocket. After Korf's division took the nearby town of Solingen, he returned to Düsseldorf, which in the meantime had been taken by the British. He informed British authorities about the safe and handed the key over. He was given a receipt, which read: "Received from Lt. Korf this date (18 April 1945) the keys to the safe of the chief of police of Düsseldorf, Germany. Joseph R. Reed, Major, CMP G-5." Korf later learned that the British uncovered valuables worth 20 million dollars in the safe. He never found out what became of them.[46]

Korf discovered that the police headquarters at Düsseldorf had been one of the last two strongholds of the German SS. He proceeded to act as an interpreter for Brigadier General Halsey and Lieutenant Colonel Fitzpatrick. By the evening of 17 April Korf's division controlled the major sections of the city. Korf's work was praised by his superiors, who told him that he would be recommended for a Bronze Star. Unfortunately, that information somehow never reached the appropriate channels, and Korf never received the award.[47]

After several hectic days, Korf and his men had completed most of their work in the Düsseldorf area. The American POWs had been evacuated, the Gestapo team had been sent to POW camps, and weapons seized from the Germans had been removed. As Korf observed these operations, he was joined by General Halsey, who asked Korf about the best place for accommodations in the city. "Lieutenant, aren't you from around here?" the general asked, adding, "Where do we go next?" Korf replied, "The Park Hotel, follow me." Korf was the first to enter the hotel. He found the general manager and two of his executives standing at the top of the main stairway, flapping a bedsheet as a sign of surrender. Korf assumed that he would be staying in a grand room on the second floor once occupied by German Field Marshal Walther Model. Korf went to the room and surveyed his opulent accommodations. Model had left in a hurry; his bed was still unmade. Then Korf heard a knock on the door. It was the General Halsey's adjutant, who announced that the general would be staying in the field marshal's old quarters.[48]

The next day Korf and his men tried to find Model. They had a tip that he was trying to seek asylum at the residence of the Swiss consul general outside Düsseldorf. They raced to the residence and crashed through the front gate, only to be informed by the Swiss consul that the general was not there. Though they followed more leads, they never found him. A year later Korf learned that Model had committed suicide rather than risk possible extradition to Russia.[49]

Having liberated Düsseldorf and Solingen, Korf received orders for the next mission, which would take him and his men across Germany on a southeastern route. The mission was secret: "All identification marks had to be removed from all vehicles," Korf recalled.

News of the mission forced Korf to make an important decision. His unit was only seventy-five miles from his mother's family residence in Lippstadt, but the upcoming mission would take him hundreds of miles farther away from there. Korf wanted to see her before he left. Not knowing what the future held as the war raged around him, he was determined to see her for perhaps the last time. As he told Rita: "There is a little underthought and I know that you understand it: my mother. Next to my great wish to make you happy, that is the immediate task and it will not be an easy one." From this it was clear that Korf was going to do just about anything to go to his mother's aid. Knowing that Rita would be understandably concerned about this, he added: "Do not worry about me, all our lives are in the Lord's hands and he will do what he thinks best.

I will try everything in my power and with my honor to come home to you safely."[50]

He asked Major Ramsey for a twenty-four-hour leave of absence and a jeep. It is amazing in retrospect that Ramsay even considered the possibility of allowing an intelligence officer to take a jeep behind enemy lines alone. Nonetheless, he agreed to look the other way about the jeep, but he granted him only nine hours of leave. Ramsey gave Korf instructions about where he could rejoin his unit and warned him, "Be sure that you find us, because this is a secret move."

As Korf drove through familiar territory toward Lippstadt, he thought it strange that his adopted country would soon invade it. He tried to approach Lippstadt through the Möhne valley, but he discovered that Germans had bombed the dam, which had flooded the roads. He had to go around it. The detour was time-consuming; he had to proceed quickly if he was to have any hope of rejoining his unit.[51]

Several times during his journey he was approached by German soldiers who wished to surrender to him. He responded, "No time!" and drove on. He also drove past a nice stereo-telescope that he espied at an abandoned enemy artillery site. He resolved to pick it up on his way back, but by that time it was gone.

He finally reached Lippstadt. Though denizens stared at Korf as though he were "from Mars; they had never seen an American in uniform before," they did not confront or challenge him. When he reached his family home, his mother emerged and said simply, "There you are," and threw her arms around his neck. His grandmother, his Aunt Mimi, and their servant of many years, Martha, joyously greeted him. Korf unloaded his jeep, which was full of supplies, including part of the cache of fine wines and liquors "liberated" from the cellar in Siegburg. Korf described the reunion as "wonderful; it made the whole war worthwhile." He wrote to his wife: "I found my mother. It was pretty hard, as you might imagine, but I succeeded. She looks well as ever, is healthy and has kept her old sense of humor. . . . She got pretty excited, of course, when I came through the door, but calmed down soon. . . . She is very much afraid 'to be a burden' to us, but I know that you agree with me that she comes over as qucily [*sic*] and speedily as possible."[52] All too soon, he had to leave. Though the brevity of the reunion was wrenching, he was grateful that he and his mother had found each other after so many years.[53] When Korf's friend Ernst Linde, who was serving with the Sixth Army, heard what Korf had done, he wrote to him, "I'm glad to hear that you succeeded in a mission which had been your goal since the beginning of the war."[54]

The trip back was a nightmare. Though the Germans did not confront him in any way, unexploded bombs and grenades made the roads impassable. He finally saw a long column of soldiers on the road, "miles long, moving like a blur—[it was] my division. I quickly blended into the long gray line, next to my men." In the wake of his perilous journey to see his mother and his reunion with his unit, Korf had to fight extreme exhaustion as the division moved forward: "In retrospect, it looks like I moved through a long, dark tunnel. We moved and moved. Ten-minutes breaks every hour. Night fell and the dark enveloped us. We were allowed small head-lamps to see the car in front. It started to blur and then the light seemed to fade. I stared at the ditch, directly in front of me. I must have fallen asleep. I shouldn't have. I hit myself in the face and yelled just to keep awake."[55]

The division drove across Germany into the Bavarian Forest close to the Czech border and made camp near the town of Weiden. Korf and his men had no idea about their final destination or mission. But the first German prisoner whom Korf interrogated gave him a hint: "You are two days late, he said. "We have been expecting you. We are the German 97th Infantry Division." Korf was amazed at the accuracy of their intelligence.[56]

Soon enough, more and more prominent Germans were captured and interrogated. As Korf put it, "As the net got tighter we got bigger fish." When he spoke to the mayor of the town of Marktrewitz on 26 April, Korf noticed that his interpreter's command of the English language was "a little too perfect." When Korf asked the mayor how long he had been using the interpreter, the mayor replied, "Not very long, but he is invaluable." Korf thought so as well. The interpreter wore well-tailored clothing and was a man "of great polish." But Korf soon discovered that his story "was not very polished." After extensive interrogation, Korf learned that the interpreter was a member of the highest echelon of the Office for Foreign Information and Counter-Intelligence. In other words, he was part of the same agency that had pressed Korf about his knowledge of synthetic oil back in 1936 and had forced his hand about leaving Germany.[57]

Korf and his men had been mistaken for Skorzeny men, but he had the chance to capture a contingent of the real thing after a German civilian informed him that a large contingent of about two hundred officers and noncommissioned officers were in a hideout close to Weiden. Korf believed that the civilian was in reality a member of the unit who had been dispatched as an emissary to feel out the terms of surrender. The emissary agreed to lead Korf and his men to the location of his unit. Korf had only four men available to assist him, so he asked Captain Grimes, the officer in charge of the CIC, for additional help. After clearing their mission with Major Ramsay and the G-2, Korf and Grimes put together a unit of about fifty men in two armed trucks.[58]

As they headed out to capture the Skorzeny unit, Korf, who was riding with Grimes, realized that he had forgotten his carbine. He asked if he could be dropped off at his quarters to get it. When he stepped out of his quarters, however, he was dismayed to discover that Grimes had left him behind. Grimes's mission to capture the Skorzeny unit was successful and he received a Bronze Star for his efforts.[59]

Korf's duties kept him too busy to dwell on his disappointment over his failure to be a part of the mission to capture the Skorzeny men. In late April he reported to his wife:

Never I would have thought that there is not even enough time to read letters, but it is true and I surely lived through the most interesting and exciting time of my life. We will hardly have to go to the movies, as all the long evenings are filled with stories far mor[e] interesting and catchy as any producer can think of. . . . It is amazing how well off the Germans still are. There does not seem to be a lack of anything, except coffee and oranges. And that while—or because—the rest of Europe is scraping meals out of garbage cans.[60]

Shortly after Korf made this remark, he came face to face with the horrors perpetrated by the Nazis. One day at the end of April 1945 Korf reported to Major Ramsey, who told Korf to follow him into a jeep. Nothing was said about where they were going. The major, Korf, and Captain Bucknell, the medical officer, drove over slick roads. They finally arrived at a large enclosure. The metal plate on the entrance gate said "Schutzhaftlager" (Protective Custody Camp), on the left, "Arbeit macht frei" (labor liberates). It was the infamous concentration camp Flossenbürg.[61] Korf soon learned that his mission was to help camp victims and apprehend the SS officers responsible for their suffering.

Many historians fault American forces for not specifically concentrating on liberating the camps, especially when the defeat of Nazi Germany appeared to be inevitable. This charge is valid, according to Korf. He recalled, "I don't think our own division targeted Flossenbürg. Like many other camps, Flossenbürg was opened up in the broad military sweep that was taking place at that time."[62]

For a long time Korf believed that he was one of the first to liberate the camp, but when he attended the Liberators Conference sponsored by the U.S. Holocaust Memorial Council in 1981, he learned that this was not necessarily the case. Members of the 358th and 359th Infantry Regiments of the 90th Infantry Division told Korf that they had entered the camp on 23 April—five days before Korf's arrival. Korf himself admitted in a letter to the U.S. Holocaust Memorial Council that, "considering the flux which is normal to combat and the fact that Flossenbürg was not actually defended, it is hard to say who the liberator was, the 97th or the 90th division."[63]

Korf was quite right on this point, for the question as to who precisely liberated the camp still remains a subject of dispute. The archives of the Holocaust Memorial Museum contain testimonies of several members of the 90th who claimed to have been the first to enter the camp on or around 23 April. This account clashes with a memoir of the veteran of the 97th, Bob Hacker, who claims that members of *both* the 90th and the 97th divisions liberated the camp.[64] For Hacker it is not surprising that members of both divisions have taken credit for liberating the camp. He explains: "The 97th had just completed their move from Solingen in the Ruhr area near Düsseldorf. For most moves division patches and identification of vehicles were removed to hinder German intelligence from identifying new units in their area. Without identification, most individuals would believe that everyone was from their division."[65]

When Korf entered the camp he learned that only medics and intelligence officers were permitted. Soldiers were denied entry for fear that they might be exposed to diseases of the prisoners such as typhus and cholera.[66] Ramsey also feared the soldiers' reactions to the horrors of the camp; he reasoned that their mission to investigate the camp would be compromised if battle-hardened American troops took their vengeance on German camp guards, who were needed as witnesses. His reasoning proved to be correct, for on 29 April—the very day that he and Korf entered Flossenbürg—American soldiers went berserk while liberating Dachau. The historian Christopher Robbins reports what happened when troops saw thirty-nine railroad cars filled with rotting corpses:

GIs began to throw up. Some broke down and wept, others entered a frozen zone of deep shock, while some exploded into vengeful combat rage. "Let's kill every one of these bastards," GIs started yelling. "Don't take any SS alive!" . . . SS prisoners were herded into a coal yard, lined up and told to keep their hands above their heads. When they saw a GI load a belt of ammo into a machine gun they panicked and bolted. The machine gun opened fire and seventeen were killed. . . . It was difficult to control the men as hardened combat troops exploded under the strain.[67]

Korf, Ramsey, and the doctor went to the administration building. Korf asked an inmate to show him books containing records of prisoners' arrival and departure from the camp. The inmate emerged with a large leather book. When Korf examined it, he found entries had been made in pencil; the pages were hard to read because the paper was nearly rubbed through by erasures. A stamp in the form of a cross appeared beside most of the names. Korf immediately understood how this system worked: "The names of inmates brought to the camp were written in pencil, so that the names could and would be erased when they had died. I hardly could guess how many men were covered by a single line and when the death stamp had been added."[68]

When Korf asked for files on the inmates, he was informed that files of deceased inmates were burned; only a few files of discharged prisoners remained. Korf read the camp record of a young Czech man who was arrested and sent to Flossenbürg. His arrest was part of a large-scale purge that occurred after the 1942 assassination of Reinhard Heydrich, the Nazi ruler of occupied Czechoslovakia and architect of the annihilation of Jews in Poland. The inmate's papers included a telegram to the Flossenbürg commander from Himmler, ordering that the Czech receive twenty-five lashes with a whip upon arrival at the camp. In what Korf describes as "typical Germanic order," the follow-up document to the punishment was a statement from the camp physician to the effect that the prisoner had been beaten according to protocol in such matters. He was subsequently put to work at the stone quarry. The file also contained several petitions to the commandant from the prisoner's mother, who wished to send packages of socks and sweaters to her son. Most petitions were denied.[69] The man was ultimately released and admonished never to speak about prison conditions.

As he toured the camp, Korf met a young camp inmate. When Korf asked who he was, the man replied that he was the son of the Michelin tire manufacturing family. He had been sent to the camp as a hostage. He weighed only ninety-five pounds. Korf arranged to have food sent to him.[70]

Korf also found that the inmates had been neatly grouped according to categories of "offense." There were religious offenders, habitual criminals, political prisoners, homosexuals, and racial offenders. The last category was subdivided into four groups: Jews, Aryans who had relationships with Jews, Jews who had relationships with Aryans, and gypsies.

The next shock that Korf received was his tour to the crematorium:

I saw piles to my right and left as I entered. I looked closer in the dim light. They were corpses. They looked very much like railroad ties, dark and close together, hands on their sides, skeletal legs straight. At that moment I felt that I should lose my mind. But a miracle happened. It was like a veil was suddenly put before my eyes. I saw clearly, but did not feel. . . . I seemed to be in a haze for the next few days. The terrible things I saw did not seem to penetrate until much later, but the views were needle-sharp.[71]

He later recalled how he was able to deal with the shocking scene: "At that moment, I must say, well, the good Lord took over and I was like a bear, I saw everything, and it [was] just [as if I] was immunized. I functioned beautifully, but I did not . . . fully absorb the events until much later."[72]

Other liberators felt the same way. Victor Wegard, a member of the War Crimes Investigation Team on Flossenbürg, recalled: "It was as if a specter of death was floating through the air and ready to strike us all. . . . The shock of the first sight of humans in the camp is a blow; thereafter quick recovery is required. You can't let it get to you."[73] William McConahey, a physician with the 90th Infantry Division who entered the camp on 23 April, observed, "I'll never forget the visit. . . . What a cesspool of human suffering and degradation! One who has not seen it cannot visualize it in his mind, and I am sure that one who has not lived through the never-ending days and nights of terror in such a place cannot possibly comprehend a fraction of its misery."[74] General Dwight Eisenhower summed up the feelings of all these men when he observed that "of all the distressing memories that will forever live with American veterans of the war in Europe, none will be sharper or more enduring that those of the DPs and of the horror camps established by the Nazis."[75]

When Korf was able to process his feelings later on, his distress was even more pronounced because he was born a German. He was ashamed about what had happened. "I mean, I knew there were decent Germans, but that a whole country could participate in the dirtiest, filthiest, shameless acts the world has ever seen! It's still beyond my comprehension. And it wounded me deeply. Aside from anything else, it was a deep hurt."[76]

As Korf continued his tour of the camp, it became clear that the camp henchmen had left in haste; though the fire of the crematorium was out, there were still corpses ready to be burned. In the back of the crematorium was a room with a concrete table; it was here that gold teeth were removed from corpses. Korf was amazed by a sign on the wall over the sink that read, "Do not forget to wash your hands." Korf saw the places were camp victims were hanged. He could tell from the crude construction of the gallows that the victims died in agony. He later learned that Dietrich Bonhoeffer, one of the leading Protestant theologians and a vocal opponent of the Nazi regime, was hanged at Flossenbürg just before the American troops arrived.[77] Admiral Wilhelm Canaris, the head of the Reich's counterintelligence who had participated in the 1944 plot to kill Hitler, had suffered a similar fate a few weeks earlier.

Other prominent prisoners were housed in a VIP barracks. Korf discovered that "it originally had been built as a bordello . . . [but] when the commandant received a wire telling him to ready a building for the King of Belgium, King Leopold, and his wife, the former countess Rhety, this was the only place available. They threw the girls out and put the royal couple in." The royal couple were later evacuated but liberated in Tirol. The former Austrian chancellor Kurt von Schuschnigg, his wife, and their four-year-old daughter spent three months there. It was also "home" to one of Winston Churchill's relatives. As Korf toured the building, he opened a closet door and a corpse tumbled out. He commented, "Good thing that the weather was cold or the stench would have been unimaginable."[78]

Korf did not have time to dwell on the horrors that the Nazis had perpetrated at the camp. The survivors needed help. The first priority was to dispose of the corpses to prevent the spread of disease. Dr. Bucknell assured Korf that the most sanitary means of disposal was to burn them in the ovens of the crematorium. With understandable reluctance, Korf gave the order to reactivate the crematorium.[79] Korf also enlisted the help of the locals in disposal of the bodies. He spoke to the mayor of Flossenbürg, who told Korf that his citizens were innocent of any wrongdoing. He insisted that they had no idea what was happening in the camp. Korf did not accept ignorance as an excuse. He ordered the mayor to round up able-bodied men to dig graves to prevent the outbreak of disease.[80] The people did as they were told. Korf recorded the scene with his camera.

Despite this precaution and the medical assistance of Dr. Bucknell, survivors were still dying of typhus and cholera at the rate of up to sixty per day. To keep up their strength, survivors needed food, but Korf's division had little food to spare for such a drastic relief effort. After one of the inmates told him that the SS families living near the camp had hoarded food and supplies, Korf decided to go to their homes to procure food for camp inmates.[81]

Korf was amazed to discover that the SS families lived just outside the gates of the camp. The pleasant housing conditions were as surreal as the horrors of the camp. The families lived in "pretty little houses in the style of the Black Forest and the Alps. Boxes contain-

ing blooming flowers decorated them. . . . The nurseries were decorated with Hummel prints and pictures." The wives of SS officers
were generally isolated from the goings-on at the camp. They employed camp inmates as domestics, but they were instructed not to
consider the inmates as fellow humans. Korf observed, "It defied
the imagination that they could exist and serve the same humans
who had not a shred of humanity a few hundred yards down the
road." From these homes Korf and his men procured wool blankets,
coffee, and meat. Shortly thereafter he ordered SS women to cook a
decent meal for the inmates.[82]

Having done all that he could for the camp inmates, Korf could
now turn to finding the people responsible for their misery. He
received a tip that a top SS officer was hiding out in the woods
nearby, and he set out with three other officers to find him. They
came upon a small building in the woods. A major told Korf to go
in first. "So I went through the window," Korf recalled, "into a hall
and into the living room. Pistol drawn. They were having dinner.
My 'friend' [was] in the middle. I told him to raise his hands [and]
later let him rest them on his neck. We took [him] along into the
jeep."[83]

As Korf tried to discern who was most responsible for the atrocities at Flossenbürg, "one name crept up again and again, Adjutant
Baumgartner." Korf learned that he, rather than Commandant Max
Kögel, had truly run the camp. Though Ludwig Baumgartner had
escaped, Korf was eager to find out what made this man tick. He
tracked down Baumgartner's wife and spoke to her for several
hours. Korf learned that Baumgartner had been one of the original
"elite" of the SS. He was trained in Oranienburg, near Berlin, the
first concentration camp in Germany, opened in 1933 by Hermann
Göring. The camp also served as the "Harvard of the concentration
camp training programs for the SS. Its 'alumni' all advanced quickly
and held key positions in the many camps which followed it. [At
Oranienburg] Baumgartner was taught to suppress any and all feelings. At the beginning of the [training] he was given a German shep-

herd dog who stayed with him at all times. After 45 days he was told to kill it. He did. He passed."[84]

Korf learned that Baumgartner's influence quickly surpassed that of his commandant. He learned from Baumgartner's wife that the camp commandant was

a sadist by nature; he liked to see blood. In the evening, when [he and his wife] sat at the dinner table with their kids, he suddenly became uneasy and disappeared. His wife knew that he went over to the camp and looked over the execution orders for the next day. He then would have the prisoners brought before him and shoot them himself with his Waithur PBK. He then would return to the dinner table like nothing had happened, but he would be relaxed. He never talked about this, but his wife knew.[85]

Korf asked Frau Baumgartner if she feared her husband. She replied that she did not, and that he was good to her and their children. Korf concluded that "Baumgartner . . . clearly was a sadist and he would have been a sadist in any society which would have given him a chance."[86]

In his report to the assistant chief of staff, G-2 of the 97th Infantry Division, Korf tallied the dismal statistics of the concentration camp Flossenbürg. He noted that the camp had housed around 65,000 prisoners between 1939 and 1945. He added that in the year before the end of the war alone, approximately "14,000 inmates died as a consequence of exhaustion, undernourishment, mistreatment, and diseases, [or] were killed by order of SS Reichsführer Himmler through firing squads, hanging, or the injection of poisons."[87] The approach of American troops in mid-April 1945 resulted in only more slaughter: The SS men evacuated several thousand inmates in the direction of Dachau. Prisoners who could not withstand the march were shot on the spot and hastily buried on the sides of the road. A War Crimes Investigation Team later concluded that 1,800 inmates perished on the death march. By the time that the Americans liberated the camp—which had a capacity for 10,000 to 15,000 inmates—only 2,000 survivors remained.[88]

The report that Korf filed on Flossenbürg shows that few of the guilty parties were apprehended. The camp's commandant, Kögel, and his adjutant, Baumgartner, were last reported heading toward Dachau. Kögel was later captured and executed; Baumgartner was never found. Moved and horrified by what he had seen at Flossenbürg, Korf accumulated evidence of Nazi atrocities. He took pictures of the camp with his camera and seized prisoner files for his own records. His wife later recalled that he acquired this evidence "because he was a reporter. He did not want anyone to doubt what he had seen or had been through; he wanted to have his own proof."[89]

Korf gained further insight into the minds of mass murderers such as Baumgartner some time later when he interrogated the head of an Einsatzgruppe (special commando) who was assigned to the Kiev area in Ukraine. He had orders to kill as many Jews in the Kiev area as he could get his hands on. Though he had only 120 men under his command, he accomplished his task with brutal efficiency; Korf recalled:

He first posted signs in villages ordering all Jewish villagers to present themselves at a clearing near their respective villages. When they came, in groups of several thousands, he would have them surrounded and order them to dig trenches, long and deep, two parallel and one connecting them, about the shape of a straight horseshoe. He would then order them to undress and to put their clothing and belongings into the middle of the trenches. After that, they were order to lie down, belly down, faces facing the trenches. He would then make the round to make sure that everything was as ordered. He then had his men go from victim to victim and shoot them into the neck. . . . Then the next wave had to cover the victims with dirt and the same thing happened to them.[90]

The commando remembered: "There was an elderly Jew lying there, he turned his head to me and said, 'Am I lying just right?' I said 'yes' and shot him in the neck." Korf asked whether the Jews did anything to resist, especially considering the fact that they outnumbered the Einsatzgruppe. The commando observed: "No, they did not resist. They knew what was coming and many of them sang the Kolniderer [Kol Nidre], the song of death. There was a calm about them that was hard to understand."[91]

What disturbed Korf most about the commando was the fact that he was very proud of the fact that he and his small contingent of 120 had been able to do away with 100,000 Jews. He asked Korf, "Don't you think it was a great success?" Korf was shocked at how the man was proud of his efficiency as a killing machine. He observed: "Here I had the ultimate bureaucrat . . . he followed orders. A man who organized death, counted victims, and was only sorry that he had not been decorated for his 'heroism.' He honestly tried to get praise out of me . . . had no feeling of any kind, except doing his job superbly. He was the perfect tool of a system bent on annihilation."[92]

By the beginning of May 1945 the German army was falling apart. Korf's job was to encourage this process by composing leaflets informing German soldiers that Germany had lost the war and that surrender was their best recourse.[93] Many did. When Korf was driving along a road one day, he stopped to relieve himself. A German soldier in full uniform and fully armed suddenly confronted him. He asked Korf if the war was over. Korf replied, "For you, it is! Where are your men?" The soldier gave a command, and very quickly a large contingent of German soldiers emerged from the bushes. The soldiers' first priority was food. Korf recalled, "They had not eaten in days, and wanted to know how the American food was. I led them to the road, and told them to dump their weapons into my jeep. I then gave them directions on how to march into captivity. In the evening, I found them in the camp quite satisfied after a good meal."[94]

Korf and his men crossed into Eger, the capital of the Sudentenland. Hitler had annexed this area from Czechoslovakia in 1938.

Korf went to the Gestapo headquarters looking for "customers." They were gone; only a safe remained. Wires sticking out of the safe convinced Korf that it was probably booby-trapped. Korf found a German safe expert to disarm it. After several hours Korf and his whole team assembled to view the contents. They were unimpressive: a picture of Hitler and a copy of the German penal code stamped "Gestapo Eger." Korf took the latter and later gave it to the Library of Congress, which he thought the "proper place" for it. After securing Eger, Korf and his men requisitioned a house. They couldn't help snickering at a German radio report that announced: "The heroic efforts of our glorious Army today have succeeded in cleansing Eger from the American enemy."[95]

As they crossed from the Sudetenland into Czechoslovakia proper, Hitler's "glorious army" was nowhere in sight. Korf noted that German resistance seemed to evaporate. Weapons were abandoned in the woods. One weapon was particularly impressive; it was "the largest gun we had ever seen and probably the largest Germany had ever produced: the barrel stretched over [the length of] two railroad cars and the grooves alone were over an inch deep." Korf later learned that this type of weapon had been fired at Sevastopol in the Soviet Union, and it could have reached Paris from Germany. Though the size of the gun was truly impressive, Korf called it an "instant relic" because it was too large and immobile to be used effectively in combat.[96]

As Germany's defeat became more imminent, army leaders began to surrender. One day Korf was informed that a group of very important German officers wished to surrender to General Halsey. Korf's division created a half-circle formation to meet the new arrivals. A large group of cars, motorcycles, and sidecars drove into the formation. The first to surrender was the chief of staff to Infantry General Karl Weisburger.[97]

Korf recalled: "He stepped forward and saluted. I did not return the salute." After introducing the rest of his staff, the prisoner told Korf that they had come from the Elbe region. He added that the rest of his division was still fighting the Russians. With pride, he noted, "We eluded the enemy. We carried ourselves well, like Lettow-Vorbeck." Korf recalled that Paul Emil von Lettow-Vorbeck was a German general who eluded the British in Africa during World War I and was never captured, but who honorably surrendered. Korf did not see the similarity. Though the British received Lettow-Vorbeck with military honors, Korf was not inclined to do the same for his self-styled successor, and told him so: "You took the last gasoline and left your troops facing the Russians. You just wanted to [avoid being] captured by the Russians." The general only shrugged in reply.[98]

The general then told Korf that he wished to surrender his sword to Halsey. Halsey was not interested, and he then said to Korf, "Fine, you take his sword." Halsey did not speak to his German counterpart; he merely "looked at him squarely in the face, made an about face and left."[99]

As the war neared its end Korf was eager to secure promotions for his team, but this did not come easily. When Korf discussed the matter with Major Ramsey, he replied that he could do nothing since Korf and his men were only "attached" to his unit; they were not under his direct command. Korf and his men were assigned to ETOUSA (European Theater of Operations of the United States of America), and they received promotions only through that institution. But since Korf and his men were in the field, ETOUSA did not know of their work and had little incentive to act on their behalf. Halsey nonetheless sent recommendations for promotions and decorations to Intelligence Headquarters for immediate action. Unfortunately, the letters disappeared in the postwar disarray.

Not satisfied with this situation, Korf decided to take matters into his own hands. In late April 1945 he simply handed the divisional personnel officer a recommendation to promote his men to the next highest rank. To his surprise, "it worked, though it was strictly illegal." The promotions went through, but a letter from Headquarters of Military Intelligence to Korf did not approve of the tactics used to obtain them. Though the letter approved the promotions, it also added, "It is to be noted that action taken by 97th Infantry Division was contrary to ETOUSA letter (copy enclosed) in regard to promotion of Military Intelligence personnel, and retroactive action taken by this headquarters in this particular case is not to be considered as establishing a precedent."[100]

Though Korf was able to promote his men, he was never able to secure a promotion for himself. He was told that no the letters on his behalf had ever reached ETOUSA. He later speculated that his failure to receive a promotion might have had something to do with the departure of his commanding officer in ETOUSA, Colonel Hochstetter, who had been discharged in December 1944 in the "interest of the Government." What this meant, Korf speculated, "was that he was permitted to take back the reins of America Metal, one of the largest metal companies in the U.S." Hochstetter was replaced by junior officers, who, in Korf's opinion, "formed some sort of clique which served their own interests better than those of the service." This point was made clear to Korf when one of them offered to sell him any quantity of Chanel No. 5 at black market prices.[101]

There were other factors that probably inhibited his promotion. First, the army generally bestowed accolades more frequently upon men who had served longer than Korf. There were also incidents that may have worked against him: the fact that he had forgotten his weapon en route to capture the Skorzeny unit may have rankled his superiors. It is also quite possible that Korf's contretemps with a powerful and influential man—the Pentagon general—may have blackened his reputation in higher circles. The unorthodox way in which he snagged promotions for his men may have aroused criticism as well.

But these factors should not diminish the significance of the contribution that Korf and his men made to the war effort. A formal evaluation of military intelligence specialist teams written just after the war duly notes the value of the information obtained particularly by those who interrogated German prisoners of war:

The information gathered by IPW [interrogators of prisoners of war] teams was generally rated highest in importance of all MIS information. Vital tactical and strategic information on enemy losses, replacements, training, supply, equipment, dispositions, movements, caliber of troops, morale, and even intentions was secured by the IPW team, and, in many cases, by the IPW team only. Important information was also picked up by the IPWs on enemy artillery, positions, command posts, supply dumps, and minefields.[102]

News of the progress of Allied troops in the war did not travel easily or quickly to soldiers at the front, and Korf's division was no exception. Korf remembered, "There was a long-standing joke in the army that if peace were ever declared, it would take six months for the news to come down through channels." Fortunately, news of Germany's unconditional surrender on 7 May in fact traveled swiftly. The transition from war to peace was awkward at first. Korf remembered: "We removed the blinds and the blackout stuff and felt kind of naked. If the enemy had not gotten the message, we were sitting ducks. But no more shots were fired."[103]

Korf described the day not as jubilant, but as "eerie. . . . It was like you suddenly had come out of a wind tunnel; the impact of the noise, the rush of the movement, the intense pressure were gone."

He wrote to his wife:

Now it looks like there is peace. . . . It is strange, for so many year[s] I promised myself that I [was] going to get drunk on VE [Victory in Europe] day and right now I do not feel like it. I want to go home, like a little boy wants home. I stayed in this war because I felt I had to, and I think I did my share and my duty. But now I want to go home, come back to you, in your arms and in our house which will have trophies [so] that we can say: "remember when pop was fighting in Europe?" . . . I saw an awful lot and

I have enough of war, killings, concentration camp country, hatred, lying and ridicule. I want to sleep like normal people, not with one loaded pistol on each side and the gun in reach. Not moving like a gypsy every day, packing and unpacking, smelling the stale smell of other people's homes. . . . VE has come and lots of our boys, many personal friends of mine are in a cool grave. Women are crying, but let's hope that in years from now they will say, "his death helped to [shape] a better world." Then all sacrifices will have been worthwhile.[104]

He also told her how difficult the last days of the war had been:

The last weeks were not easy. We went over the Rhine when the fight for the bridgeheads still raged. We took Siegburg and it was not easy. The 88s picked the houses all around us; we just lay in bed and listened to the bricks flying closer and closer in the dark of the night. A friend of mine hit a mine and empty will be the hearts of his wife and kid on VE day. We cleaned out the Ruhr pocket and took Düsseldorf without a fight, we crossed the whole of Germany, fought the battle of Bavaria and then that of Czechoslovakia. We felt no rain, nor cold, not hunger or sleep. We did not live in foxholes but comfortably, even under shambles. Today we are tired.[105]

Fatigue at war's end was compounded by a sense of emptiness: "Suddenly there was nothing. You felt numb. It took a long time for me to deal with the psychological after effects of the war; the sudden change from pressure to decompression." Korf later learned that the end of the war caused more nervous breakdowns than any other single incident.[106]

Some of the GIs eased the "boredom" of peacetime by relieving the Germans of their valuables. Korf opposed the idea of his men taking the property of German civilians. When Rita wrote once that her female colleagues at work were flaunting expensive jewelry that their husbands had "liberated" from the Germans, Korf told her that this was stealing.[107]

Korf practiced what he preached. One day he was approached by GIs who declared that they had "found" some diamonds. Since Korf had studied gemology as a young man, he could see that they were not precious stones. He asked where they came from, and he was led to a farmhouse where he discovered GIs dragging out boxes of jewelry. He was approached by an agitated woman who explained that she had stored the goods from her Dresden costume jewelry store in the farmhouse for safekeeping. The GIs then lifted a crate out of a wall. Korf asked if it also contained costume jewelry. She explained that she also collected glass from the Phoenician period to modern times. After thoroughly examining the crate's contents, Korf concluded, "The collection was her property and had no Nazi connection." He declared the farmhouse off limits and posted two guards for the night.[108]

Though Korf opposed seizure of civilian property, he had no qualms about relieving captured German military personnel of their military hardware. In fact, the army permitted the confiscation of captured enemy equipment, provided that items seized did not include "explosives or firearms capable of being concealed on the person."[109] Shortly after VE day, he reported to Rita: "Right now I am sifting [through] my stuff, looking over the papers and admiring my souvenirs. I got the most beautiful collection of German military and Nazi daggers, medals and decorations, swastika flags and Gestapo blackjacks—all gotten directly where the getting is tough and you might trade a bullet for it. I don't know whether we might spoil our beautiful walls with it or whether you will insist upon putting it in the drawer where it is deepest."[110] He justified his acquisitions in a letter to her a few weeks later: "They were acquired under many dangers and each of them has a story to tell. . . . You see, when time shrivels down the war to some fleeting memories, these souvenirs will be the only thing I can show for years of your life and mine wasted but for the little bit of use the Army had out of me. We ourselves will not have acquired any fortune—just souvenirs to show for [our time], and gray hair on the temples."[111]

Along with the military hardware, Korf shipped home hard evidence of Nazi atrocities. After he told his wife that he was sending some more "souvenirs," he warned, "One book, please, do not look over. . . . I rather would not like you to see the faces of murdered people, people the Germans killed themselves and then tried to pass the guilt on the Poles. Put it away unseen."[112]

Korf's sense of relief by war's end was soon replaced by uncertainty about what would happen next. Korf and his men had no idea whether they would be sent home, remain as part of the army of occupation, or be shipped off to fight the Japanese, who had not yet surrendered. Korf wrote to his wife: "The longing for home has had time now to settle; it eases itself onto us. Hardly anybody speaks about home. It is too obvious, too self understood and too hopeless."[113]

A few days after Korf wrote these words, he learned what the immediate future would hold. Though he was just as eager to leave Germany as he had been eight years before, the army had other plans for him.

Margarete and Kurt Korf,
K. Frank Korf's parents, circa
1907.

Hildegarde Korf, K. Frank Korf's
sister, circa 1927.

Kurt F. Korf and Rita Korf at the time of their marriage, 1943.

The reunion of K. Frank Korf and his mother in Lippstadt, Germany, April 1945.

A lighthearted moment between mother and son, April 1945.

Soldiers captured by Korf in the woods near Karlsbad, April 1945.

General Karl Weisburger, who
surrendered to Korf.

Contents of a safe at Gestapo headquarters in Eger, Czechoslovakia.

Major Ramsay and Captain Bucknell investigating the concentration camp at Flossenbürg, April 1945.

Liberated prisoners emerge from the gangway between the lower and upper parts of Flossenbürg concentration camp, April 1945.

The liberated prisoner Michelin in the courtyard where prisoners were hanged, Flossenbürg, April 1945.

Local residents were forced to dig graves at Flossenbürg concentration camp, April 1945.

Former SS men sweeping the streets of Munich, summer 1945.

Korf in front of the ruins of Reichsparteitag in Nuremberg, summer 1945.

Korf on the stand used by Hitler at the Nuremberg parade ground, summer 1945.

Korf wrote on the back of this photograph, "Germany's fate—people on the road," April 1945.

A Gestapo spy from Zagreb, Yugoslavia, after a night of interrogation by Korf.

Korf in front of the POW enclosure, summer 1945.

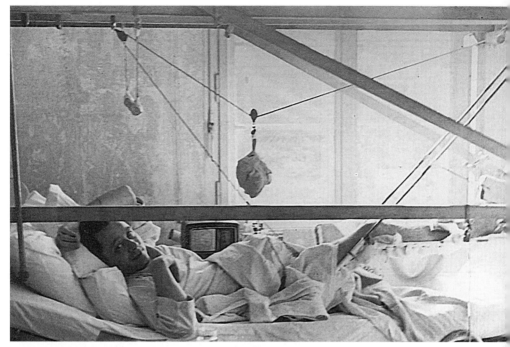

Korf in a hospital near Bayreuth, Germany, spring 1946.

Frank and Rita Korf in Germany, 1948.

Patricia Kollander, K. Frank Korf, and John O'Sullivan in 2000. Author's collection.

5   The Hunt for War Criminals: 1945-1946

Shortly after VE day Korf and his men were ordered to move west. No destination was announced. They stopped at Schloss Seehof, an ornate seventeenth-century castle built on the outskirts of Bamberg, a town about sixty miles north of Nuremberg. The men looked forward to staying in the beautiful castle, but were dismayed when they were ordered to pitch tents outside it. Korf and his men were miffed: "Were we Boy Scouts? The indignation ran high. This was a nice way to start the peace." But the general was adamant; he wanted the castle unoccupied in order to "respect private property." Later, however, Korf heard that the general "wanted to try out his sumptuous trailer, which had been running along unused all through the campaign."[1]

While some of the soldiers explored the castle, Korf dutifully pitched his tent. When he finished he went inside, only to have the tent collapse on him. He soon found out why: a soldier had found a samurai sword in the castle and was testing its sharpness by slicing the tent pegs. After he finished repairing his tent, Korf was handed several large picture albums found in the castle. As a security officer, he had to determine whether they had a "Nazi connection." They most certainly did not. The albums contained nothing but pornographic photographs. Korf was then approached by the general's aide, who said, "The general understands that you have material with security aspects. He wants to see it." Korf handed over the albums. He never saw them again.[2]

After the men settled into their tents, they were called to a staff meeting. They learned that the 97th Infantry Division was to be transferred to the Pacific to fight against Japan—but Korf and his men would be detached from the 97th and remain in Germany to process prisoners of war.

Before this work began, Korf and his men toured southern and central Germany. In less than two weeks they covered a distance of over a thousand miles. The trip gave Korf an excellent opportunity to observe the extent of wartime destruction in Germany. He observed: "All bridges around Frankfurt had been blown up, by order of the Nazi High Command, to make it impossible for us to cross the Main. Thanks to our engineers, our troops quickly crossed it. But it took the Germans years to rebuild the bridges. Many roads had been [rendered] 'impassible' by blocking them with fallen trees and other obstacles. We put the Germans to work removing them. The same people who had put them up had to remove them."[3]

Korf had the opportunity to assess the emotional damage the war had inflicted on ordinary Germans as well. In Frankfurt he met a crying woman who was standing in front of a deep hole. Korf asked, "Was this your house?" She nodded and then added, "The furniture was all new." Korf asked, "Where is your husband?" "He is in there too," she replied. Korf remembered standing in front of a similar hole in Lippstadt where his uncle had been buried. Korf "felt no emotion. I had known how terrible the war would be for its victims, but I also knew that there had been no way to avoid bloodshed."[4]

He related his feelings about seeing his homeland in ruins to his wife:

As I indicated in my last letter, we were recalled from the division and called back to an advanced echelon of our Headquarters in Germany. It was quite a trip. . . . At HQ, we were alerted the next hour, but actually had to wait a while until everything was halfways straightened out. Then we were back on the road and saw the whole Rhineland. It is one heap of ashes and rubble. You come into a town and think it cannot be any worse, and then you find a town which is much worse.[5]

He also marveled at the attitude of the Germans toward war and defeat:

The people look surprisingly healthy, well-fed and well clad. . . . They smile at us Americans and ask us whe[n] we are going to liberate the other half of Germany from the Russians for them. They are still under the ban of Goebbels propaganda that they cannot see straight, though the majority seems to be well willing to learn from us. . . . In back of all of this is the ever-present fear of the Russians which seems to govern all their waking hours. The bad conscience is also there, but only too willing to be put to sleep again.[6]

In Frankfurt, amid destruction and desolation, there were faint signs of postwar recovery as people set up makeshift shops in the rubble and sold what they could. He saw signs that read, "Mueller's Bakery or Pfeiffer's Butcher Shop: the sale goes on."

In Nuremberg Korf made a point of going to the huge stadium where Nazi party meetings had taken place. "I stood on the platform where Hitler had stood and had my photo taken, like a tourist. . . . My mind replayed the huge parade, the pomp and the crescendo of the speeches that were held here. I saw the triumvirate of Hitler, Himmler and Göring strutting about and [then] looked at the garbage at my feet." Korf found that the Justice Building had not been heavily damaged. Shortly thereafter the building was used for the famous Nuremberg trials of Nazi war criminals. Munich, where Korf had studied law for two semesters, "was badly bombed, but still showed a lot of life." He found that the U.S. troops put the SS to good use by having them sweep the streets. Korf snapped a picture of the new street sweepers doing what he called the "best work they had ever done."[7]

In late May 1945 Korf's work began in earnest when he became one of the officers in charge of the international prisoner-of-war screening team at the prisoner-of-war enclosure near Third Army Headquarters in Bad Aibling, a small town about thirty miles east of Munich, in Bavaria. The job ahead was daunting. American military leaders expected that they would have to process about 3 million German soldiers, but up to 5 million were in American hands by June 1945.[8] The prisoner-of-war enclosure at Aibling was equipped for about sixteen thousand prisoners, but by May 1945 the number contained had swelled to over thirty-five thousand.[9]

When prisoners began to stream into Bad Aibling, Korf and his men soon discovered that there were not nearly enough U.S. Army soldiers to guard the massive number of prisoners. The camp commandant had to resort to employing discharged German soldiers to help with this task. Korf had no qualms about using them or their performance: "They did a good job," he later recalled. To provide the Germans with an incentive to cooperate, the occupation forces decreed that only lawfully discharged personnel could qualify for ration stamps.

The next major problem Korf faced was how to feed the prisoners adequately. He learned that up to thirty prisoners a day were dying. Korf asked his commandant to send a physician from the Third Army to the camp, who concluded that nearly all the prisoners were malnourished. They received the same rations as the civilians, amounting to 850 calories per day, but the Americans failed to take into account that civilians were able to supplement rations with black market goods. The prisoners, of course, did not have access to such sources, and the meager rations left them hungry and therefore more susceptible to disease. One American soldier remembered that the citizens of Aibling tried to help prisoners by throwing bread over the barbed wire fences, but this practice had to be discontinued when prisoners began to fight over the food. The problem was solved by the camp commandant, who, according to Korf, did a "courageous thing" by ordering the prisoners' rations to be doubled.

Korf added, "This not only helped to save lives, it also helped to secure the cooperation of many prisoners: I think [the additional rations] helped allay the fears of the Germans."[10]

During a 1999 interview Korf was asked to comment on the work of the journalist James Bacque, who charged in his 1989 book, *Other Losses*, that Eisenhower deliberately starved the Germans as a means of retaliation. Korf replied, "We saw no such thing. As a matter of fact, we saw necessary the survival of these people. Our job was to get these people back into their jobs and into the economy . . . as fast as we could, as safely as we could."[11]

This observation has been corroborated by the historian Lee Kennett, who observes, "On balance the American presence proved in the end to be a beneficent one." He adds that "Eisenhower's orders were to be 'just and humane' in treatment of the German people, and by and large the GI's he commanded adhered to that policy."[12]

Korf also believed that fraternization between American GIs and German women helped to better relations between Germans and Americans. Korf referred to this as the "sex angle" of reconciliation. He recalled that in spite of a ban against fraternization, "There was a great deal of fraternization going on between the American soldiers and the German girls, which certainly got in the way of hatred. . . . I think it was . . . positive that the relationship between the women and the soldiers was there."[13]

Once the basic needs of the prisoners were attended to, Korf and his men had to ferret out possible war criminals, moles, and hard-core members of the Nazi party, the SS and Gestapo. To separate the German troops into the proper categories, Korf and his men designed a questionnaire. Generally, they looked for well-educated people who spoke several languages. This method worked to draw out an interesting suspect. As Korf recalled, "I remember a very good-looking girl who admitted to speaking seven languages. She was elegantly dressed and carried an alligator suitcase. I questioned her for hours and she finally admitted that she had worked as the assistant to the Gestapo chief in Zagreb (the capital of Croatia, a Nazi client state during the war), with responsibilities for most of the Balkans. She was an automatic arrest. I asked her why she had voluntarily come in and she simply answered, 'I needed the food stamps, and I did not think the Americans would be this thorough.'"[14]

Screening was difficult as a general rule. The blacklists were "woefully inadequate," Korf recalled. "Many individuals were listed without first names, occupation, or domicile. If a [common] name like 'Mueller' appeared, we would have to hold several hundred Germans, knowing that perhaps only one would be the right one. Or a high-ranking Nazi could be a possible war criminal . . . and have intelligence value, though these 'virtues' did not always overlap."[15]

Screening was also made difficult by the fact that many members of the SS had altered their identification papers. Some of them were pretty creative about it. Korf recalled, "We discovered that an amazing number of soldiers had been on duty with the 44th division until we put their army passports under the magnifying glass and discovered that the insignia 'SS' had been converted into the number 44."[16]

Korf had many methods for sniffing out suspects: "At personal interviews I always looked at the hands. Anyone who had been a coal miner had bluish coal dust under the wrinkles of his hands. If he did not, he was faking it." Men who claimed to be factory workers but had no calluses were also suspect; many turned out to be desk officers who had what Korf referred to as "intelligence value."

The business of processing the prisoners and finding guilty parties as quickly as possible was not easy, but Korf felt that he had done a thorough job. Long after the war, Korf met a former German prisoner of war who told him that no one had ever asked him any questions at Aibling. Korf observed, "[The prisoners] did not know that even without an interrogation, I could tell a lot. And I said to him, 'Are you a subversive?' He said, 'Of course not.' I replied, 'Well, that's why we let you through.'"[17]

Once discharged, however, former detainees found that they could not go home because of territorial changes wrought by the end of World War II. Germans who had settled in Eastern Europe before 1945 were forced to leave their homes and go west under the terms of the wartime agreements between the Soviet Union and the Allies.[18] Those who were forced out were classified as displaced persons, or DPs. Millions of ethnic Germans fleeing Eastern Europe after the war fit into this category.[19] A system to handle the DPs had just been developed. Those who had someplace to go in Western Europe were allowed to leave; the rest were sent to displaced person camps that were run by the United Nations Relief and Rehabilitation Administration (UNRRA).[20]

Enforcement of the terms of the wartime agreements regarding prisoners was not easy. The arrival of a Soviet team at Aibling created difficulties for Korf. It was headed by a full colonel and accompanied by an interpreter who, Korf suspected, was an agent with the KGB, the Soviet secret police. First the team requested that prisoners from the Baltic States be handed over. Citing chapter and verse from wartime agreements regarding those prisoners, Korf replied that only men from the Baltic States who volunteered to leave for the USSR could do so. None did. But the Soviets did not leave empty-handed. They asked Korf to hand over the Vlasov men, anticommunist Russians who fought with the Germans against Stalin's Soviet Union. Korf knew that the Soviets considered the Vlasov men traitors, and he knew how the Soviets dealt with traitors. This time there was little that Korf could do, because he knew that repatriation of the Vlasov men was indeed mandated by wartime agreements between the United States and the Soviet Union.[21]

Knowing what lay in store for the Vlasov men, Korf tried to stall the repatriation process. He told the Soviet colonel that he could not comply "without specific orders." Soon thereafter Korf received a call from SHAEF (Supreme Headquarters Allied Expeditionary Forces) about the Vlasov men. Korf was instructed to hand the Vlasov men over to the Soviets. Korf now tried to use his expertise as a lawyer to help them. He told the colonel that because the orders from SHAEF were verbal, they were therefore "nonbinding." Exasperated, the Soviet colonel took the initiative and contacted SHAEF himself. SHAEF in turn ordered Korf to hand over the men. Sadly, Korf observed, "There were about 12 men and they went quietly, though in other camps some of them committed suicide rather than going. I later learned from our men that the Soviets killed every one as soon as they had crossed the border."[22]

Korf's experiences processing prisoners and detainees taught him a great deal about the impact of war not only on soldiers, but also on women and children. "We met every type of human that the six-year war had created," he recalled. Korf found the German women who answered the call to arms in the final days of the war "hardly distinguishable from the men; they were hardened and full of lice . . . [and] coarse. If there ever was an argument against women serving in combat, this was it." He was also dismayed when he discovered that children as young as thirteen had served in the German army. After the women and children were processed, Korf and his men did what they could to help them. Korf himself took one of the boys under his wing. He was from Silesia, had no idea where his parents were, and had no place to go. He performed odd jobs for Korf until the latter found a carpenter to employ the boy as an apprentice. When the carpenter asked who the boy's parent was, Korf replied, "I am," and signed the employment contract "in loco parentis."[23]

Korf received a respite from his duties when he was assigned to do intelligence work for General Maxwell Taylor of the 101st Airborne Division. Taylor's mission was to investigate Hitler's mountaintop home at Berchtesgaden in southern Bavaria, the so-called Eagle's Nest. Korf drove to Berchtesgaden with Koref. They rode up to Hitler's compound in an elevator that had been made with the labor of thousands of foreign workers. Korf learned that the laborers were killed after they had finished the work so that the location of the elevator would be kept secret.[24]

Korf described the interior of Hitler's dwelling:

The interior rooms on the top were out of proportion. The furniture was too massive for the low ceilings. I took photos (when I went back years later, I was told by the guide that there never had been furniture and that we had found it empty). Hitler's kitchen was downstairs. I examined the kitchen carefully, but found only a few bottles of Fachinger. No alcohol. There was a large butcher block, but it did not show a single mark. The rumor of Hitler being a vegetarian apparently was true.[25]

Korf came upon a telephone book for the Berchtesgaden compound and discovered that it included not only Hitler's quarters but also several nearby cottages where some of his top aides were housed. Korf also saw Hitler's Mercedes: "This is where Hitler took the ovations of the masses. I opened the door. It had bulletproof glass, which was an inch thick and enormously heavy. I had to press my shoulder against the door to close it."[26]

Korf also went to Hitler's nearby mountain home, Haus Wachenfeld. The top floor contained a large room with a "huge picture window, but it was bare down to the naked walls. I was told that the SS had tried to blast the villa with dynamite, but they only [succeeded in bending] the huge pillars in the cellar bearing the metal beams. It was strange to look out of nothing into the alpine landscape." On the floor Korf found some meal vouchers for members of the SS and took them, along with the Berchtesgaden compound telephone book, as mementos of the visit.[27]

Though his experiences were remarkable, foremost on Korf's mind was his desire to return home. Shortly after the end of the war, he confided to his wife:

It is no fun [being] in a country with blown up bridge[s] and streets full of bomb holes, where the roadsides are still littered with burned-out vehicles, homeless families and returning German soldiers. If I only had a chance to go home. I got enough of war and mental stupidity, of curfew and hidden truths. [I am a] strange bird in a country which has become strange to me, and it is not home any more. My home is in the States, in New York with all her ugliness and smoke. . . . I want to breathe again as a free man and not in a slave's country. I want to go back to you, darling.[28]

It was ironic to Korf that his primary job was to discharge German soldiers, while he was not allowed to go home. He noted with bitterness: "If I could only discharge myself! Sometimes, I wonder who won this war." In late June he added, "Oh, Rita, why do they punish us so much after this war in Europe is over, why do they not send over those who stayed snugly at home during the fighting?"[29]

To add to the frustration of not being able to go home, Korf was not receiving promotions and awards that he felt he had earned. His frustration became even more acute when he learned that Ritchie graduates who spent the war on desk duty—as opposed to combat—had been promoted above his rank of second lieutenant. He wrote to Rita:

I held back long enough, but today I got to do some bitching. Around the first of May, my old division put in the promotion for me (the General himself signed it), it was approved all the way up, but until today, there is no news and I think I have to resign myself to the idea of remaining a permanent second Louis [Lieutenant]. You know that I have held the position of a capt[ain] all through combat and still hold it. . . . My Bronce [sic] star medal also was messed up because I left right after it was put in and such a thing always stays in the outfit. It would have meant five points towards discharge and now I only got my two combat stars. . . . What will I have to show for all this fighting when I come home?[30]

But shortly after making these observations, Korf backtracked a bit: "As to my bitching, forget about it, it is not important, as long as we two are satisfied with our achievements and I do not have the idea of making the Army a career." And although he resented the fact that many of his army colleagues had secured promotions without having to endure the rigors of combat, Korf was grateful for the experiences he had gained: "I saw many friends recently," he told Rita. "They were all 1st Lts [lieutenants] and none of them ever smelled [gun]powder, but I do not want to change places with them and I do not care whether [they] got the softest jobs in the world."[31] Korf retained this sense of satisfaction for the rest of his life. When asked what his war experience would have been like had he made it through Transportation OCS instead of becoming an intelligence officer, Korf summed up his feelings in one word: "Dull."[32]

Still, Korf made clear his disdain for anyone who implied that his service was not noteworthy. When an old colleague from the *Staatszeitung* wrote to Korf that his wartime experience was "easier" than that of soldiers who had fought in Africa and Sicily, Korf was irate. "My blood is boiling," he wrote to Rita. He resented "this fellow, who never set foot outside his office all during the war and has been making heaps of dough with a typewriter dripping with patriotism."[33]

Though Korf was working hard, and felt bitter about having to stay in Germany after the war was over, his lifestyle was far more comfortable than it had been just a few months earlier. As he reported to his wife:

I am here near a PW camp and house[d] in a barrack with my boys. We fixed two large rooms very nicely; one for the boys; the other one is divided by a partition and [I] house myself and the office–day room combination. I got some orderly to keep the place clean and it really sparkles. There is always something around to wet the throat, also food and two radios. The Bavarian mountains are very pretty. . . . The work is not hard and I am trying to weed out mistakes as much as possible. We have to be conscious of the responsibility.[34]

His needs were well attended: "Aside from my general discontent about not [being] able to get home nor to get work which promises something for the future—there is not much to complain [about]. I have service more than the Rockefellers in the States: men to clean my room, polish my boots, wash my clothing, shave my beard, tend my cars. I hardly spend a nickel and send everything home."[35]

Since Korf and his men could not go home, Korf wished to keep his team intact because they worked so well together. When in late June 1945 he discovered that the only other Third Army prisoner-of-war enclosure near Auerbach desperately needed German-speaking officers and personnel, he arranged to have his team transferred to that location. Auerbach was a town about a hundred miles northeast of Nuremberg, on the former German army training grounds. Korf found that about twenty thousand prisoners of war were housed in former German army barracks.[36]

The prisoners were separated into four cages: the first housed five thousand men, the second housed five thousand Hungarians, the third held assorted German military men, and the last accommodated twelve hundred women who had served in the army, but in noncombat positions. Korf and his men took housing inside the camp perimeter. The camp was headed by Colonel Andrew J. Schriver, Jr., whom Korf described as "a good soldier and a good man." The camp was understaffed: "There were only several officers and one hundred military police to guard the large group of battle hardened prisoners," Korf recalled.[37]

Korf devised a system to keep track of those he interviewed: he made out file cards for each of them, and made notes on them, such as "possible war criminal" or "possible concentration camp guard." In this way, he recollected, "we quickly learned to know our customers and could put the finger on each of them within minutes."[38]

Keeping order in the camp was not easy. "The SS men were a problem," Korf recalled. "These men were the best Germany had to offer and supposedly the most fanatical [Nazis]." After interviewing several of them, he found that "most of them were human though somewhat hardened by indoctrination and six years of fighting." Korf tried to make them see the error of their ways: "I had the

photos from Flossenbürg enlarged and posted them on a board outside the main SS barracks. [The caption] above them read: 'See what
you have done.' It made an impression."³⁹

One SS man made an impression on Korf. "He was well over six
feet tall and extremely intelligent. He had been an adjutant to Hitler." When Korf asked him why he became an SS man, he replied,
"I was tall, I was interested in sports and I was ambitious. I picked
the best military outfit there was, the Waffen SS." Korf remembered, "I could understand him. He made no excuses. He was a
soldier, not a cowardly murderer." Convinced that the man was not
a war criminal, Korf "put him in charge of the SS cage and in short
order he restored discipline. [He posted] good-humored signs telling
the men what to do and what not to do. There were no reports of
bribery or black marketeering, though I had installed little boxes in
out of the way corners where anybody could deposit a complaint."⁴⁰

In the late summer of 1945 Korf received special orders from
SHAEF to ferret out SS prisoners who had served in a regiment
commanded by Colonel Joachim Peiper, who had ordered the mas-
sacre of ninety-eight American soldiers at Malmédy during the Battle of the Bulge in late 1944. To his chagrin, Korf discovered that he
was not allowed to use his own interrogation techniques for this
special operation. The switch did more harm than good. "The
method for finding the culprits was so complex that it took us three
days to find two SS men" Korf's job was made a bit easier by an SS
colonel. "On the first day of interrogations, an SS colonel sidled up
to me and said casually: 'You are looking for [Peiper's] boys?' I did
not answer. He gave me a sealed envelope and said, 'When you are
through [with your interrogations], look at it.'" After three days Korf
opened the letter, thinking that he had perhaps overlooked one
guilty party. The letter revealed that he had missed three of them.⁴¹

The twelve hundred women at the camp created special challenges for Korf. "They had been captured or surrendered during the
warmer months. Now it became colder, so they needed clothing."
Korf found tablecloths and the women made dresses out of them.

Many women had been pregnant when they were captured. After they delivered their babies, they needed milk and baby food. Korf went to the townspeople of Auerbach for help. He appointed the mayor's wife president of the Auerbach chapter of the German Red Cross and charged her to secure goods that the prisoners needed from the townspeople. Thereafter the prisoners went into town every week—under guard—to pick up what they needed.[42]

On another occasion several women prisoners claimed that German physicians who examined them for venereal diseases had "taken liberties with them." They now refused to be examined. Korf recalled, "It looked like a mutiny." Korf removed the ringleader of the rebellion to a remote corner of the camp, but then rumors began to spread that she had been shot. So Korf "stopped all examinations by German doctors and asked the army to send down a team of our own physicians. After they took over, the complaints stopped. The rebel leader came back, to the surprise of all her [fellow prisoners]. The rebellion was over."[43]

Dealing with the problems of these people was not easy. As he reported to his wife:

I see much human misery every day and try to do the best. Being with prisoners daily is not too cheerful. You need a thorough belief in your mission of avoiding another war in 20 years from now, a deep interest in human nature and a sincere will to guide those who still might be guided and are not too deep in guilt. It is not easy, but somebody [has] to do it who can do it. There are lots of bright sights too, and I make myself see them. It is a kind of training and it needs lots of self-discipline, but the feeling that you moved the huge rock of our mission in Europe just a tiny bit is a reward even if you have to give up many personal pleasures, like being with the ones you love. I do not think you are in the habit yet to select the waves of our times which might uplift you, but you more or less stick to the little circle you are in.[44]

Korf's uncertainty about the length of his service in Europe muted his happiness over the victory of the United States over

Japan in August 1945. Korf, who was on furlough in Paris, wrote to his wife: "Today is VJ Day [Victory in Japan]. Celebrations are going on. I hardly feel like it. It has been too long and costly to enjoy it."[45] When Korf visited army headquarters shortly thereafter, he hoped to find out when he could be shipped home, and whether he could secure a promotion to first lieutenant. He came up empty on both counts. "My last trip to HQ was pretty disappointing," he wrote to Rita. He learned that second lieutenants had to be eighteen months in grade in order to be promoted. Korf was bitterly disappointed. He wrote to Rita, "I am too mad to spit."[46]

The Paris sojourn failed to lift his spirits. "I came back from Paris last Wednesday," he wrote to his wife. "Funny enough, I was glad to get out of there. For the first time, I did not like it too much. The egoism of the French I felt too strongly."[47]

Across the Atlantic, his wife had a more joyous experience when the war ended:

Well, it's over at last! The official announcement of the Japanese surrender was made by President Truman last night at 7 o'clock. People went crazy! Even in our little corner of the world! I don't think I ever heard such noise, in some cases almost hysterical; all kinds of noise-makers, automobile horns blowing and blowing, people shouting and singing: all kinds of decorations on houses—flags, papers, etc., and the largest crowd ever assembled in Times Square. . . . Around here cars were racing around with all kinds of ribbons and streamers and horns blowing. . . . We had a little something to drink, but mainly, we thanked God that it was all over.[48]

Korf resigned himself to an extension of his army duty. In late August 1945 he wrote to Rita, "All we can do is . . . sweat it out." He tried to make the best of an unfavorable situation by sending home as much money as possible, and by cultivating a newly found appreciation for nature. "I go hunting a lot," he reported to Rita. "I got a little shack out in the woods where I daydream. . . . My thirst for people is pretty small, especially since I am handling a very large number professionally. I am amazed that I can stand so much nature, but after so many unnatural things, this might be the normal reaction."[49]

Korf's situation at the camp took a turn for the worse upon the arrival of a new commandant, who "was a West Pointer, straight as a ramrod and just as flexible." Shortly after he took command, it was clear that he and Korf were going to be at cross-purposes. Their differences came to a head when the commandant ordered Korf to evacuate the children and infants in the camp. Korf objected, not only noting that it was wrong to remove children from their mothers; he also feared that the prisoners would riot: "We have 200 mothers and only 120 GI's [to guard them]; there will be a bloodbath!" he told the commandant. The West Pointer did not budge. He said, "Do as I told you, that is an order."[50]

Korf, however, balked: "I got on the horn and talked to Army and explained the situation. Fortunately, Army listened and within three hours the Commandant was recalled to the Army. He left before 1700 [hours]." Korf later learned that the West Pointer had been assigned to Auerbach in the first place as punishment for "conduct unbecoming to an officer and a gentleman"; rumor had it that the misconduct had involved violent behavior toward an army nurse.[51]

Korf's reputation as someone who could help people eventually caught up with him. As he reported to his wife:

Everybody thinks we are the only place on earth to carry their troubles to. In the various cages I listen to . . . stories [for] many hours and [when] I come back, the civilians are already waiting on the street in front of my house. Everybody seems to labor under the illusion that just seeing me absolves [them] of ever thinking for himself again and that, besides, everything will be wonderful immediately. People are sent by MG [military government] and other agencies too lazy to settle their own problems. A big sign in front of my house "Entry strictly forbidden" has no effect, neither [does] the strict order to the Bürgermeister [mayor] and Police neither to send up anybody nor to allow anybody around. A woman claimed today that she traveled 100 km just to speak to me. It is high time for redeployment or there will be some kind of pilgrimage for purely selfish reasons.[52]

Prisoners showed their appreciation in a number of ways. "German WACS . . . made me a pillow in [the] shape of a heart and I am going to send it soon. Also a few little drawings and paintings. It is surprising how many talents are behind [the] wire. But they [the prisoners] live better than they did for quite a while."[53]

Korf's work was made more difficult by the fact that many members of his staff were sent home, leaving him to do their work along with his own. As he told his wife, "Since I lost my other two boys, my work has more than doubled. It is openly admitted that I run the whole Camp, but that is a poor consolation for the amount of work we put in, and I wished somebody else would take over. Sometimes, it threatens to wear even me down to be the whole day among people behind barbed wire, to listen to their complaints and sorrows and to try to better things."[54]

Korf was also concerned about the welfare of his mother and his other relatives. His half-Jewish relatives on his mother's side had a hard time of it. He learned that his mother's sister Lili and her husband, Theobald, had been sent to Mauthausen concentration camp in Austria.[55] After the war Korf located his Aunt Lili. He reported to Rita, "My aunt looks terrible; life in the concentration camp has left marks which never will disappear. Her husband has not been found yet and it looks like he has been killed just before we [the American army] arrived."[56] Korf later had the chance to interrogate an SS officer who signed the order transferring his uncle to Mauthausen. Korf asked why he had been arrested. Unlike his wife, Theobald did not have Jewish blood. Korf asked the SS officer, "How much evidence did you have against him?" And he replied, "How much do we need?" Korf was stunned that his uncle had been sacrificed for no apparent reason: "You can't think yourself into these people."[57]

Ironically, Lili's two brothers—Korf's uncles Julius and Karl Mossner—were drafted into the German army at the end of the war.

Both men were in their fifties, in ill health, and had no inclination to serve. But neither their age mattered nor the fact that they were half Jews, or Mischlinge. As the historian Bryan Mark Rigg explains: "The Wehrmacht's policies dealing with Mischlinge were complicated and perplexing. . . . Yet, [they] resulted in tens of thousands of Mischlinge wearing the Wehrmacht's uniform."[58]

The trauma of war was compounded by a drastic shortage of food. A report sent to the chief of staff at SHAEF in June 1945 noted that food shortages had been caused by "military destruction, by an almost complete disruption of transport facilities, by . . . the need to feed millions of Displaced Persons. . . . These conditions . . . are resulting in ration levels in cities that are below the requirements needed for normal economic activity. This situation, if prolonged unduly, will lead to disease, unrest and a generally chaotic situation."[59]

Korf became acutely aware of this problem when he went to see his mother in November. This reunion was not as joyous as the one seven months before, because the privations of the postwar situation made themselves now felt. As Korf reported to his wife:

I am still pretty much shaken up by my experiences, as I found things much different from what I expected. They hunger. My mother lost much weight and what she still got on roundings is pretty much potatoes, starch and soup water. The hair is falling out from lack of fat and the teeth do not look good either. They get 1/8 of a pound of margarine a week for eating, baking, etc. No eggs, no milk, not much bread. She aged more the last couple of months than all the years before. . . . My grandmother also looks so thin, but has lost none of her dignity. For 85 she is carrying on magnificently. I feel like a criminal whenever I eat thinking how much they starve and I will be back at the next opportunity with plenty of eats.[60]

Korf's contributions were supplemented by packages of food and clothing sent by Rita. Korf and his wife also began to process the papers necessary to bring Margarete Korf to the United States.

Korf's relatives in Berlin were not faring much better. He wrote to his wife, "There are close relatives [in Berlin] who are starving and who lost everything they had [and are] exposed to a cold winter. Persecuted by the Nazis, ravished by war, struck by bombs."[61] When he was finally able to visit them, he reported to Rita:

In Berlin I found all my relatives, though I hardly recognized some of them. These people went through sheer hell. One uncle was buried under the debries [sic] of his house for 8 days and still thinks he was lucky that "he missed the fighting." They have aged very much and scars will be left in their minds which will never heal. Our own apartment, strangely enough, was . . . about the only house still standing in the street. Some stuff was pilfered by the Germans themselves, but much is left and I mailed you some boxes of it. . . . There is much more coming, silver, for 20 years in the family, linnen [sic] old china, more beautiful than we ever could afford to buy. As for the rest of Berlin, I better tell [you] when I come home or maybe never. It is good that you never have seen so much misery, so much physical and moral damage.[62]

In addition to his duties at Auerbach, Korf was also called upon to supply information to prosecutors of major Nazi war criminals concerning the structure of the SS. Korf was selected as an expert because he had studied the SS on his own for several years, and because he had learned much from his interrogations of SS prisoners. Nonetheless, creating the deposition for the upcoming trials at Nuremberg was not easy: "It took hours to lay out this extremely complex organization with its hidden branches," he recalled. Impressed with his efforts, Nuremberg prosecutors offered him a job as a trial interpreter. There was also talk of a promotion. The offer was attractive because the work was certainly less demanding than his current assignment. But because he felt that he could truly help the people in the Auerbach prison camp, Korf turned down the offer.

Even though Korf turned down the job offer, Nuremberg prosecutors nonetheless showed their gratitude to him by inviting him to observe the trials for a few days. As much as Korf supported the idea of trying important war criminals, he felt that some of the work of the prosecution had been done too hastily. He recalled hearing that Alfred Krupp von Bohlen und Halbach would be tried for exploiting slave labor. Krupp wasn't guilty, as far as Korf was concerned: "He was an elegant man in his mid-forties. . . . They had the wrong man. His father was guilty but had not been indicted because he was too old and sick." Korf believed he was being prosecuted simply because he was the symbol of the great Krupp arms manufacturing dynasty. He also found it disconcerting that the only war crimes that were going to be prosecuted at Nuremberg were those committed by the Germans. Though he himself had uncovered strong evidence that the Russians had committed atrocities against German civilians at the end of the war, the Nuremberg prosecution was not interested. Korf recalled that the prosecutor looked at his evidence and said, "They also won [the war], didn't they?"[64]

Korf's decision to remain at Auerbach was soon validated as he continued to sniff out important prisoners. One evening a woman came to Korf to inquire whether her husband was an inmate at the camp. It soon came out that the husband was no average prisoner; he was Hitler's loyal SS adjutant Otto Günsche, who was with Hitler during his final days in his Berlin bunker. He had told his wife everything that had happened during Hitler's last hours. Her story, remembers Korf, was "big news," since U.S. forces to that date had only the sketchiest information about Hitler's death. The wife said that Günsche was present when Hitler and his wife, Eva Braun, committed suicide on 30 April. Günsche and Hitler's valet, Heinz Linge, had helped carry the bodies out of the bunker into the courtyard for incineration. Günsche poured gas over the bodies and set them on fire, only to realize that he did not have enough fuel to complete the process. As a result, the bodies were barely singed. As Günsche and Linge contemplated what to do next, Russian sniper fire broke out. The men scurried away. Günsche ran home, told his wife what had happened, dumped his uniform, and headed for Bavaria.[65]

Korf promised the woman he would look into her story. He then immediately contacted the G-2 of the Third Army. The G-2 soon found Günsche in the prisoner-of-war enclosure in Aibling. Somehow he had been overlooked as an important witness. He was interrogated, and he confirmed his wife's story in all details. Korf later learned that the Russians had captured Linge. Years later, after he was released from a Soviet prison camp, he also confirmed the story.[66]

Korf also stumbled upon a prisoner who turned out to be an important scientist. The prisoner asked Korf to be released to his family. Scrutinizing his papers, Korf saw that the prisoner was an officer assigned to the Kaiser Wilhelm Institute in Berlin. Korf thought this unusual. The institute was a place for scientists, not for officers. Korf interrogated him, and it became clear that the officer was both an officer and a scientist: "With some coaxing, I got the story out of him that he had been working on 'Kampfstoffe,' [a] euphemistic term for poison gas." Though Korf released him to his family, he sent two of his men to keep the scientist under observation.[67]

Korf duly reported the scientist to the chemical warfare section of the army. An official told Korf, "We want the guy right away. We have been looking for him all over. Get him down here!" Korf complied. He picked up the scientist himself, and he assured the man's wife that he would be all right. He later learned that he was sent to Chemical Warfare Headquarters in Maryland. Korf followed up on his promise to the scientist's wife: "I called his wife and told her that her husband was safe and that she probably could follow him later. I believe that he got into the US under 'Operation Paper Clip' which gave German scientists immediate access to the United States."[68]

As head intelligence officer at the prisoner-of-war camp in Auerbach, Korf was directly under the command of the general of the Third Army, George S. Patton, Jr. In the fall of 1945 Patton asked Korf to present to him information he had elicited from German POWs regarding German weaponry. Korf was to fly to the meeting at Bad Tölz, near Third Army Headquarters at Aibling, in a Piper Cub L-4. His pilot lived in a tent that had a sign above it that read, "Housekeeper Wanted."[69]

The pilot's flying was as slipshod as his accommodations. He began the flight by asking Korf if he had ever been airsick. When Korf replied in the negative, the pilot nonchalantly said, "You will be." Korf recalled, "It sounded like a promise." The pilot was as good as his word. When he took off,

the nose of his plane went straight up and up and up. Then he did an Immelmann and turned around to look at me. I still looked healthy, not green. He turned the plane upside down and flew over a house so close that I thought I could touch the shingles. Still not a moan out of me. He became desperate, went straight up again and then flew low over the Autobahn, so low that his wheels touched the tarmac. The road bent slightly uphill. In that moment a truck came over the hill and bore down on us. He cleared the truck by inches.[70]

The arrival was no smoother than the flight. When Korf disembarked an MP immediately arrested Korf for being out of uniform; he was wearing not his steel helmet but his overseas cap. Korf did not have the chance to explain that he had been excused from wearing his steel helmet because it pressed painfully on his cracked neck vertebrae, an injury that had occurred at Düsseldorf. As Korf was trying to explain, the phone rang. The voice yelled over the wire, "Where is Korf? I want him here on the double." It was Patton. Korf's breach of uniform etiquette was forgotten, and he was sent to the general immediately.

Thanks to the information that Korf was able to elicit from his prisoners, he duly supplied Patton with a detailed report on specific German weapons. "He wanted to know the effect of new artillery shells that had a radar tip and exploded about fifty feet before impact," Korf recalled. He told the general that the shells were very effective, and he gave the general the names of two prisoners at Auerbach—both generals—who were well acquainted with how they worked.

Korf was impressed with Patton's mastery of minute details and with his German language skills. He observed that for Patton "the world was divided into good soldiers and poor soldiers." By Korf's lights, this explained why Patton hit a soldier who didn't want to fight, but attended the wedding of a soldier who did fight—to the daughter of a German general at the height of the fraternization ban. Meeting with Patton also made Korf understand that soldiers did not approach the business of killing the same way: "A soldier is trained to kill, he does it professionally and without passion. He may not hate the enemy, but destroys him." Korf considered himself to be the kind of soldier who "had compunctions about killing and tried to avoid it."[71]

Korf celebrated Christmas 1945 with his mother in Lippstadt. But familiar surroundings did not ease his homesickness. He wrote to his wife that he felt a bit guilty for wanting to abandon people who needed him in Germany so that he could have a normal life in the United States. Rita hastened to console her husband:

I must disagree with you when you call our wanting to live normal lives "little selfish wishes." They are not little and most certainly not selfish. After all, the primary thing in life is to have a home and family—ambitions notwithstanding. Even truly great men have families—and perhaps their homes and families enabled them to have success and achieve greatness. And isn't it important that people with at least a certain amount of intelligence contribute something to the next generation—or do we want them to be a bunch of "dum[b]bells"? Wouldn't this world come to a speedy end if people didn't live a "normal life"? Even the best inventors can't invent a human being with just chemicals.[72]

Korf's homesickness was no longer mitigated by his work: "I am slowly getting tired of seeing SS-men all day," he wrote to his wife. His superiors also made his job harder because they sent members of his team home without sending in replacements.[73] When he went to army headquarters to inquire about his discharge, the reply was discouraging. As he reported to Rita: "Now my redeployment. While EM [enlisted men] down to 55 points are already going back, the officer's score is only lowered to 70 points. . . . I went up to Army [headquarters] to find out when I finally can go home, and they said they do not know. This discrimination against officers stinks to high heaven. An emergency furlough to the States seems to be the only thing which can get you out fast and there seem to be people who succeed."[74]

Korf's situation changed a few weeks later, but not in the way he had hoped. He reported to his wife: "We are being detached from Army and assigned to XVth Corps, after MIS has decided to go out of existence. It does not mean an actual change, as we are supposed to stay right on where we are. But slowly I am getting fed up with things and Third Army inefficiency."[75] Since the Third Army had done nothing to facilitate his discharge, he asked for transfer to the Fourth Armored Division, which was approved in early 1946.

Korf soon discovered that his transfer did not help as he had hoped it would. Ironically, his wife had better information about the subject than he did. After making some inquiries, she reported: "'Ike' gave out following discharge scores for officers today: 'Discharge points will drop to 67 points or 45 months by April 30 and 65 points or 42 months on June 30.' Since you'll be in the army 42 months on May 30, that June business should apply to you. It's a long way off, but at least it's something to go by."[76]

Korf did not want to wait until June 1946 to go home. He was now willing to explore alternative means of getting out of the army.

He asked his wife to contact his former employer, Victor Ridder, to see if he had any connections that could be of use to him:

After the latest redeployment announcement, I am little willing to wait until the brass hats screw things up even worse. I am sick and tired of being away from home and of waiting patiently. Therefore, I ask you to go to Mr. Victor Ridder and tell him that I asked you to see him and to inquire from him how I could get out of the Army. Either by being declared non-essential over here, or by being declared essential over there; by emergency furlough or any other legal means. . . . It is time that something is being done and the smarties are wriggling themselves out of it while we get stuck. I sent Ridder some time ago a sword which was pretty valuable and I think he could do something, or at least, he could give some workable advice.[77]

Korf did indeed return to the United States in June 1946. But neither Ridder nor the army was responsible for making this long-awaited return possible.

6

From World War to Cold War

In late January 1946 Korf was sent to Regensburg by his commandant. Koref drove him. The skies were overcast, and visibility was poor. As they drove into Regensburg the two discovered an overturned jeep. The driver, an American officer, was lying in the snow, bleeding profusely. Korf and Koref resolved to transport him to a nearby hospital in their jeep. But as they tried to lift the victim, Korf's leg began to slip on the ice. Rather than let go of the injured man, Korf held on to him, but he could not maintain his balance. As Korf fell, his leg twisted and gave way underneath him. Korf heard his leg bone crack, felt unbearable pain, and fell to the ground. Thinking quickly, he slipped out of his raincoat and wrapped it around his leg in order to immobilize the injury.[1]

Koref somehow managed to get them both to the hospital. The pain was so intense that Korf was struggling to remain conscious. He told himself, "If I lose consciousness, my foot will be lost." The risk was quite real. The doctor informed Korf that he had broken the two lower bones of his right leg, the tibia and fibia, in a spiral fracture, and he advised immediate amputation below the knee.[2] He added, "You will be out of here in a month and get a prosthesis." Korf adamantly refused: "My 'NO' was so firm that he seemed surprised." The doctor acquiesced, but he warned Korf as they entered the operating room that they were short on anesthesia. He would have to be held down by two men as the operation was performed. "Without ceremony, [the doctor] started drilling, without so much as a local. I yelled, but the two sergeants were strong, as strong as any anesthetics. I fainted. When it was over I found that they drilled a hole straight through the flesh and bones of the foot and fed a wire through it. The wire was fitted into a horseshoe-like contraption, called Kirscher wire."[3]

After the harrowing surgery, Korf remained concerned about losing his leg. As soon as he could, he summoned a friend who was a physician in the medical corps. The physician warned Korf that he could still lose his leg if it became infected, and he advised a transfer to superior facilities in Bayreuth. The transfer was duly granted, but the trip was very painful for the patient. "The ambulance driver," Korf recalled, "found every shell hole in the road from Regensburg to Bayreuth. I could feel my bones rattle. . . . I passed out again."[4] The facility in Bayreuth was somewhat better, but Korf was disarmed by its architecture. "It was built with Richard Wagner's dough and all [the discomfort] of modern times," he observed.[5]

When Korf wrote to his wife about his injury, he downplayed its seriousness. "I am sorry that my handwriting is so bad, but I am in bed at the hospital. A week ago I slipped on ice and broke my right lower leg, both bones. I guess I will be laid up for a little while, but the doctor thinks in a few days I will be on the way to recuperation again."[6] But subsequent letters made it quite clear that he would not be walking any time soon. At Bayreuth, Korf's leg was placed in traction. He explained to his wife: "My leg is in quite an apparatus, 17 pounds on the silver wire through my ankle, 3 pounds lateral drag, one pound on the shinbone, 25 pounds counterweight. You cannot move even a fraction of an inch."[7]

The process was more painful than it should have been: "My foot . . . was supported by a canvas sheet on which my Achilles [tendon] rested. Slowly the [area] turned pink, then red. . . . I was in excruciating pain. One day a doctor came and said: 'Where is the doughnut?' The heel was supposed to be lying in a ring of cotton to lift it off the canvas to prevent inflammation. They had just plum forgotten about it. I thought this was just part of the overall pain package." As a result of the omission, Korf's Achilles tendon was permanently affected.[8]

Since enlisted men did not share rooms with officers, Korf had a room to himself. Soon this privacy gave way to loneliness. He was heartened by a visit from his mother's younger brother, Günther Mossner, in February. He was only seven years Korf's senior, and the two had attended the same school and always had been very close. Mossner was busy trying to revitalize the family publishing company. Before the Nazis came to power, Mossner publications had controlled a sizable majority of publications in Berlin. But the Nazis had forced the Mossners to give up their newspapers because ownership was forbidden to half Jews. The defeat of Nazism brought new complications to their business dealings, thanks to the postwar division of both Germany and the city of Berlin into American, French, British, and Soviet sectors of occupation. The Mossners' business was concentrated in the Soviet sector, and Günther complained that the Soviets were trying to seize German businesses as part of an effort to get the Allies out of Berlin.[9] He also told his nephew that he had been under observation by the Soviet secret police, the KGB.

Since prospects for Mossner publishing looked bleak in Berlin, Günther wished to move a large portion of the company into the French sector of occupied Germany. He had purchased a large building there and planned to start transferring all printing presses, machines, and personnel to the French zone as soon as he got home. Korf agreed with his uncle's strategy, and bid him a fond farewell.[10]

Only two days after the visit, Korf received a telegram from Mossner's wife stating that Günther had died in an automobile accident in Mellrichstadt, near Bayreuth, the day after he visited his nephew. Foul play was suspected, as Mossner carried a large sum of cash and was trying to move his operations away from the Russians. Korf did what he could to investigate his uncle's death, but he could find no evidence that incriminated the Russians.[11] After Günther's death, Korf insisted that none of his relatives risk coming to see him. "I would not like anybody to take the risk of these roads and transportation system," he wrote to his wife.[12]

It took a very long time for Rita to receive these words. Because of a serious lull in the efficiency of the postwar mail service, Korf's letters to Rita failed to reach their destination. Up to that point, she had been "living from letter to letter." And then, she remembered, "I didn't hear from him for a long, long time and I didn't know what had happened."[13] Nearly four months passed before Rita, frantic with worry, went to the Red Cross for information. She finally learned that her husband was alive and in the hospital, though the Red Cross was unable to supply information regarding the extent of his injuries.

Bereft of visitors, Korf had little to do but reflect on his pain. He wrote: "Pain is a strange thing and as relative as all the other emotions of life. A small pressure of any part of our body for a prolonged time seems to be able to arouse in us as much the feeling of pain as the crushing of bones and the tearing of tissue in a sudden accident. As a matter of fact, the latter we seldom feel in its full impact; excitement, fear, and other feelings seem to be strong enough to dull momentarily the strongest pain. Our spirit rises to its fullest height in such moments."[14]

Apart from reflecting on his condition, Korf passed the time by observing the goings-on in the hall outside his room. His room was between the wards for enlisted men and military prisoners. "All prisoners marched past my door," Korf recalled. "One of them stopped to be examined by a doctor, just a few feet away from me: Well soldier, where is your pain? The soldier was deeply bent over 'Just in my back, Sir. I cannot straighten up.' The captain examined him closely, the back, his legs, his arms. All of a sudden, he gave him a kick in the rear end. The soldier straightened up, straight as an arrow. 'Well,' said the captain genially. 'You are healed, you can go back to your outfit.'"[15]

Get-well letters from staff as well as inmates from the prisoner-of-war enclosures lifted his spirits. He recalled, "The German Red

Cross of Auerbach named me an honorary member and sent me a Rosenthal vase. They said they missed me."[16] He was missed at the POW camp as well. Only a few days after his injury, a riot broke out and four prisoners were killed. Korf could not help thinking that the incident might have been avoided had he been there. "I knew their problems and could solve them. I had very touching letters from them."[17]

As Korf began to recover, he spent his time reading books on history and politics. He prophetically observed to his wife that the Soviet Union "will be our main problem for the near future and we actually know very little about it."[18] He played chess occasionally with an officer. He also began to enjoy a steady stream of visits from his sergeant, as well as the corporal who took over Korf's duties. "He cries on my shoulder how difficult it [the job] is," Korf wrote to his wife.[19]

Apart from writing letters, Rita Korf could do little to help her husband. She could not travel abroad to see him, because "compassionate visits" were not allowed from the United States to the Theater of Operations. Nor was Korf allowed to go home, because in his present state he was not transportable.[20] In mid-March he wrote to his wife, "The healing progresses normally. There is sufficient growth to bridge the gap between the bones, but it is still soft. As the whole leg is being stretched to contract the pull of muscles, the latter would pull the leg out of shape if I were taken out of traction now, the doctor tells me."[21]

In May 1946 Korf was finally pronounced fit to travel home.[22] The long trip began with his transfer from Bayreuth to Wiesbaden General Hospital via train. He made the journey in a body cast. "Injured soldiers were carried into the car, their stretchers lifted onto the hooks in the walls." During the trip, Korf was approached by a strange young man who asked:

"Do you believe in God?" The young soldier clutched his blue bathrobe over his light GI pajamas. [The metal] on his combat boots tinkled as he bent down to my stretcher just above the floor of the hospital car. He looked imploringly at me, though his watery blue eyes did not seem to take in any objects. "Yes," I said. He seemed satisfied while he tried to keep his balance over the swerving of the train. . . . "Did you ever see a saint?" Again the whisper, the tense, pleading voices, the empty, sightless look. He did not wait for me to answer. He continued pushing the words out of his hoarse throat into my face. "I had never seen a saint myself, until last week. Gosh, it's funny to be one myself. But I won't talk about it unless you want me to." His voice had become so low that I hardly could understand him. An inner drive seemed to overcome him and I wondered what he might do next. He stopped as abruptly as he had started, turned around and walked down the aisle of the train, his unlaced combat boots tinkling at every step.[23]

Others walked in and gathered momentarily around the GI in the blue bathrobe who now shrilly announced: "I will not force any GI to listen when I talk about God. But I will help you if you want me to—for I am a saint." No one paid much attention to the delusional man. It was soon quite clear to Korf that his fellow passengers were not battle casualties, but personnel who had suffered mental breakdowns.[24]

As the train reached its destination, he pulled himself up in his bunk so that he could look out of the window. He was able to get "a glimpse of the neat brown houses of the German flats, brown cows and moist green grass." When the train reached the station, the patients got their first glimpse of the hospital ship that would ferry them home—the SS *Stafford*. As the wounded waited for transport, a demented WAC said, "It's a dirty rotten shame. They will never get me on the boat." She spouted obscenities and began to tear up her travel ticket.[25] When a medical officer tried to stop her, "she jumped from her bunk and with all her might she drove her knee into the captain's groin. The captain doubled up [in pain] and in a soft voice, he sputtered, 'Bad mental case.' Presently two husky GIs appeared and carried the kicking and screaming [woman] away."[26]

Exit from the train was difficult. Korf had to grab the springs of the bunk above him, hoist himself up, and slide over the side of the bunk.[27] After his ticket was checked at the gangplank, two GIs lifted his litter and took him on board. Korf's space aboard the SS *Stafford* was cramped: "My bunk was one of 33. I was close to the floor so I could roll out and get at my crutches. The transportation cast was very heavy."[28]

Accommodations on board were far from luxurious, but Korf was at least relieved when he was separated from the mental patients who had accompanied him on his rail journey. His sailing companions were interesting, particularly a captain who had commanded the prison watch in Nuremberg. He showed Korf several documents he had received from prisoners, including Göring. He generously allowed Korf to photograph the documents, but unfortunately none of the photos came out. He told Korf that Göring was wearing a "ten-karat diamond ring on his pinky when he was captured. There was quite a struggle to bag it. The highest rank won."[29]

The captain's penchant for liquor cost him his job. One morning he found himself in the hospital after a hard drinking bout with his colonel standing over him. When the captain asked the colonel what had happened, the latter replied, "You are in the hospital and you are sick." When the captain protested, the colonel said, "You [will say that you] are sick, or do you prefer a court-martial?" The captain chose to be sick.

Korf's homecoming "seemed to be in a haze." Because of the continued disruption of mail service between Europe and America, Rita had no idea that her husband was on his way home. She was washing her husband's car one evening when her mother ran out and said that he was on the phone—from New Jersey. He informed his wife that because of his injury, he was unable to go home to her. Instead, he was dispatched to Tilton General Hospital at Fort Dix for rehabilitation. Joyously, Rita and her father drove to Fort Dix for the long-awaited reunion, only to discover that it could not take place because visiting hours were over. Since there were no motels nearby, Rita and her father were forced to drive all the way back to New York, and Rita could not see her husband until the following day. Korf was proud of the way in which his wife kept their household affairs in order during his extended absence: "She had done wonderfully well and kept everything together with work, dedication and love."[30]

Unable to go home, Korf had to adjust to life in yet another hospital. He found Tilton Hospital to be a rather businesslike institution. "There was no self-pity or desperation," he recalled. "Everything was matter of fact. If a fellow was going to die, they put a screen around his bed and then they took him out. . . . The wounds often were horrible and many fellows were incredibly maimed." Despite this depressing atmosphere, Korf was surprised that the soldiers "talked about themselves . . . with a slight sense of humor. They had youth, resilience and optimism." When Korf passed by the ward for amputees and paraplegics on his crutches, he saw that "mattresses replaced the beds because none of them could have gotten out of a bed. Most of them were bouncing around on the mattresses, in good humor. It was a sight I will never forget."[31]

Shortly after his arrival at Fort Dix, Korf was transferred to Halloran General Hospital on Staten Island, which was closer to the home of his wife's parents in Queens. There was no question about his returning to duty, as army officials had concluded that his injury made him unfit for duty. But the extent of Korf's disability could not be determined. The board opted to recall him in six months to determine whether he was permanently disabled.[32]

While he was recuperating, he and Rita went to visit his friend Dean Wilkinson at Fordham Law School. Korf recalled, "I dragged my body, in uniform, with cast and crutches, into his office. He was jovial, as always." When the dean asked Korf what he had been doing since arriving home, Korf replied that he was recuperating at Halloran Hospital. Wilkinson retorted, "In other words, you are not doing a thing." He told Korf to hobble over to the next building to register for courses to complete his law degree. Korf later observed that this was one of the quickest decisions he had ever made.[33]

Though the decision to return to law school was easy, the daily commute between the hospital and the law school was not. Rita had to pick up her husband in New Jersey, drive him to school, wait until he was finished, drive him back to New Jersey, and then drive herself home to Queens. "She drove endlessly and waited endlessly," Korf recalled. Rita remembered leaving the house at six in the morning and not returning until midnight. She feared that she would fall asleep behind the wheel. She ultimately took the advice of friends and drove in her bare feet with the windows open and sang at the top of her lungs in order to stay awake.[34] Korf wasted no time in finishing his degree. He completed two years' worth of course work in one year, and made the dean's list in the process. His leg began to improve; soon the cast was replaced by a brace, which made him far more mobile.[35]

After Korf was finally released from the hospital, he needed two things: a job and a home of his own. He resumed his old job at the *Staatszeitung*, but his injury made this difficult. Although he had a vehicle equipped with special controls to compensate for his handicapped leg, the car could not give him the same mobility as he had had before the war. Korf was relegated to deskwork as a "rewrite man." The work was not interesting, which made Korf all the more eager to pursue a career in law upon completion of his degree at Fordham.

Finding a home was even more difficult. The postwar boom had left housing at an absolute premium. "The war had unhinged the economy," Korf recalled. "Everything had become a racket and black market was rampant."[36] He visited several organizations that were supposed to help veterans find housing, with no luck. Finally, he told a veterans' housing coordinator that he would "do anything" to get an apartment. The coordinator asked, "Well, would you go on the radio? There is a program on [radio station] WOR called 'Veteran of the Day,' would you be on it?"[37]

Korf agreed, and he found himself on a radio soundstage several days later in full uniform and on crutches. The host of the program, Jack Barry (who later hosted the TV shows *21* and *The Joker Is Wild*), asked Korf questions about his overseas exploits. His answers were well received by the audience. Barry made the following appeal to his audience: "If you have an apartment for this worthy veteran, call the station." After the show, the Korfs were offered a one-bedroom apartment in Harlem, but the price was twenty thousand dollars.[38]

No better offers came that day, but a week later Barry called the Korfs. He had "a letter from a woman in Queens. She offered to let me have her rental apartment if we would buy the furniture." The location of the Elmhurst apartment suited the Korfs, but the furniture did not. After Korf bargained with the landlord, he secured the lease for the apartment and sold off the furniture as quickly as he could.[39]

In the meantime, Korf was recalled before army officials. This time, they determined that his leg injury had rendered him permanently disabled. The board asked the Veterans Administration to determine the extent of Korf's disability. He was given an initial disability rating of 10 percent, subject to later review. Korf then requested an honorable discharge from the First Infantry Division, and it was granted on 15 March 1947.[40]

After his graduation from law school a few months later, Korf applied for admission to the New York bar. The application process was more difficult than he had anticipated. Though he had been warned that applicants for admission to the bar had to have "high moral standards," the paperwork involved was formidable, to say the least. He had to supply records for every school he had attended. Most of those records were located in war-torn Germany and were not recoverable. He also had to file affidavits attesting to the good moral character of his mother, sister, and wife. But the affidavits were initially rejected because they were based on insufficient evidence of "good moral character."

Miffed, Korf wondered what kind of evidence the authorities wanted to prove that his mother possessed such a thing: "How do you prove an elderly lady's good moral character when she led a sheltered life, never was employed and lived on a fixed income? It took me weeks to convince the [New York bar] that my mother was not a gun moll, that my wife had good morals and that my sister was an honest to goodness physicist."[41] His efforts bore fruit, and he was finally admitted to the bar on 25 June 1947.

With diploma in hand, Korf expected to get a job with good law firm in New York, but he soon learned that his lack of connections and his German background were obstacles to success. All the connections he had carefully cultivated before his departure for war were gone: "Four years of absence in New York is a lifetime. Nobody knew me now." He also found it ironic that his service in the American army did nothing to erase his German-born background: "Strangely enough, the fact that I fought against the Nazis . . . did not dispel that fact that I was German born, therefore a 'Nazi.' The doors politely were slammed in my face." Unable to secure a job in a New York law firm, Korf contemplated a move to California, where his sister lived. But he balked when he learned that he would have to establish a yearlong residency before he could apply for admission to the California bar; this he could not afford.[42]

The best option left to Korf appeared to be employment with the federal government. He went to Washington and applied for a job in the State Department. Though he was labeled "too old" for career service, he was offered a seven-year contract as an embassy counselor overseas. Korf was not inclined to accept the offer, since he knew that it would make little use of his legal training; he would have been more of a problem solver than a lawyer. As he contemplated the job offer, he paid a visit to Ludwig Oberndorf, the son of his old *Staatszeitung* boss who now worked for the FBI. Oberndorfer told Korf that he could easily gain employment with the FBI.[43]

Korf was not interested. As he told Oberndorf: "After all the years in Intelligence, I want to go straight. Work from 9 to 5." Oberndorfer suggested that Korf try the Justice Department. Korf went directly to the Justice Department and arrived there just before its offices were to close for the weekend. He filled out an application but was told by the secretary that she was leaving for the day and that it would not be considered at the present moment. As she covered her typewriter, Korf asked her to throw his application away.[44]

Frustrated, Korf went back to New York, and he and Rita left immediately for a vacation in Canada. Their sojourn was interrupted by a long-distance call from Washington, which was "quite an event in those days." The call was from the Justice Department, asking for an immediate interview. The application had not been thrown away after all. The right thing had happened, but at the wrong moment, for Korf had no intention of ending his long-awaited vacation prematurely. He and his wife had enjoyed little time alone since his return from the war. They had lived in a small home with Rita's parents after his return from Europe. And even after they managed to find a tiny apartment, they soon found themselves sharing it with Korf's mother when she emigrated from Germany. This being the case, Korf told the Justice Department that he would consent to being interviewed after his return from Canada.[45]

After his return Korf discovered that a division of the Justice Department known as the Office of Alien Property (OAP) was interested in his services. The position would make use of Korf's expertise as a lawyer, his familiarity with German law, and his investigative abilities as a former reporter. His first posting would be with the OAP's Overseas Mission in Berlin.[46] His work would involve ferreting out German enemies of the United States and seizing property they held in the United States. Since the U.S. government had "seized, but not expropriated all German assets" in the country when the war began, the Overseas Mission had to determine which Germans were eligible to reclaim their property in the United States. As Korf put it, "Who was an enemy of the United States? We had to find out. While it had been easy to seize enemy property, it proved to be difficult to return it to those who were held not to be enemy aliens and to finally confiscate it from those who were held to be enemies."[47]

Though the job was tailor-made for Korf's abilities, he balked at the idea of returning to Germany. As he told Henry Leroy Jones, a member of the upper echelon of the OAP who interviewed him for the job, "No, not Berlin, not Germany. I just came from there and I swore I would never go back. I can still smell the stench of the corpses coming out of the rain-drenched rubble. I want a job in Washington, over here."[48] Jones compromised. Korf would spend one year with the Overseas Mission in Berlin and then receive a permanent post in Washington. The OAP would also pay for shipment of his specially equipped car to Berlin. Korf was to leave the country as soon as possible. Rita would be allowed to join him within a month.

The subject of salary was never discussed. "That," remembered Korf, "turned out to be a big mistake. I got a GS-9, while my qualifications called for at least a GS-12."[49] In hindsight, Korf had made the mistake of equating the American civil service with the Prussian civil service, when the two in fact were quite different. He recalled:

The Prussian civil service remained basically unchanged from the early eighteenth century until the Nazis came to power. It was founded in merit and duty. The government would do its best for you if you did the best for it. But despite the fact that the United States civil service had been based on the principles of Karl Schurz, a German liberal who left Germany in the aftermath of the 1848 revolution, the agency that evolved never really matched the ideals of the founder. It took me almost 25 years to fully realize that pay and promotions were not based on merit, my work and my dedication to duty, but my connections and my charm.[50]

Korf was sworn in as a Justice Department official in December 1947. A few weeks later he was in Berlin. Though Korf was underpaid, his job was far from dull: his work in Berlin put him at the forefront of the cold war. Agreements made by the Allies during

World War II had divided Germany and the city of Berlin into American, British, French, and Soviet zones of occupation. Berlin was inside the Soviet zone of occupation, and the Soviets had promised the Western powers unfettered access to the city.

Soon tensions rose between the Soviets and their former wartime allies over the eventual disposition of Germany in general, and travel in and out of Berlin in particular. The Americans, wary of increasing Soviet influence in Eastern Europe, wanted to keep West Berlin and the western zones of Germany firmly under Western influence; they did not want to see them fall to Soviet influence. The Soviets, for their part, wished to end the four-power occupation and secure the creation of a united, neutral Germany that would eventually drift into the Soviet orbit. The more the Western powers refused to give ground on the subject of Germany, the more the Soviets complicated westerners' travel through their zone. They required the westerners to obtain interzone passes to traverse the zone. Korf recalled that the Soviets also "stopped any traffic into their zone and the three allied forces had to agree to traffic on Soviet terms."[51]

Korf once discussed the question of access to Berlin with Ambassador Armour, who had advised President Truman at the Potsdam conference in 1945, which had dealt with the Berlin question. When Korf asked Armour why the United States had not insisted upon the establishment of a neutral corridor between the western zone and Berlin that would have been open to all, Armour replied: "You have to understand the atmosphere in Potsdam at the time. The [question of] access to Berlin was discussed, but Stalin said to Truman, 'That is a question which can easily [be] handled between [Soviet Marshal Georgy] Zhukov and Eisenhower.' Everybody nodded and [we] went on with the agenda. Frankly, none of us thought that there would be problems."[52]

But problems had indeed arisen, and they became more acute after the United States began to pump money into the war-torn

German economy, which the Soviets perceived as an extension of U.S. capitalist influence in Germany. Korf thought of it otherwise.

Two events created a healthier West Germany: the Currency Reform and the Marshall Plan. . . . Today, few remember the Currency Reform, which overnight gave life to the German economy, at our expense and great sacrifice. All German Marks in the hands of the Americans were declared void, except for the 50 DM. This killed the black market. In Frankfurt I discussed the situation created by the Marshall Plan with Herman Abs, the foremost banker and president of the Bank Für Wiederaufbau, which distributed Marshall Plan money into the German economy. . . . Abs said to me, "The fact that there are no political strings attached, I consider the most outstanding feature of the plan. It will be of lasting benefit for the whole country and for Europe."[53]

Korf certainly agreed with Abs's assessment. As far as Korf was concerned, the Marshall Plan showed that the Americans had learned from the lessons of history:

After World War I, Germany had been similarly bled white. On top of the Treaty of Versailles [the allies] decreed reparations. For years Germany exported without getting any considerations. Its economy was hollowed out and there were no values created to restore it. This led to the inflation, which wiped out any savings and all fortunes. Then, under the Dawes Plan, Germany got loans from the United States at rather high interest rates. This money was not always wisely invested and did not fully replace what had been lost. After the crash of 1929, our banks recalled their loans on short term and the German banking system collapsed. In 1932 Germany was bankrupt again. It seems rather clear today that the hopelessness of 1932 translated into the insanity of 1933 and the formation of the Hitler government. While consequences hardly could have been foreseen, I believe that our government took the economic despair of a defeated nation into consideration. Like a blood transfusion, the American money slowly fed into the German economy and created an "Economic Miracle" (Wirtschafts-wunder).

He later wrote: "While the Currency Reform gave Germany a currency which today is one of the most stable currencies . . . the Marshall Plan brought an infusion of capital vitally necessary to revive the German economy, which had almost been totally destroyed by the disastrous war and the subsequent defeat. In my opinion, it was a master-stroke as there are few in world history."[54] But although Korf praised the currency reform and the Marshall Plan, in the short run they both exacerbated tensions between the Soviets and their former allies.

Amid rising cold war tensions, Korf found himself working with many other "former Germans who had not yet found a real job in the United States," along with "a small group of American lawyers who were not too familiar with Germany and its laws. I quickly learned that all the lawyers had been getting a considerably higher salary than I did."[55] Frustrations with his salary and rising cold war tensions aside, Korf lived a rather solitary existence in postwar Berlin. He wrote to his wife: "I get up at 7.30 AM, make my own breakfast, tea and a sandwich. At 9 AM I am in the office and eat at Truman Hall for lunch. Supper I mostly prepare myself and stay at home a good deal of the time or go to Harhack House for a movie. . . . After the lecture you gave me on spending and drawing on the checking account, I decided to cook my own meals [like] the obedient husband I am. . . . I always try to oblige."[56]

He also confided that he missed her: "Life is a little lonesome alone and I spend a lot of time home evenings reading my law books and writing. . . . I would like to have you here right now."[57]

His loneliness was not to be mitigated soon. Though Rita was supposed to join her husband only weeks after his arrival in Berlin, she soon encountered several roadblocks to her trip. It took her far longer to arrange for the shipment of her husband's specially equipped car than she had expected. When she was finally ready to leave, her husband told her to postpone her trip because of rising tensions between the Russians and their former allies. As Korf explained to his wife:

I had a long talk with my new . . . boss about your sailing and he advised me to cable you to delay your trip until things have cleared up a bit. . . . The Russians are trying to get us out of here and they are trying to make life a bit tougher. I do not believe that the Russians want war and I do not even think that they could wage a war successfully right now. But I also think that they are trying to do anything short of war to reach their goal— domination of Europe—as quickly and as safely as they know how. They only will stop when and if they are convinced that the next step means war. . . . All the little things you read about are steps in the war of nerves, but I do not want to expose you to any unnecessary risks and nobody knows what the Russians are going to do next. That is the reason why I thought it better for you to wait a few days. . . . Just be patient for a while and see what Joe [Stalin] is doing.[58]

He told Rita that she had no reason to worry about him: "I am kind of used to a risky life and my Army education comes in handy. That means that we watch our step and take one at a time, without being stirred up or nervous."[59]

Korf's frustrations with the delays in his wife's travel plans were somewhat mitigated by his work, which he found fascinating. Korf reported to his wife, "I am . . . as satisfied with my work—in spite of everything—as I have not been in years."[60] He was particularly fascinated with his work on the diaries of Hitler's propaganda minister, Dr. Joseph Goebbels. (The details of this case will be discussed in the next chapter.)

In the middle of investigating the Goebbels case, Korf found himself entangled in the U.S.–Russian antagonism that was boiling over into the cold war. In March 1948 he wrote to Rita, "I must tell you that I expect some things to happen in the very near future . . . it will probably take the form of some new Russian fait accompli."

He speculated that the Russians would somehow try to push the Americans, British, and French out of Berlin. But although many members of his office were moving to Frankfurt, he felt that the United States would not give in to Russian pressure: "I think that [the] U.S. [will] stay in Berlin and only will yield as the very last resort."[61]

He was right. A few weeks after Korf penned this letter, General Lucius Clay, the American military governor of occupied Germany, wrote to General Omar Bradley: "Why are we in Europe. . . . We retreat from Berlin. After Berlin comes western Germany. . . . If we mean to hold Europe against communism, we must not budge. We can take humiliation and pressure short of war in Berlin without losing face. If we move, our position in Europe is threatened."[62]

By early April 1948 the Russians were making matters more difficult for the Americans in Berlin. Korf boarded a night train from Berlin to Hamburg on official business for the Justice Department, but the train was delayed by a Russian roadblock. Korf weathered the delay by retiring to his sleeper car. After the train finally left, Korf was awakened from a deep sleep by an American train transportation officer, who asked Korf for his passport. Korf replied, "I am on an American train on official business and you have no right to ask for my passport." The officer replied that he had to proceed, because there were Russian officers aboard the train who insisted on examining all passports. Just as Korf replied, "To hell with the Soviets," he espied two Russian officers standing behind the American officer. Though they were polite, Korf was angry at the situation in general and the American officer in particular. He later read that the officer was court-martialed for allowing the Russians on the train.[63]

Tensions between the Soviets and their wartime allies escalated over the next few months. The Western powers felt threatened by the extension of Soviet influence in Eastern Europe. The Soviets, in turn, resented the introduction of powerful Western currency both in the western zones of Germany and in West Berlin. They felt their position in Germany was further undermined when the Western powers announced plans to unify and rebuild the three western zones of occupation in Germany. In protest, on 22 June 1948 the Soviets imposed a blockade on all land and water routes to Berlin. Korf recalled, "The Russians never admitted that they blocked Berlin, they just said they had to repair the bridges leading to the West." The purpose of the blockade was to starve the Berliners and force the West to come up with a solution to the German problem.

Rather than give in to such pressure, the Western powers airlifted supplies to the people of Berlin over the next year. The project was enormous. Korf recalled: "The planes, most C47's, barely touched the ground before they were flown back for a new load. The strain on the pilots was enormous. But it had its rewards. Most of them took dollars in American Express checks out, or vice versa. Each turn-around guaranteed a 10% profit. Everybody knew, nobody ever told. It was felt that the boys earned it. As big as the Berlin Airlift was, it covered only parts of the needs of the population. They suffered."[64]

Members of Korf's family were not immune to the hardships imposed by the blockade. He learned that one of his cousins was in the hospital in Berlin with a severe ear infection, and there was no penicillin available to treat it. Without penicillin, his life was in danger. Fortunately, Korf was able to use his connections to get the drug to his cousin.[65]

Korf managed to get out of Berlin before the blockade was imposed, and he moved to the new location of the Overseas Mission in Munich. He wrote to his wife: "An investigator and myself got out of Berlin OK. In Nowawes [now Babelsberg] near Berlin we took an English guard with a tommy gun in our car as a passenger and felt much safer after that. These trips through the Russian zone are not exactly fun."[66]

The closure of land routes to Berlin left Korf at a bit of a loss because his car and chauffeur were still in Berlin. He traveled back to Berlin via airplane and made plans to get the car and chauffeur out. He first secured an interzone pass, or "Interzonenpass," which gave him permission to travel from Berlin to Helmstedt in the western zone via the Soviet zone. He knew that the Interzonenpass would be honored by the British, French, and Americans, but he feared that the Russians would give him trouble about it. Knowing that Russian officials were impressed by documents that had a lot of official stamps on them, Korf sought to secure as many stamps as possible. To his chagrin, the headquarters of the military government in Berlin did not have the kinds of stamps that the Russians liked. But then he was fortunate enough to run into an old friend who was president of a German heritage club. The club used many symbols and had a lot of stamps to represent them. Korf recalled, "I collected all the stamp pads I could find, red, yellow, blue, black and stamped the Inerzonenpass."[67] In addition to the stamp-laden pass, Korf also wrote out a permit for himself, his car, and his chauffeur to cross the Soviet zone. Both documents, he recalled, "looked impressive."[68]

The next task Korf had to face as he headed out of Berlin was to cross the Elbe River. This was not easy, because the Soviets had closed all the bridges over the river "for repairs." Fortunately, Korf noticed a small sign near the bridge indicating that a ferry was close by. As he came to the dock of the ferry, however, he encountered another problem: the ferry was unable to move because a French bus had partially slipped off it; two wheels were in the water, and two wheels were on the ferry. The scene had drawn a small crowd of onlookers onshore, who observed the disabled ferry and the occupants of the bus, who were "wailing and gesticulating wildly." Korf espied a local farmer witnessing the scene and thought of a solution to the problem. He offered the farmer a pack of American cigarettes in exchange for the use of his tractor to get the bus off the ferry. "He disappeared like lightning," Korf recalled. In short order, the farmer returned with his tractor. He then tied a rope to the undercarriage of the bus and pulled it off the ferry. "The farmer got his cigarettes and I was the first one on the ferry," Korf remembered.

The incident with the ferry delayed Korf and his chauffeur; they had to get to the border of the Soviet zone before it closed at nine that evening. They reached the border outpost minutes before closing time. Korf provided something extra for the border guard: "I took out my two passes, folded them in half and put into each of them several hundred eastmarks [currency in the Soviet zone]. A very grouchy border patrolman, a Russian, sat behind the counter. 'Papers,' he said. I handed him my privately authorized papers, with the money. . . . He then looked at my driver and me. Nobody spoke. It seemed ages until he put his stamp on the paper. We left the hut. It was exactly nine."[69]

Korf's pride in his accomplishment shows in this letter to his wife: "I am about the only American on record who dared to take along a German driver through the Russian Zone by car and one of the few who had the guts to make the trip by land lately, at all. But I had my car and driver in Berlin, and I had to get them out. And I did. It was not easy and I will tell you the details later."[70]

Though Korf got his chauffeur and car out of Berlin, Rita was still having problems getting out of the United States. In the summer of 1948 her trip was once again delayed by her bad reaction to the inoculations she had to receive for residency abroad. When she recovered she had trouble securing signatures on visas and other travel documents, and then she found that there was no space available for her on transatlantic ships. She finally made the journey overseas in August 1948.[71]

She arrived in France, looking forward to a brief vacation with her husband in Paris. When her ship docked, however, Korf was nowhere in sight. She learned that he was hospitalized back in Munich with a kidney infection. The illness was the result of travel from Berlin to Munich in a rickety airplane that had no heat. When she finally met her husband in Munich, he insisted that the first thing they had to do was to tour the city. After witnessing the appalling devastation wrought by the war, she cried bitterly. Once she was settled in her Munich home, Rita decided to get a job. "The other wives played bridge and went shopping; that was not for me," she recalled.[72] She secured a position as an administrative assistant to the commanding officer of the Munich quartermaster depot.

Her husband found himself working harder than ever after his office was transferred from Berlin to Munich:

Our territory included Germany (to the extent that we could operate there), Switzerland, Holland, France, and to some extent Italy. Our mission was to solve post-war legal problems for the United States. These were primarily in the field of [uncovering] Nazi assets in countries other than Germany, in short [dealing with] legal questions arising out of the Trading with the Enemy Act. But we also represented the U.S. Government in citizenship questions and practically every question affecting U.S. interests in Central Europe outside of the domain of the department of State. . . . The status of the Mission, in view of the extended workload and authority, was raised to that of a "Branch."

The transfer to Munich did not isolate Korf from the tensions of the cold war. Korf traveled frequently to Berlin on business for the Overseas Mission or to visit with his family. At a reception for one of his family's publishing concerns, located in the Soviet zone of Berlin, Korf met the minister-president of Saxony, a German state in the Soviet zone. The minister was a member of the Liberal Democratic Party, which was then tolerated by the Soviets. Korf recalled, "We had a pleasant talk and he casually asked me where I lived in Munich. I told him and added casually, 'There is plenty of room under the roof for you.' He smiled and nodded and said something like 'thank you.'"

This brief exchange brought unforeseen consequences. Months after it took place, an American counterintelligence agent asked Korf if he knew the minister-president of Saxony. When Korf replied that he had met the minister briefly, the agent requested that Korf notify the CIC in the event that the minister contacted him again. Korf replied, "No, I will notify my superiors and let them make the decisions." The agent left, miffed. A mere half hour later, Korf was approached by an agent from the CIA, who asked him the same questions. Korf refused to pass on any information without the approval of his superiors at the Justice Department.

A few days after these curious visits Korf read in the newspaper that the minister-president had planned to take a vacation in the West, but had died unexpectedly. Suicide was suspected, but Korf thought it likely that the man had been murdered by the Soviets to prevent his defection to the West. Korf learned the following from this episode: "Any diversion from Soviet policy or planned desertion from the Soviet zone was deadly. Our intelligence agencies had moles in the East who fed both the CIC and the CIA, probably independently. The CIC and the CIA spied on each other and were in fierce competition."[73]

Korf had to confront cold war tensions in Berlin once more when he was doing work on his next major case, which dealt with the assets of the German dye company IG Farben. In the late twenties the company had established a subsidiary in Basel, Switzerland, which, as Korf recalled, "controlled its subsidiaries in the United States, General Film and Analine, GAF, among them. The Germans retained a 40 percent interest and a 48 percent interest was transferred to Swiss interests. The remaining 12 percent was held by a Swiss banker, Sturzenegger, who was close to IG Farben. It was the Department's task to show that this was a cloaking arrangement."[74]

The OAP in Washington informed Korf's office that one of the witnesses to the creation of the subsidiaries was a resident of Berlin. Korf was instructed to get to Berlin, find him, and get him to testify to the arrangement. Korf soon learned that his quarry was the deputy finance minister for the German Democratic Republic. His office was located in East Berlin. Korf placed a call to him and left the following message: "I am Frank Korf of the American Justice Department and I would like to see you in your office tomorrow at 10 AM. I hope that this does not inconvenience you." Korf's next task was to get to East Berlin. Although the Justice Department needed the evidence from East Berlin for the lawsuit, it could not order Korf to go there to get it. Korf understood this to mean that if he went to East Berlin, he was doing so at his own risk.

Risks there were. He had heard rumors that the Russians permanently detained "undesirable" foreigners by arresting them under names different from their actual ones; this way they could deny to authorities of their prisoners' home countries that they were holding those people in custody. Korf believed that "hundreds of Americans and Westerners . . . disappeared and [never] again were heard [from]."[75]

Korf found an ingenious way to avoid risks by arranging for special transportation into East Berlin. He contacted the offices of General Clay, who was head of American military forces in Berlin. He asked whether Clay's "automobile no. 2" would be available for a trip to East Berlin. He reasoned that the Soviets would recognize the VIP car and not stop and question its occupants. Korf knew that Clay's wife usually used the number 2 car for shopping, and that she happened to be out of town. He mused, "If her car disappeared, she would be more distressed than General Clay. They could stand the loss of an American civilian, but not the loss of her Cadillac." The request was granted. The car, with a civilian driver, picked him up the following morning and transported Korf through the Brandenburg Gate into East Berlin.

Korf soon found himself at the headquarters for the East German government. When he went inside, he found his interviewee standing nervously next to the open door: "He wore an open shirt (a tie would have made him look too much like a capitalist). He sat behind his desk, with [pictures of] Lenin and Stalin looking down on him from the frames on the wall behind him. He said, 'My chief, of course, is interested in the matter and he would like to be present, you understand.' I understood. We went next door to the Finance Minister, who was equally unimpressive and also wore an open shirt."

Korf discovered that his quarry indeed had connections to IG Farben and was present at the conference at which the subsidiaries were created. Korf then asked about the quality of the secretarial service at the ministry. "Excellent," the minister replied, and added, "We have everything the West has and can do everything as well, if not better." Korf then requested that a secretary produce a transcription of their meeting. After the secretary typed up the proceedings of the meeting, Korf quickly had his interviewee sign the document. Hastily, Korf then took the paper, folded it, and put it in his pocket. He thanked his interviewee and walked out. His exit was not quite as easy as he hoped it would be: "Two Russian soldiers with submachine guns stood in front of the door, and were confused when I opened it suddenly. 'Call back your dogs,' I yelled as I ran down the steps. My driver, a German, trembled as he heard the commotion behind me but he put the car in gear and we left, rather abruptly. The document was on its way to Washington the same day."[76]

Although the document that Korf obtained was important to the case, he received no acknowledgment of the fact that he had accomplished his mission under very risky circumstances. "I never heard a 'thank you,' from Washington or my boss," he complained.

This lack of recognition was mitigated by his fascination with his ongoing investigation into the diaries of Dr. Joseph Goebbels. The investigation yielded more than information concerning their origins and authenticity: Korf's interest in the diaries and his work on them lasted for the rest of his life.

7 The Goebbels Diaries

Without question, the highlight of Korf's tenure with the Overseas Mission—if not his entire career with the Justice Department—was his investigation into the diaries of Hitler's propaganda minister, Dr. Joseph Goebbels. His search for evidence took him through all four zones of occupation, camps for displaced persons, and the prisons for Nuremberg war criminals. He met highly placed members of the Third Reich and members of Goebbels's family. Korf not only uncovered previously unknown facts about Goebbels's personal life, but also discovered that the history of the diaries was as fascinating as the career of their author.

Throughout the investigation, Korf kept careful records of his research and his interviews. In 1987 Korf donated copies of these records to the Hoover Institution on War, Revolution and Peace at Stanford University and to the Institute of Contemporary History in Munich.[1] Since then Goebbels's biographers have made use of Korf's work.[2]

The Goebbels diary case was Korf's first assignment after he arrived at the Overseas Mission in Berlin in 1948. The case was controversial because an American publishing company, Doubleday, had acquired documents that should have been seized by American occupation authorities in Germany—Goebbels's diaries from the period January 1942 to December 1943. Contents of the diaries included Goebbels's responses to the German debacle at Stalingrad and the subsequent Soviet push to the west, the Allied invasion of Sicily, and the fall of the Italian fascist dictator, Benito Mussolini.

The copyright to the diaries had been given to Doubleday by the former U.S. president Herbert Hoover. Doubleday announced that diary excerpts would be serialized in newspapers all over the world.

The 1948 publication of the excerpts from the diaries of Goebbels—a major war criminal—created a sensation in the United States and embarrassed the U.S. government. Officials wanted to know how the former president and a private company had gotten their hands on documents that should have fallen into the hands of occupation forces. The Justice Department therefore ordered the Overseas Mission in Berlin to find out whether the Doubleday excerpts were genuine, and how they had come into Hoover's possession in the first place.

There were other important issues at stake concerning the copyrights to the diaries. Whoever creates a work owns the copyright to it. Since Goebbels had written his diaries, the copyright to his work belonged to him. In the event of his death, the copyright should have gone to his closest living relative. But the rights of that relative to benefit from publication of the diaries were limited because of Germany's status after the Second World War. Germany had no sovereign government; it was divided into American, British, French, and Soviet zones of occupation. The government of each occupying power exercised complete authority in its zone of occupation.[3] If Goebbels's surviving relative was a German living in the American zone of occupation in Germany, that relative was an "enemy alien" in the eyes of the American government, and his or her property could be classified as "enemy property." As such, the diaries, along with any moneys collected under the diary copyrights—were subject to seizure by the U.S. government.[4]

Korf was intrigued by the case because of his fascination with Goebbels in general and the power of the Nazi party in particular. He felt that the diaries would supply crucial information about the Nazi era. He wrote: "Since Goebbels was the man who controlled not only the centrally owned German press but also the news which he distorted daily, he was the only man who really knew what was going on in Nazi Germany before he shaped it to suit the Nazi cause. His diaries are the only cohesive Nazi records of the years 1933–45."[5]

To answer the crucial questions concerning the diaries' copyrights, Korf first had to confirm that Goebbels was dead and that he had kept a diary. He interviewed the famous aviator Hanna Reitsch, who had visited Hitler's famous bunker in April 1945. She was the undisputed star of aviation during the Third Reich. In 1932 she had been one of the very first pilots to cross the Swiss Alps in a glider. She was also known as the first woman test pilot; she successfully tested the Messerschmidt 163 and the aircraft that became the prototype of the V-1 bomber.

But for all her brilliance as a pilot, Reitsch was politically naïve. She was fanatically devoted to Hitler, and she believed the SS chief and Holocaust front man Heinrich Himmler when he told her that rumors of mass murders of Jews were just so much Allied propaganda. When the Russians were closing in on Berlin, she gamely flew into the city and visited Hitler at his bunker. She offered her airplane as a means of escape. Hitler refused, gave her a vial of poison, and said, "Hanna, you belong to those who will die with me. . . . I do not wish that one of us falls into the hands of the Russians alive, nor do I wish our bodies to be found by them."[6] Hitler later changed his mind; he ordered Reitsch and the Luftwaffe chief, Robert Ritter von Greim, to escape Berlin and arrest Himmler, who had betrayed Hitler by offering to make a separate peace with the Allies.[7] The two escaped Berlin amid a hail of Russian artillery fire. They reached the headquarters of Hitler's successor, Karl Dönitz, where they were finally arrested.

Reitsch was held at an American interrogation center for fifteen months and released in 1946. Korf met the thirty-four-year-old flying ace in her Wiesbaden apartment. She told him that she had also offered to fly Goebbels and his family out of Berlin, but they too had declined, saying that they preferred to die together. Korf noted that Reitsch still had the capsule that Hitler had given her. He observed, "She played with a cartridge shell. I asked to see it. It contained a cyanide capsule, which I knew so well from the encounters with the Gestapo and Nazi top brass." When Korf asked her what she needed it for, she was evasive: "'Just in case,' she shrugged."[8]

From the interview with Reitsch, Korf suspected that Goebbels and his family were dead. Any lingering doubts on this score were erased when he interrogated Hans Fritzsche, who had been Goebbels's deputy in the Propaganda Ministry. When Korf met Fritzsche, he was serving his sentence at the prison of the palace of justice in Nuremberg. Fritzsche was very cooperative. He recalled in detail the events of 4 May 1945, when he was captured by the Russians and ordered to identify Goebbels's corpse:

Accompanied by numerous high Russian officers, I was led into the garden of a small house and to a spot on which a door was lying. . . . On it was a corpse. It was almost entirely disrobed and only around the neck it had the remnants of a brown jacket, which obviously had been burned. The trunk of the corpse did not show traces of burning; the head, however, was very much destroyed by the fire. . . . My convictions that this was the corpse of Dr Goebbels was gained by reason of the figure of the dead man; by reason of the shape of the head on which the back was very conspicuous . . . and finally from the deformed leg. . . . I asked to have the golden party badge, which was still on the remnants of the clothing, taken off. On the back was engraved a number 24, which was Dr. Goebbels' membership number in the party. This was the body of Goebbels.[9]

In addition to the corpse, the Russians had stumbled upon notes in what appeared to be Goebbels's handwriting. Fritzsche duly identified a page of Goebbels's handwriting that appeared to be part of a diary. He added, "The page was on top of a stack of paper on the desk, I saw about 20 volumes bound."[10] Thanks to the Fritzsche interview, Korf could confirm that Goebbels was dead and that he had kept a diary.

Korf now had to determine whether the diaries mentioned by Fritzsche and the Doubleday excerpts were one and the same, and how Doubleday had come into possession of the excerpts in the first place. As a starting point in their research, Korf and his associates at the Overseas Mission consulted the "Publisher's Notice" in the recently published Doubleday version for clues. The notice stated:

Considerable fragments of the Goebbels diaries . . . were found in the court-yard of his [Propaganda] Ministry. . . . The unburned papers were taken away by . . . amateur junk dealers who carefully salvaged the binders and discarded the contents—leaving more than 7000 sheets of loose paper. . . . Most of the pages were tied up in bundles as waste paper. In looking over the material offered for sale or barter, a customer was struck by the impressive quality of the paper and sensed that he must have fallen on something of . . . importance. He acquired the lot for its value as scrap paper. The bundles, roughly roped together, passed through several hands, and eventually came into the possession of Mr. Frank E. Mason, who has made a number of visits to Germany since the war.[11]

Korf and his colleagues had to verify the accuracy of this account. They began by questioning junk dealers all over Berlin. They finally zeroed in on one by the name of Breier. On a cold and dreary afternoon in March 1948, Korf drove to Breier's flat in the American sector of Berlin. Korf found Breier at home. "He looked as ragged as the old paper he bought and sold," Korf noted.[12] Breier remembered acquiring the bundle of heavy paper—about seven thousand pages—in October 1946. He stated that he had purchased it from a man hawking materials found in the basement of the former Transportation Ministry in the Soviet sector of the city. Chaotic conditions in the wake of Germany's defeat help to explain why these important papers were simply lying about. One account from a German newspaper explains the chaos quite well:

When Soviet troops occupied Berlin in April 1945, they searched through the official German archives with greater vehemence than thoroughness.

[They] dispatched quite a good lot to Russia, destroyed some things, and left the rest lying about. As [was] done frequently on other occasions, they just emptied the file cabinets of the Propaganda Ministry on the courtyard and took the cabinets with them. Considerable portions of Goebbels's diary—unfortunately not the complete 23 volumes . . . were found in the courtyard of his ministry, where they evidently just missed getting burned to cinders. Many pages were scorched; many were missing altogether. . . . In those days the whole of Berlin was just one big junk shop. Everybody picked up what was lying about.[13]

Breier was one of those who "picked up what was lying about"—he took a number of reams of paper.

Neither Breier nor the man who sold him the paper recognized its value. Breier bound his purchase with string and paid 176 marks for it. As he loaded the paper on his cart, he noticed that it was of top quality, and that there was large-faced typewriting on it. On his way home he stopped in a pub for beer. He spotted a friend, a paint dealer named Erwin Richter, and showed him sample pages of the papers he had just purchased.

During questioning, Richter stated that Breier's find was conspicuous for several reasons. First, it contained the kind of information that was not printed in German newspapers during the war. According to Richter, the sample "had something about an air raid on Dortmund. . . . Details were described as we could never read in our newspapers." Second, the paper was top quality; the kind of paper used for government documents. Finally, Richter recalled that the large type on the papers was the kind of lettering used only by the highest Nazi officials.[14]

Although he knew that government documents could be sold at a substantial profit on the black market, Richter wanted to turn the papers over to the Americans. Richter explained: "I am going to tell you something: when those papers got into my hands, I said to myself as a businessman that they might turn out to be a very profitable business. One could have made a lot of money with it.

But I didn't want that; I said immediately that these papers ought to get into American hands. . . . The past few years had taught us, indeed, to meddle as little as possible with politics. We had burnt our hands before with that kind of business."[15]

Richter had connections with the Americans. His employee's daughter was dating an American counterintelligence agent, who in turn was acquainted with William Heimlich, deputy chief of the Civilian Administration Branch of OMGUS (Office of the Military Government of the United States) in Berlin and chief of RIAS (Radio Berlin in the American sector).[16]

Heimlich went to Richter's flat and looked the papers over. There is good reason to believe that he knew that these were Goebbels's diaries from the start, for he had extensive experience with Nazi documents. In the fall of 1945 Heimlich was a member of the Counter Intelligence Branch of the Berlin Command and head of the Documents Section of G-2. Heimlich had searched Hitler's Reich Chancellery for documents at that time and had stumbled upon documents that were identified as Goebbels's diaries from the years 1925–1926.[17]

In exchange for the papers, Heimlich compensated Breier and Richter with several cartons of cigarettes, valuable currency in post-war Berlin. Breier did particularly well with the exchange; he sold one carton for one thousand marks.[18]

When Korf and other members of the Overseas Mission interrogated Heimlich, it soon became clear that he was the key to solving the case because he admitted giving the diaries to Hoover. But Heimlich was evasive about all other matters pertaining to the transfer of the diaries. The accounts of Germans involved in the affair coincided on key points, but such was not the case with Heimlich's testimony. Though the Germans claimed that Heimlich paid them several cartons of cigarettes for the diaries, Heimlich insisted that he had given only "a few packages" of cigarettes as a gesture of gratitude to the men who had discovered the papers.[19]

Other inconsistencies surfaced as well. Although Heimlich admitted he had given the diaries to Hoover, he had a hard time convincing investigators that he had done this because officials in Berlin were "not interested" in them. Further investigation revealed that it was in fact Heimlich who had labeled the documents as "unimportant." In November 1947 he told George Elkan, a member of the Overseas Mission, that he had some papers that had belonged to Goebbels, but that they were "insignificant." Heimlich offered to produce copies of the papers for Elkan, but he never did.[20] Investigators from the Overseas Mission were "unable to verify that Heimlich properly reported these documents within a reasonable time after their acquisition."[21]

Not only did Heimlich fail to report the documents, but it is also possible that he tried to smuggle them out of the country. He was accused of attempting to hide them in packages of clothing and mailing them to a friend in the United States. The documents did not get very far. U.S. officials in Berlin opened them and suspected Heimlich of foul play. He was not prosecuted; news that a highly placed official was trying to smuggle documents would have no doubt compromised the reputation of U.S. occupation forces. Instead, the packages were sent back to Heimlich, along with a stern warning that another false step would cost him his job.

Since Heimlich was unable to get the diaries out of Berlin, he had to find someone to do this for him. A golden opportunity arose when Herbert Hoover visited Berlin in February 1947 as head of a commission to looking into the nutritional needs of postwar Germany. As a visiting dignitary, Hoover was exempt from having his baggage searched. If Heimlich could get the diaries into the baggage, they could leave Germany undetected. His next task was to talk Hoover into taking them. Fortunately for Heimlich, Hoover's entourage included Heimlich's friend Hugh Gibson, who worked for Doubleday. Heimlich contacted Gibson, and the latter arranged for Heimlich and Hoover to have breakfast together. During the meal, Heimlich informed the former president that he had found Goebbels's diaries from 1942–1943. He offered them to Hoover as an addition to the collection of the Hoover Institution on War, Revolution and Peace at Stanford University in California.

Heimlich also asked Hoover to have the diaries copied in New York and published. In this way, said Heimlich, "the world will know the horrors of the Nazi regime." Hoover accepted this logic. The diaries became part of Hoover's diplomatic baggage. In New York Hoover met with a representative of Doubleday, who copied the papers for publication. The originals subsequently were housed in the Hoover Institution.[22]

Korf's papers show that Heimlich wanted to get something in exchange for his donation of the diaries. According to Korf's brief on the subject, Hoover "confirmed to Heimlich the understanding of the Hoover Library that the publication and usual collateral rights under the author's league contract would be held by the Hoover Library as Heimlich's property for the duration of the copyright. Hoover also agreed to protect Heimlich's publication rights by agreeing not to make the diaries accessible to research students or others for quotation without Heimlich's permission for three years."[23]

In a lengthy brief to his superior at the Overseas Mission, Korf essentially proved that this transaction was invalid: "Mr. Heimlich's statement that former President Hoover had granted him certain publishing rights in connection with the transfer of the manuscript sheets, need, in my opinion, not to be considered here, as Mr. Heimlich must have known that Mr. Hoover had no such rights and could convey none."

More than forty years after the investigation, Heimlich continued to insist that he had done nothing wrong. In 1990 Heimlich contributed an oral history interview about his experiences during the war and its aftermath to none other than the Hoover Institution. Heimlich repeated that there were no takers for the diaries. The International Document Center was interested only in documents that related to the Nuremberg trials. Heimlich said he was unaware

that Hoover oversaw an eponymous institute that would be interested in the documents until he met him in 1947. Heimlich said that
if he was doing something wrong in giving the documents to Hoover, the chief of U.S. intelligence, who was present at his meeting
with Hoover, certainly would have stopped the transaction.[24]

Korf duly tracked down the intelligence chief, but he found him
to be less than cooperative about the meeting with Hoover and the
discussion about the diaries. As Korf recalled:

I learned that a CIA agent (station chief) had been present at the dinner
for the former President Hoover. I agreed to contact him. I was told that
he had no office, but a phone number. I called the number and a "colonel"
answered. I do not remember his name. I asked to meet him and he said
he would come to my office; I could not come to his. He came and he
acknowledged that he had been at the dinner and witnessed the presenta-
tion of the papers designated as part of Goebbels diaries. I asked him to
sign a paper to that effect. He refused. I asked him whether he was an
American citizen. He was upset. "Well, if you are an American citizen, you
are subject to American law. Sign." He did. I then destroyed the paper in
his presence.[25]

Heimlich's account is evasive when it comes to the question of
copyrights. He made no mention of copyrights to the diaries in the
1990 interview, and he was also murky on the subject when Korf
interrogated him in 1948. When Korf asked Heimlich, "Why do you
think Mr. Hoover thought he could not publish anything from these
documents without your consent?" Heimlich replied, "I haven't the
slightest idea. I don't think Mr. Hoover thought of it." Korf then
asked, "You think he considers you the owner of the papers?" Heimlich replied, "I don't think so."[26]

Korf's brief used articles in both German and American law to
prove that the diaries, and the copyrights to them, belonged not to
Heimlich but to Goebbels's legal heirs. From there on, however, the
U.S. government could exploit a clever loophole to acquire the copy-

rights: in view of the fact that Germany had no official government in 1948, as the occupying force in Germany the U.S. government had special rights to the diaries. Korf's brief concluded that since Goebbels's heirs were enemy aliens, residing in enemy territory, the Office of Alien Property could vest its interests in the copyrights and could pursue a lawsuit for damages caused by violation of its rights to the diary.[27]

Korf's next mission was to locate the surviving legitimate heir to the diaries and their copyrights. At the time of Korf's investigation, it was not known which of Goebbels's direct heirs had survived the war. Korf therefore had to find and question survivors of Hitler's last days at his bunker, particularly those who had been close to Goebbels and his wife, Magda.[28] Korf managed to track down Goebbels's mother, two sisters, brother, and stepson, Harold Quandt. He also questioned Max Winkler, Goebbels's longtime economic adviser, and the Hitler Youth leader, Artur Axmann.[29]

These interviews supplied not only the answer to the question of copyright, but also fascinating information about how and why the diaries were created in the first place. Max Winkler told Korf that Goebbels began keeping a diary in the 1920s. In 1933 Goebbels told Winkler about his dream of acquiring a large farm outside Berlin someday. Winkler suggested that his friend could sell some of his writings to the Eher Verlag, the official publishing house of the Nazi party. Goebbels duly complied, and his account of the Nazi rise to power was published the following year. But the sale of the writings did not generate enough money for Goebbels. According to Winkler, Goebbels was a poor businessman: "He had a good income from his royalties and his articles, [but] he largely spent it as he made it."[30]

Eleven years later Goebbels told Winkler that he had another plan to get his farm: as Gauleiter (head) of the city of Berlin, Goebbels controlled its finances and real estate. Goebbels wanted to sell city property and use the profits to fill his depleted bank accounts.[31] Goebbels added that Göring had done the same thing. Winkler advised his friend not to proceed; Göring was closer to Hitler and could use Goebbels's questionable property sales as a means by which to blacken Goebbels's reputation.[32]

Goebbels had good reason to worry about this. He had already run afoul of Hitler's graces thanks to his adulterous affair with the actress Lilli Barowa. The married lovers managed to keep the affair secret until the day when Barowa's husband, the famed actor Gustav Frölich, found his wife in bed with Goebbels. Frölich punched Goebbels. When he recovered, Goebbels went straight to Hitler and told him what had happened.[33]

Hitler was enraged when he found out about the affair and threatened to fire Goebbels if he continued to "shame" the Nazi movement by his behavior. The Führer phoned Magda Goebbels and told her about the affair. Hitler then sent Goebbels home with instructions to pacify his wife and salvage his marriage. The humiliated Goebbels chose not to face his wife. Instead, he went to his summer home outside Berlin and wrote letters to his wife and his mother intimating that he wished to end his life. He sent the letters by special courier. But at the last minute he had a change of heart. He took only two sleeping pills and went to bed.[34] Magda received the letter and rushed to his side. She was relieved to find her husband asleep but very much alive. Ironically, the melodramatic incident served to strengthen the marriage, for Magda never let her husband leave her sight thereafter, and she took greater interest in his career and activities.

But although Goebbels's personal life was stabilized, his political career was not. As a result of the Barowa affair, Göring's stock with Hitler rose, and all of Goebbels's transactions came under greater scrutiny. Goebbels and Winkler therefore agreed to drop the shady real estate project and focus on raising money via legitimate means, such as the sale of Goebbels's diary rights.[35]

Goebbels discussed the matter with his good friend Artur Axmann. When Korf interviewed Axmann at Nuremberg prison in the summer of 1948, Axmann was a little hazy about the details of the agreement with Goebbels. But he did confirm that Goebbels would be paid for writing a diary, and that Axmann would make a down payment when Goebbels particularly needed the money.[36] Since his diaries were his only true asset, he kept them religiously. Surviving members of his staff confirm that he thought of them as his most valuable possession.[37]

Harold Quandt, Goebbels's stepson, also had important information about the diaries. When Korf interrogated Quandt in 1948, he found him surprisingly cooperative. "He talked readily and seemed to make every effort to answer all the questions put to him as fully as possible," Korf wrote. Quandt, born in 1921, was the only issue of Magda Goebbels's first marriage, to the German industrialist Günther Quandt. Quandt told Korf that he lived with his mother and stepfather until he was drafted into the German army during World War II. Quandt and Goebbels were close; Quandt stated that Goebbels had treated him like his own son.[38]

Quandt told Korf that he came upon his stepfather writing in a book during the 1930s. Goebbels told Quandt that this was his diary and it consisted of several volumes. Quandt added, "I am sure all his diaries were his personal property and that he did not write them in his official capacity. They contained a lot of personal material which was not suited for publication without severe editing."[39] Quandt also stated that Goebbels's diary entries were later transcribed via a special typewriter that featured large type. Two such typewriters were found at Goebbels's residence and in his offices in Berlin.[40]

Because of Germany's declining military fortunes by 1945, Goebbels never had the opportunity to make money from publishing his diaries. When he realized that Germany was losing the war, he knew that his life was over. He therefore tried to hide the diary by scattering volumes in basements of official buildings in Berlin.[41] The ruse failed. The Soviets found about twenty volumes—covering the years 1935–1941—in the safe of the Reichsbank in Berlin in 1945. Fragments of his diary from the 1920s were located in Hitler's bunker by the Americans, and the 1942–1943 diary was discovered by Breier in the Transportation Ministry.

Korf's extensive research enabled him to create a narrative of Goebbels's final days. Goebbels and his family resided close to Hitler in the Chancellery. After Hitler committed suicide, Goebbels decided to do the same rather than face prosecution by the Allies as a war criminal. Goebbels tried to arrange for his wife and children to leave Berlin, but Magda decided that it was better that they all die rather than live with the onus of the defeat of the Third Reich. By the time Hanna Reitsch offered to fly the family out of Berlin, they had resolved to die with their leader. But Reitsch did not leave Berlin empty-handed. She took a farewell letter from Magda Goebbels to Harold Quandt, who was serving with the army in Egypt.

Goebbels and his wife and six children made their final exit one day after the death of their leader. Korf's investigation enabled him to provide the following account of the events of 1 May 1945:

Magda called Dr. Stumpfegger, Hitler's personal physician, and asked him to give the children lethal injections. They were clad in little nightgowns and pajamas. The physician used a strong sedative (Evipan) and they probably felt no pain. They died one by one. Magda then took out a cigarette lighter with a poison vial. The lighter-cum-vial had been a recent gift from Artur Axmann, the Nazi youth leader. The cyanide vial worked quickly. Joseph Goebbels slowly died in the adjoining room shortly afterwards, by all accounts from a self- inflicted bullet wound.[42]

The farewell letter from Magda Goebbels to Harold Quandt was confiscated by the Americans. Korf had the letter with him when he interviewed Quandt in Hanover in the middle of 1948, and he gave it to Quandt, who read it for the first time. In the letter Magda wrote: "Our splendid idea is being destroyed, and with it everything beautiful, admirable, noble, and good that I have known. The world that will come after the Führer and national socialism won't be worth living in, and that's why I've brought the children here.

They're too good for the life that will come after us, and a merciful god will understand me when I give them salvation myself."[43] It was in this way that Magda justified killing her six children, who ranged in age from twelve to three. The first names of all six began with the letter "H," to honor Hitler.

As a result of his interviews with Goebbels's former associates, Korf knew that since Goebbels's wife and children were dead, Goebbels's heirs clearly were his mother and sister, his only surviving blood relatives. Goebbels's mother had been located in Bachhausen, Germany. She had falsely registered her name with occupation authorities as "Giebes" in order to avoid possible prosecution. She was fined fifty marks for registering under a false name. Once she was properly identified, she received the copyrights to her son's diaries, only to see them vested by the U.S. government as specified by the terms of the Trading with the Enemy Act.

Though the government now controlled the copyrights to the diaries, it allowed Doubleday to continue publication of the diary entries and to serialize excerpts. But the government insisted that all royalties be held in escrow until the government could decide whether Doubleday was entitled to any compensation beyond printing costs.[44]

This resolution left several parties dissatisfied. First, there was Heimlich, who had given the diaries to Doubleday, Louis Lochner, a journalist who edited and translated them, and Frank Mason of Fireside Press. The trio contested the seizure of the copyrights and ultimately settled with the Office of Alien Property. Korf's papers contain a copy of a notarized agreement made in late 1950 between Heimlich, Mason, and Lochner on the one hand and the Office of Alien Property on the other. In exchange for $55,000, the three agreed to transfer their rights to the Goebbels diaries to the Office of Alien Property. They also agreed to transfer nearly $133,000, which constituted the profits from sales of the work from the time of its publication in 1948 to the Office of Alien Property.[45]

In the 1990 interview that he contributed to the Hoover Institution, Heimlich insists he did not profit from the diaries:

Well, the President [Hoover] came home with the diaries, they were turned over to Louis Lochner for translation, the book of the month club selected them, etc. etc. And then all hell broke loose over my head in Berlin. Oh, the rumors were fantastic. The President had paid me fifty thousand dollars for the documents, that I was not only unethical and a crook but rich. All of it was not true. . . . But it was a great flap, and it all got into the newspapers of course, and it was directed as part of an attempt to smear Mr. Hoover.[46]

But the 1950 agreement between Heimlich, Lochner, and Mason and the Office of Alien Property clearly shows that although he did not make fifty thousand dollars, Heimlich did profit from his business with the diaries.

The copyrights were later returned to the Goebbels heirs, but the saga over the ownership of copyrights to Goebbels's 1942–1943 diaries and profits from their publication continued. In March 1956 Goebbels's estate transferred the copyrights to the publisher François Genoud in exchange for 50 percent of the profits from publication of the diaries.[47] Shortly thereafter Genoud learned that a Swiss branch of Doubleday intended to publish the diaries in German. Genoud sued for copyright infringement. In September 1956 Doubleday settled the suit by paying Genoud fifteen thousand dollars in exchange for the copyrights.[48] The original documents—the seven thousand pages discovered by Breier—remained in the Hoover Institution in California.

The Goebbels diary case was closed after a two-year investigation. But Korf's fascination with the case did not end. From his research on the diaries he knew that the collection at the Hoover Institution was incomplete; it did not include all the daily entries from 1942–1943. From his contacts with the French liaison in Berlin, he learned that the French had located part of the typewritten diaries in Berlin. French sources also informed Korf that a CIC agent had found about six hundred pages of the diary in a trash heap near Hitler's bunker in 1945. The agent handed over the pages to the U.S. government four years later, but they somehow never made their way to the Hoover Institution.

After his retirement Korf searched for these missing pages. During a visit to the National Archives in Washington, D.C., in the 1970s, he stumbled upon a bundle of paper classified as "Misc Goebbels." When Korf opened the bundle, he found original diary fragments from 1942–1943 that had been picked up in Hitler's bunker by a CIC agent. He also tracked down about sixty pages of the diaries that had been discovered by the French. The papers were subsequently transferred from the National Archives to the Hoover Institution. As a reward for tracking down the missing pages, Korf was given permission to copy them for his own use.[49]

Korf's extensive experience with the diaries eventually brought him in contact with the Goebbels diary expert Dr. Elke Fröhlich, of the Institute for Contemporary History in Munich, a nonprofit organization dedicated to historical research of the Nazi period. Fröhlich dedicated her career to an exhaustive search for the missing portions of the diaries. In 1987 Korf donated copies of his papers on the Goebbels diary case to the Hoover Institution and to the Institute for Contemporary History in Munich. Fröhlich traveled to Boca Raton, Florida, to work with Korf on the material before she took it back to Munich.[50]

After the fall of the Berlin Wall and the subsequent end of the cold war, Fröhlich's search for diary fragments picked up significant speed. She wrote to Korf that she had found a "mildewed box buried near the Bunker in East Berlin, which contained new pages of the diary." She eventually learned that the Nazis had microfilmed the complete run of the diaries in early 1945, and she unearthed the entire microfilm collection in the archives of the former Soviet Union in Moscow in 1992. Fröhlich became the chief editor of the complete diaries. Published during the 1990s by the Institute for

Contemporary History, the collection comprises twenty-three volumes.

Korf's donations of documents to the Hoover Institution aroused the interest of the controversial revisionist historian David Irving. When Irving was working on a biography of Goebbels during the late 1980s, he wrote to Korf asking him if he had any other unpublished material about Goebbels in his collection.[51] Before consenting to share information with Irving, Korf contacted Dr. Fröhlich, who informed Korf that Irving was disreputable.[52] "Stay away from him," she warned. In his reply to Irving's request for an interview, Korf told Irving that he wanted to be paid a significant amount of money to be interviewed, knowing full well that Irving would not take the bait. "I knew damn well I would never hear from him again," he recalled. He never did.[53]

Korf's preoccupation with the Goebbels case—which lasted from 1948 until his death more than a half century later—is understandable in view of the fact that Goebbels was one of the architects of a policy that disgraced his family and brought war, destruction, and havoc upon the land of his birth. Korf's work on the diaries was intended to expose the misdeeds of Goebbels and his Nazi cohorts so that they could never be repeated. In the end, Korf was a true grandson of Curt Mossner, who firmly believed that evil could be averted if journalists were ethical and told the truth.

Conclusion

The comfort and security that eluded Korf and members of his immediate family during the Nazi era were provided for them in the United States. Korf's mother, Margarete, came to the United States in 1947 and lived with her son and daughter-in-law. When Frank and Rita Korf went to Germany in 1948, Margarete moved to California to be with her daughter, Hilde. Margarete became a citizen of the United States in the early 1950s. She died during a visit to Germany in 1958 at the age of seventy.

Hilde Korf became a renowned person in her own right. She pursued her study of physics, and in 1955 she became the first woman to receive a doctorate in physics from the University of California at Los Angeles. Thereafter she divided her employment between the UCLA Physics Department and the newly founded RAND Corporation, where she pursued her research on the upper atmosphere. She authored several articles on the subject and conducted studies on upper atmosphere physics for the U.S. Air Force.[1] RAND recommended her to NATO, and she became a scientific advisor to Greece and Turkey.

Hilde ended her marriage to Curt Kallmann in 1956. In 1957 she married Jan Bijl, vice president of Fokker Aviation. During World War II Bijl had been a member of the Dutch Resistance and served as a courier for the queen of Holland. He was captured and suffered imprisonment in a concentration camp. After her marriage to Bijl, Hilde moved back to Europe and became a visiting professor at the

University of Utrecht. Bijl died in a car accident in 1963. Heart disease claimed Hilde's life five years later.[2]

After Frank and Rita Korf returned to the United States in 1951, he continued his work for the Department of Justice. Following his stint with the Office of Alien Property, he moved on to the Admiralty and Anti-Trust sections of the Civil Division. Rita also obtained employment at the Department of Justice; she worked for its Office of Salary Stabilization before moving on to the Civil Division, where she worked as a legal secretary. In addition to her work, she became a member of the prestigious Capital Speakers Club, a noted women's organization. After sustaining injuries in a car accident, she retired on a disability pension in 1965.

Frank Korf found the remainder of his career with Justice rather frustrating. He struggled long and hard to secure a promotion to the highest grade, G-15. Because he felt his slightly accented English might be a liability in the courtroom, he took lessons with a linguistics professor for over a year to get rid of his accent. The lessons worked. Thanks to the professor's tutelage, people meeting him for the first time never suspected that he was born in Germany. But though his accent was gone, his German background remained, and Korf suspected that it served as an obstacle to promotions that he felt he deserved. He was finally promoted to G-15 only shortly before a heart condition forced the issue of his retirement in the early 1970s. The Korfs moved to Boca Raton, Florida, in the early 1980s. During his retirement, Frank Korf remained extraordinarily active as a freelance legal consultant and as a patron of education and the arts in the area. In 1999 he permitted my colleague John O'Sullivan and me to interview him about his life. Korf also donated his papers to Florida Atlantic University shortly before his death at the age of ninety on 6 September 2000.[3]

In the decade before his death Korf did a lot of writing and thinking about everything he had been through, and he came to some poignant conclusions. Although he regretted that he and his wife never had children, he otherwise felt satisfied with what he had accomplished during his life. He admitted that leaving Germany in 1937 was difficult, because it led him to fight fellow Germans, but this was his only alternative to a life "with and under Hitler." He did not regret going to the battlefront, because this enabled him to save American and German lives. As he put it, "I did contribute a little bit towards our victory."

From his experiences in the war he concluded: "In war, many men and women are killed because they do not understand each other. . . . I learned that much blood is shed out of fear and that understanding kills fear." He had his own way of putting the violence of war into perspective. He recalled:

Sometimes I would give my men a little talk before engagements. "You have many lives in your hands and nobody will question whom and how you will kill." But when you kill you must ask yourself, "Is this in the best interest of my country?" The other question is: "Can I look myself in the mirror five years from now and say this was the right thing to do?" It is fearsome when you consider the power over life and death which . . . a lonely soldier has. If he does wrong he can wound himself forever. In the heat of battle you go on. [But] when the battle is over, you can crumble. I have seen many men crumbled by peace. They called it battle fatigue, but very often it was guilt.[4]

K. Frank Korf donated his papers in order to draw attention to the experiences of German Americans such as himself. The papers indeed show that these experiences were significant and provide a contribution to the history of Nazi Germany as well as the history of the Second World War. On the surface Korf was a typical member of the U.S. forces fighting in Germany during World War II. He was drafted, went through the rigors of basic training, and complained about the food and ill-fitting uniforms. He expressed exasperation with the army's way of doing things. He resented the fact that the army kept him in Germany long after the war ended. He also witnessed the horrors of war from the fields of combat to the crematoria of Flossenbürg concentration camp. Like many, he disassociated himself from his wartime experiences after he was discharged from the army. He did not stay in touch with his former comrades in arms and shied away from movies and programs about the war.

But in many more ways, Korf was not the same as the others; he had qualities and experiences that make his story stand apart from that of the average World War II soldier. He was older and far better educated than the vast majority of men with whom he served. Indeed, he became something of a father figure to fellow recruits who frequently sought his advice. He also had contact with many famous people of his era, such as Maria von Trapp, Thomas Mann, Pablo Picasso, Anthony Eden, George Marshall, and George Patton.

Most important, Korf's direct contact with and opposition to the Nazi movement made him different from his fellow soldiers. He witnessed speeches by Hitler and Goebbels. He was victimized by the Nuremberg laws, which made him a "Mischling zweiten Grades." To be sure, what he and others like him suffered underscores the precariousness of the existence of the Mischlinge in the Third Reich. Work by the historians James Tent and Bryan Rigg shows that Mischlinge were vulnerable to a dizzying gamut of risks. Tent has shown that their Jewish heritage made them eligible to suffer the fate of their more "full-blooded" Jewish relatives in concentration camps.[5] On the other hand, Rigg has proven how the shortage of manpower at the end of the Second World War in Germany forced Mischlinge to fight in the army of a government that actively discriminated against them. As we have seen, Korf left Germany precisely to avoid these possible scenarios. Had Korf stayed, he could have suffered either the fate of his half-Jewish uncles, who were forced into the German army at the end of the war, or that of his mother's sister Lili, who was arrested and spent months at the Austrian concentration camp Mauthausen.

Unlike most of his fellow soldiers who were born in the United States, Korf actively fought against Nazism as a journalist and as an informant for the FBI. Unlike many men, Korf was also eager to join the army to continue his battle. As he put it, "I felt very strongly that I should go into combat, because these boys, they came from Pennsylvania and South Dakota, they didn't even know what a Nazi was. They had no idea what they were fighting for, and they were going to get killed for it, too. I felt I had a much higher obligation."[6]

Korf's German background made him different as well. It worked both as a liability in the case of his experience in the OCS, and as an asset in the case of his experience in military intelligence. And while military personnel who saw the horrors of Hitler's regime were duly shocked, Korf's shock was compounded by shame because of the fact that he was born a German.

Korf's commitment to fight Nazism—along with his linguistic skills and connections to German culture—not only made him different from the others; it also enabled him to make important and heretofore unacknowledged contributions to the war effort. First, had it not been for Korf and others like him, the Americans obviously would have been hampered in their efforts to obtain intelligence from the Germans during the war and to search for war criminals in its aftermath. Second, we may recall that Korf's treatment of the Germans was aboveboard and fair and that he was highly regarded by many of them. Because he could speak the German language and understand German culture, he was able to impart to them the idea that the American presence was a benevolent one. In this sense, he and his peers contributed to the speedy postwar reconciliation between Germans and Americans, which in turn contributed to the strong cold war partnership between West Germany and the United States.[7]

In the end Korf's mission to fight Nazism not only set him apart from his fellow soldiers, but also made him and others like him members of the resistance movement against Hitler. In recent decades the historiography of Nazism in general and resistance in particular has changed. As the historian James Sheehan puts it, "Whereas once [scholars] studied the source of the Nazis' apparently limitless power, scholars are now increasingly concerned with the multiplicity of opinion and the variety of resistance that existed behind the regime's monolithic façade."[8] The historian Martin Broszat insists that the number of resisters should be far higher than those tens of thousands who were imprisoned and executed for defying Nazism.[9] As he puts it: "We must include in our revised resistance canon the many instances of civil courage and steadfast maintenance of democratic convictions during the Third Reich. Many Social Democrats, liberals, and Christian Democrats were able to remain true to their political convictions during the Nazi period through acts of non-conformity and passive resistance."[10] If we accept Broszat's definition, Korf was a member of the resistance movement. His opposition to Nazism before he left Germany easily surpassed the minimalist definition of resistance. He exhibited civil courage when he ridiculed Goebbels at the Nazi rally and when he refused to have himself Aryanized. He maintained his democratic convictions by leaving Germany rather than staying and possibly being forced to join the Nazi party or the German army.

Some might argue that Korf's departure from Germany would disqualify him from membership in the resistance movement. One anti-Nazi political activist, Carl von Ossietzky, argued that "when someone who opposes the government leaves his country, his words sound hollow to those who remain. . . . In the long run, the pamphleteer cannot survive if dissociated from everything he is fighting against. . . . To be really effective in combating the contamination of a country's spirit, one must share its destiny."[11] Two points need to be made here. First, Korf did not dissociate himself from what he was fighting against after he left Germany. He resisted Nazism in the United States by investigating pro-Nazi organizations and by spying on the German-American Bund leader, Fritz Kuhn. His resistance to Nazism also ultimately defined his experience in the armed forces.

Second, although Ossietzky courageously fought against Nazism in the early 1930s, his insistence upon remaining in Germany restricted his ability to resist Hitler; he was imprisoned in 1933 and died of tuberculosis in Oranienburg five years later. But by leaving Germany, Korf was able to continue his resistance as a member of the U.S. armed forces. In the end the contributions of Korf—and other recent German émigrés of similar bent—to the resistance movement should not be necessarily obscured by the fact that they wore American uniforms and had the weight of the American army behind them. As victims of the Nazi movement, they shared the experiences and goals of their former German brethren in the resistance movement. And even though they were less defenseless than their counterparts within Germany, they undertook many of the same risks as those who openly confronted the regime, and they certainly put themselves at far greater risk than those who passively opposed it.

Martin Broszat has also observed that the spirit of wartime resistance carried over into the successor government to the Third Reich, the Federal Republic of Germany. As he puts it, those who resisted Hitler within Germany exercised a sense of "political and moral responsibility that constitutes one of the most valuable traditions inherited by the new democracy of the Federal Republic."[12] To be sure, those who resisted Hitler soon rose to the leadership of the democratic government that succeeded him, and they were committed to preventing a resuscitation of Nazism. Korf carried on this sense of political and moral responsibility outside Germany because he continued to wage his own battle against Nazism long after the war ended. He kept concentration camp documents to prove that the evils of Nazism were by no means exaggerated. His work on the Goebbels diaries—which he conducted over a period of several decades—shows that he remained committed to disseminating knowledge about the evils of Nazism in the hope that they could never be repeated.

It was not the resistance movement within Germany but the force of arms of the American, British, and Soviet armies that defeated Nazi Germany. Viewed from this perspective, the German émigré soldiers were more successful in their objective to defeat

Nazism than their counterparts within Germany. That their success was dependent upon leaving Germany and joining the American army once again underscores the overall difficulty of resisting Nazism.

But although Nazi power was quite formidable, it was not limitless in the sense that it did not deprive Germans of their ability to choose what to do about it. Korf's story supports Sheehan's view that varieties of resistance were possible during the Nazi era. Under Nazism, the Germans had choices. These choices may not have been enviable ones, but they were choices all the same. Some freely adhered to Nazi doctrines. Some who were in principle opposed to them nonetheless cooperated with the regime. Some who left supported the regime from abroad.[13] Some opposed passively, others actively. Others who left Germany continued their resistance from abroad in writing.[14] Others, like Korf, resisted Nazism during his years in Germany and as a member of the U.S. armed forces. As Korf put it, "I knew that the cancer of [the] Nazis had to be cut out and that people would be killed who did not [think] that they had a choice. But they did have a choice and did not make it. Without war and total disaster, totalitarianism could not be uprooted."[15]

Korf's story opens the door to many avenues of future research. He was but one of over thirty thousand German-born men who served in the U.S. forces during World War II. Of this number thousands were recent German immigrants who had some firsthand experience with Nazism. More research—including oral histories—needs to be done on men who escaped Nazism and then confronted its apocalypse as members of the U.S. Army. The views of this group of men on Germany under Nazism and Germany under defeat are worthy of further exploration.[16] Their precise motives for fleeing Nazi Germany and joining the American armed forces to defeat Nazism also need to be elucidated.

We also need to recognize the extent of the prejudice these men experienced during and after the war because of their backgrounds. Korf felt that his German background worked against him at OCS, cost him a postwar job as a lawyer on Wall Street, and stood in the way of promotions at the Department of Justice. In the end one of the bitter ironies of Korf's life was that he was penalized as a Mischling zweiten Grades in Germany, and he left Germany only to end up feeling penalized for being a German in the United States. While the racial characteristics of German Americans and Italian Americans may have made them less subject to discrimination than Japanese Americans and African Americans, the fact remains that both former groups were nonetheless victims of ethnic prejudice. The extent of this prejudice needs to be explored.

Notes

Introduction

1. Kurt Korf to Margarete Korf, 24 November 1942, K. Frank and Rita Korf Collection, Florida Atlantic University Library (hereafter Korf Collection).

2. Stephen Ambrose, *Citizen Soldiers: The U.S. Army from the Normandy Beaches to the Bulge to the Surrender of Germany* (New York: Simon and Schuster, 1997), and Paul Fussell, *Wartime: Understanding and Behavior in the Second World War* (New York: Oxford University Press, 1989).

3. Timothy J. Holian, *The German-Americans and World War II: An Ethnic Experience* (New York: Peter Lang, 1998); Don H. Tolzmann, ed., *German-Americans in the World Wars* (Munich: K. G. Saur, 1995–1998); and Arnold Krammer, *Undue Process: The Untold Story of American's German Alien Internees* (Lanham, Md.: Rowman and Littlefield, 1997).

4. Watson B. Miller, commissioner of Immigration and Naturalization, "Foreign Born in the US Army during World War II, with Special Reference to the Alien" (Carlisle Barracks, Pa.: U.S. Military History Library, 1948), Table 1, "United States Citizenship Status of Foreign Born Who Enlisted or Were Inducted, United States Army: July 1, 1940, to June 30, 1945." The table reports that 33,396 men who served were born in Germany. Of this group 18,944 were citizens and 14,452 were noncitizens.

5. Memoirs by German-born veterans include Joachim von Elbe, *Witness to History: A Refugee from the Third Reich Remembers* (Madison: University of Wisconsin Press, 1988); Tom Frazier, *Between the Lines* (Oakland, Calif.: Regent Press, 2001); Kurt Gabel, *The Making of a Paratrooper: Airborne Training and Combat in World War II* (Lawrence: University Press of Kansas, 1990); and Hans Schmitt, *Lucky Victim: An Ordinary Life in Extraordinary Times, 1933–1946* (Baton Rouge: Louisiana State University

Press, 1989). The most prominent German-born veteran is former U.S. secretary of state Henry Kissinger, who, like Korf and Elbe, emigrated from Germany in the 1930s and returned to Germany with the U.S. Army. Recalling his experiences, Kissinger noted, "Living as a Jew under the Nazis, then as a refugee in America, and then as a private in the army, isn't exactly an experience that builds confidence." Kissinger's biographer Walter Isaacson disagrees: "Not only did the army Americanize him, it toughened him. . . . [He had] an aura of confidence that comes from having survived in war and thrived in command" (Walter Isaacson, *Kissinger: A Biography* [New York: Simon and Schuster, 1992], p. 56). Kissinger's memoirs focus on his time as secretary of state under Nixon and have little to say about his life under the Nazis and his stint in the American army.

Chapter 1   From Patriot to Outcast: 1909–1937

1. Korf's lineage on his father's side is mentioned in the following genealogies: Patrick de Gmeline, *Dictionnaire de la Noblesse Russe* (Paris: Editions Contrepoint, 1986), p. 801; Victor Rolland, *V. and H. V. Rolland's Illustrations to the Armorial Général by J. B. Rietstap* (London: Heraldry Today, 1967), p. 1122; G. A. von Mülverstedt, *Der verstorbene Adel der Provinz Preussen* (Nuremberg: Bauer and Raspe, 1874), p. 50; *Genealogisches Handbuch des Adels*, vol. 6 (Limburg an der Lahn: C. A. Starke, 1987), pp. 424–425.

2. K. Frank Korf, unpublished memoir (hereafter Korf memoir), Korf Collection, p. 16b.

3. The Junkers were members of the landowning aristocracy of Prussia and eastern Germany who held substantial political power. The Junkers were conservative monarchists who exercised leadership in the army as well. See Gordon Craig, *Politics of the Prussian Army, 1640–1945* (New York: Oxford University Press, 1955).

4. K. Frank Korf to his cousin Berndt Mossner, 16 October 1974, Korf Collection.

5. Interview with K. Frank Korf, 24 February 2000, Korf Collection.

6. Kurt Korf, autobiography, 1928 (hereafter Korf autobiography), Korf Collection.

7. Korf memoir, p. 1.

8. Ibid., p. 2.

9. Korf autobiography.

10. Interview with Korf, 24 February 2000.

11. Korf memoir, p. 3.

12. Ibid.

13. Ibid., p. 5.

14. Korf autobiography.

15. Interview with K. Frank Korf, 17 February 2000, Korf Collection.

16. Interview with K. Frank Korf, 9 March 2000, Korf Collection.

17. Interview with K. Frank Korf, 25 July 2000, Korf Collection.
Schacht, in fact, was present at Korf's baptism. "He gave me a little pewter
thing, which wasn't worth a nickel."

18. Korf memoir, p. 6. Korf saw Albert Einstein deliver a lecture at the
University of Berlin in 1932. Korf recalled: "I remember he wore a black
sweater and he had that flaming white hair. And he wrote endless . . .
equations. And then he would turn around every fifteen minutes or so and
say, 'That's correct isn't it?' And go right on. Well, only the first three rows
stayed alive, or awake. And they were all Japanese or Chinese. They took
down every word. The rest of them were either asleep or somewhere else.
So I met him just shortly and as a teacher, he certainly was a bust. But . . .
I remember his chalk and dandruff settled on his black sweater . . . he
looked like a Christmas tree." Interview with K. Frank Korf, 6 July 2000,
Korf Collection.

19. Korf memoir, p. 6b.

20. Ibid, p. 6e.

21. Ibid., p. 6b.

22. Ibid, p. 8.

23. Ibid., p. 9.

24. K. Frank Korf to the Editor of the *Boca Raton News*, 5 January 1981,
Korf Collection.

25. Korf memoir, p. 10.

26. Interview with K. Frank Korf, 16 July 1999, Korf Collection.

27. Kurt Korf, "Admission Denied," English composition dated 17 April
1940, Korf Collection.

28. Ibid.

29. Ibid.

30. Ibid.

31. Korf memoir, p. 11b.

32. Ibid.

33. Autobiography of OCS candidate K. F. Korf, 19 November 1943, Korf Collection.

34. Interview with Korf, 9 March 2000.

35. In his book *The Destruction of the European Jews* (Chicago: Quadrangle Books, 1961), the Holocaust expert Raul Hilberg notes that as of 1939 there were 64,000 Mischlinge of the first degree and 43,000 Mischlinge of the second degree living in Germany, Austria, and the Sudetenland. The original census figures are published in *Statistik des Deutschen Reiches*, book 3: *Die Bevölkerung des Deutschen Reiches nach der Religionszugehörigkeit* (Berlin: C. H. Beck, 1942); book 4: *Die Juden und jüdischen Mischlinge im Deutschen Reich* (Berlin: C. H. Beck, 1944).

36. Korf memoir, p. 16.

37. Ibid.

38. James F. Tent, *In the Shadow of the Holocaust: Nazi Persecution of Jewish-Christian Germans* (Lawrence: University Press of Kansas, 2003), p. 233.

39. Korf memoir, pp. 16b–bb.

40. Ibid., p. 16bb.

41. Interview with Korf, 24 February 2000.

42. Korf memoir, pp. 16c–d.

43. Until fairly recently, historians assumed that all Mischlinge were exempt from military service by virtue of their "tainted" blood. But research by the historian Bryan Mark Rigg shows that up to 150,000 Mischlinge served in the German army during World War II. Rigg concludes that "the Mischling experience clearly demonstrates the complexity of life in the Third Reich. Nazi policy toward them was a maze of confusion and contradictions, which reflected the regime's uncertainty about how to deal with Germans of partial Jewish descent." See Bryan Mark Rigg, *Hitler's Jewish Soldiers: The Untold Story of Nazi Racial Laws and Men of Jewish Descent in the German Military* (Lawrence: University Press of Kansas, 2002), p. 268.

44. Interview with Korf, 24 February 2000.

45. Korf memoir, p. 18.

46. Ibid., p. 21.
47. Ibid.
48. Ibid., p. 20.
49. Ibid., p. 21.
50. Interview with K. Frank Korf, 25 June 2000, Korf Collection.

Chapter 2   How to Become an American: 1937–1942

1. Korf, memoir, pp. 23–24.
2. Richard O'Connor, *The German-Americans: An Informal History* (Boston: Little, Brown, 1968), p. 437.
3. Krammer, *Undue Process*, p. 26.
4. Korf memoir, pp. 24–25.
5. Ibid., p. 25.
6. Ibid., p. 29.
7. Ibid., pp. 26, 30.
8. Ibid., p. 26.
9. Ibid., p. 27.
10. Ibid., p. 28.
11. Kurt Korf, "Memories of an Elevator Boy," Korf Collection.
12. Korf memoir, p. 27.
13. Ibid., p. 30. Korf's correspondence with the law firm is contained in his papers.
14. Ibid.
15. Ibid., pp. 30–32.
16. Interview with K. Frank Korf, 27 January 2000, Korf Collection.
17. Kurt Korf to Werner Scheff, 1 April 1941, Korf Collection (translated from the original German by the author).
18. Interview with Korf, 27 January 2000.
19. Sander A. Diamond, *The Nazi Movement in the United States, 1924–1941* (Ithaca: Cornell University Press, 1974), p. 8.
20. Korf memoir, p. 36.
21. Ibid., p. 37.
22. Ibid.
23. Ibid., p. 38.
24. Interview with K. Frank Korf, 15 June 1999, Korf Collection.

25. Lillian D. Kozloski, *Hitch Your Wagon to a Star: Hildegarde Korf Kallmann-Bijl, Pioneer Researcher on the Space Frontier*, Works in Progress (Washington, D.C.: National Air and Space Museum, 1978), p. 3 (in Korf Collection).

26. Ibid.

27. Interview with Korf, 15 June 2000.

28. Kurt Korf to Margarete Korf, November 1942, Korf Collection.

29. Sander Diamond holds that the Bund posed an attractive alternative to the hardships of the American Depression; see Diamond, *Nazi Movement in the United States*, p. 151. Susan Canedy, however, sees the rise of the Bund as a response to the negative treatment of German Americans during World War I; see Canedy, *America's Nazis: A Democratic Dilemma* (Menlo Park, Calif.: Markgraf, 1990), pp. 214–215.

30. Korf memoir, p. 34. Korf was not the only non-Nazi investigating Bund activities. According to the historian Timothy Holian, "For several years before the war, FBI sources had been secretly sitting in on meetings of German organizations. . . . The government began keeping tabs on those members of German clubs and others attending their social functions who spoke in positive terms of Hitler, his government, or Nazism" (Holian, *The German-Americans and World War II*, p. 97).

31. LaVern J. Rippley, *The German-Americans* (Boston: Twayne, 1976), p. 204.

32. The story did not bring the fame to Korf that it should have. This was because the owner of the *Staatszeitung*, Victor Ridder, did not believe in glorifying his reporters by giving them bylines. Interview with Korf, 15 June 2000.

33. Diamond, *Nazi Movement in the United States*, p. 299.

34. Pro-Nazi movements in the United States had been under investigation by the FBI since 1934, and the House Un-American Activities Committee began its investigation of the Bund after Kuhn met with Hitler in 1936. See Richard W. Steele, "Franklin D. Roosevelt and His Foreign Policy Critics," *Political Science Quarterly* 94, 1 (Spring 1979): 17, and Rippley, *The German-Americans*, p. 206.

35. Diamond, *Nazi Movement in the United States*, p. 326.

36. Cited in ibid., p. 328.

37. Korf memoir, p. 39.

38. Although it was rumored in many circles that Henry Ford actively supported the fledgling Nazi movement in the United States, there is no evidence to back this up. See Diamond, *Nazi Movement in the United States*, pp. 96–97.

39. Interview with K. Frank Korf, 16 March 2000, Korf Collection.

40. Korf memoir, p. 40.

41. Interview with Korf, 16 March 2000.

42. Korf memoir, pp. 40–41. Oberndorf translated documents of pro-German associations in the United States for the FBI. Several documents translated by Oberndorf are housed in the National Archives. Records of the Office of Alien Property, Records of German Organizations: Deutsche-Amerikanische Berufsgemeinschaft, Records of FBI Investigations and Exhibits in Court Cases, 1936–1943, Expert Testimony, Exhibits, RG 131, Box 3, National Archives.

43. Interview with Rita Korf, 14 December 2000.

44. Douglas M. Charles, "Informing FDR: FBI Political Surveillance and the Isolationist-Interventionist Foreign Policy Debate, 1939–1945," *Diplomatic History* 24, 2 (Spring 2000): 231–232.

45. According to Douglas Charles, "Clearly, he [Roosevelt] had a low regard for his opponents' civil liberties and was apt to use surreptitious means to monitor them. . . . Roosevelt's callous approach can be understood within the context of the world crisis and his personal political style. Fearing irrevocable strategic and economic ruin in an Allied defeat, Roosevelt refused to bow to anti-interventionist pressure. See Charles, "Informing FDR," pp. 231–232, and Steele, "Franklin D. Roosevelt and His Foreign Policy Critics," pp. 15–32.

46. Holian, *The German-Americans and World War II*, p. 91. In December 1939 J. Edgar Hoover wrote bureau chiefs in major U.S. cities that the FBI was "preparing a list of individuals, both aliens and citizens of the United States, on whom there is information available to indicate that their presence at liberty in this country in time of war or national emergency would be dangerous to the public peace and safety of the United States." The full text of the letter appears in Don H. Tolzmann, ed., *German-Americans in the World Wars*, vol. 4, sec. 1, pp. 1520–1521.

47. Tolzmann, *German-Americans in the World Wars*, p. 1565.

48. Diamond, *Nazi Movement in the United States*, p. 323. The exact number of Bund members cannot be confirmed since Kuhn destroyed per-

tinent records of the organization. Kuhn claimed that the Bund had two hundred thousand members, whereas the Justice Department and FBI came up with a total of fewer than seven thousand. See Rippley, *The German-Americans*, p. 205.

49. Rippley, *The German-Americans*, p. 206.

50. Queen Victoria's son Alfred became the heir to the German duchy of Saxe-Coburg-Gotha in the late nineteenth century. Since he died without issue, the duchy was inherited by his brother Leopold, and after Leopold's death, his son Carl Eduard inherited the duchy. Because he sided with Germany in World War I, he lost his British peerages and was forced to abdicate his ducal throne. The deposed duke joined the Nazi paramilitary organization, the storm troopers, in the early 1930s and became a full-fledged member of the Nazi party in 1935.

51. Korf memoir, pp. 41–42.

52. Tent, *In the Shadow of the Holocaust*, p. 191.

53. Korf memoir, p. 42.

54. Ibid., p. 45.

55. Ibid., p. 46.

56. The letter of appointment to the Volunteer Registration Committee of the Selective Service Administration for New York City appears in the Korf Collection. According to a 1948 report of the director of the Selective Service, before 7 December 1941 "the Selective Service Act, with amendments, provided that male aliens within prescribed age limits residing in the United States were required to register, but only those aliens who had declared their intention to become citizens of the United States were eligible for training and service.... Under such provision, declarant aliens were classified in the same manner as United States citizens." After Pearl Harbor, however, Public Law No. 360 stipulated that "no citizen ... of any country proclaimed by the President to be an alien enemy of the United States could be inducted unless he was acceptable to the land or naval forces" (*Selective Service and Victory: The 4th Report of the Director of Selective Service* [Washington, D.C.: Government Printing Office, 1948], pp. 206–207).

57. Krammer, *Undue Process*, p. 27.

58. Interview with Rita Korf, 6 January 2001.

59. Kurt Korf to Margarete Korf, 2 August 1942, Korf Collection.

60. Krammer, *Undue Process*, p. 26.

61. Albert Einstein, Bruno Frank, Arturo Toscanini, and Bruno Walter also signed the letter. See Mark M. Anderson, ed., *Hitler's Exiles: Personal Stories of the Flight from Nazi Germany to America* (New York: New Press, 1998), pp. 249–252.

62. Kurt Korf to Hildegarde Korf, 3 March 1942, Korf Collection.

63. The National Archives contains records of FBI interviews with camp detainees regarding their associations with pro-German organizations in the United States, in Records of the Office of Alien Property. See also Tolzmann, *German-Americans in the World Wars*; Holian, *The German-Americans and World War II*; Stephen Fox, *America's Invisible Gulag: A Biography of German American Internment and Exclusion in World War II* (New York: Peter Lang, 2000); Arthur D. Jacobs, *The Prison Called Hohenasperg: An American Boy Betrayed by His Government during World War II* (New York: Universal, 1998). A very comprehensive work on the subject of German American detainees is Krammer's *Undue Process*.

64. *Selective Service and Victory*, pp. 206–207.

65. Interview with Rita Korf, 6 January 2001.

66. Kurt Korf to Margarete Korf, 1 August 1942, Korf Collection.

67. Ibid.

68. Ibid.

69. Ibid.

70. Ibid.

71. Ibid.

72. Elbe, *Witness to History*, p. 254.

73. Schmitt, *Lucky Victim*, pp. 185–186.

74. Gabel, *The Making of a Paratrooper*, p. 3.

75. Before shipping overseas, Ulrich Heinicke changed his name to Tom Frazier, and he later wrote a memoir. See Frazier, *Behind the Lines*, p. 120.

76. Miller, "Foreign Born in the US Army During World War II, with Special Reference to the Alien."

77. This article is in the Korf Collection.

Chapter 3   A German in the U.S. Army: 1943–1944

1. Lee Kennett, *G.I.: The American Soldier in World War II* (Norman: University of Oklahoma Press, 1987), p. 33.

2. Korf memoir, p. 49.

3. Ibid., p. 48.

4. Ibid., p. 49.

5. Kurt Korf to Hilde Kallmann, 14 February 1943, Korf Collection.

6. Korf memoir, p. 50.

7. Kurt Korf to Rita Baunach, 13 December 1942, Korf Collection.

8. Kurt Korf to Rita Baunach, 1 January 1943, Korf Collection.

9. Kurt Korf to Rita Baunach, 3 April 1943, Korf Collection.

10. Kennett, *G.I.: The American Soldier in World War II*, pp. 35–36.

11. Ibid., p. 36. According to Kennett, about twenty thousand Japanese Americans were inducted into the army. Though they were understandably bitter about being segregated, they fought bravely in Europe.

12. Kurt Korf to Rita Baunach, 17 January 1943, Korf Collection.

13. Kurt Korf to Rita Baunach, 2 February 1943, Korf Collection.

14. Kurt Korf to Hilde Kallmann, 17 January 1943, Korf Collection.

15. Korf memoir, p. 50.

16. "Advanced Student of Many Subjects Takes a New Course in Third Regiment," *Fort Bragg Post*, 20 January 1943, Korf Collection.

17. Kennett notes that local draft boards were even able to bypass orders from the Pentagon. He adds, "Nor was the Army more successful in preventing certain men from being drafted, notably, the young physicists it had working as civilians on its super-secret Manhattan project" (Kennett, *G.I.: The American Soldier in World War II*, p. 10).

18. Korf memoir, pp. 50–51.

19. Ibid, p. 51.

20. Kurt Korf to Rita Baunach, 15 February 1943, Korf Collection.

21. Korf memoir, p. 51.

22. Kurt Korf to Rita Baunach, 25 March 1943, Korf Collection.

23. Kurt Korf to Rita Baunach, 17 April 1943, Korf Collection.

24. Korf memoir, p. 52.

25. Ibid., p. 56.

26. Ibid. During the war the U.S. government made it easier for alien soldiers to become naturalized. "The Congress, in the Second War Powers Act of 1942, on the recommendation of the Immigration and Naturalization Service, provided for the expeditious naturalization of noncitizens serving honorably in the armed forces while in the United States or

abroad. . . . Judicial naturalization for the armed forces in this country began in May 1942. . . . Between 27 March 1942 . . . and 30 June 1945, a total of 110,678 members of the U.S. armed forces were naturalized" (Miller, "Foreign Born in the US Army during World War II," p. 274).

27. Kurt Korf to Rita Baunach, 17 April 1943.

28. Korf memoir, p. 56. Korf's application to OCS is housed in the Korf Collection.

29. Kurt Korf to Rita Baunach, 12 July 1943, Korf Collection.

30. Kurt Korf to Rita Baunach, 15 July 1943, Korf Collection.

31. Kurt Korf to Rita Baunach, 7 August 1943, Korf Collection.

32. Korf memoir, p. 56.

33. Kurt Korf to Rita Baunach, 11 August 1943, Korf Collection.

34. Korf memoir, p. 52.

35. Kurt Korf to Rita Baunach, 25 August 1943, Korf Collection.

36. Kurt Korf to Rita Baunach, 4 September 1943, Korf Collection.

37. Korf memoir, p. 52.

38. Ibid., p. 53.

39. Ibid., p. 54.

40. Ibid.

41. Rita Korf to Kurt Korf, 4 December 1944, Korf Collection.

42. Korf memoir, p. 55.

43. Ibid.

44. Lieutenant Colonel Stephen Ackerman, Commandant, to Rita Korf, 4 November 1943, in which he explained the rigors of OCS training; Korf Collection.

45. Kurt Korf to Rita Korf, 26 November 1943, Korf Collection.

46. Korf memoir, p. 57.

47. Ibid.

48. Kurt Korf to Rita Korf, 20 December 1943, Korf Collection.

49. Kurt Korf to Rita Korf, 25 December 1943, Korf Collection.

50. Kurt Korf to Rita Korf, 11 January 1944, Korf Collection.

51. Kurt Korf to Rita Korf, 16 January 1944, Korf Collection.

52. Korf memoir, p. 57.

53. Ibid., p. 58.

54. Ibid.

55. Ibid., p. 60.

56. Kurt Korf to Rita Korf, 16 January 1944.

57. Korf memoir, p. 60.

58. Ibid.

59. Kurt Korf to Hilde Kallmann, 27 June 1944, Korf Collection.

60. Korf memoir, p. 59.

61. Kurt Korf to Rita Korf, 4 April 1944, Korf Collection.

62. Korf memoir, p. 60.

63. Ibid.

64. John Patrick Finnegan, *Military Intelligence* (Washington, D.C.: Center of Military History, U.S. Army, 1998), p. 65.

65. See www.fas.org/irp/doddir/army/miotc/mihist.htm; see also Oscar Koch, *G-2 Intelligence for Patton* (1971; repr., Atglen, Pa.: Schiffer, 1999).

66. Interview with K. Frank Korf, 8 June 2000, Korf Collection.

67. Korf memoir, p. 61. Another graduate of Camp Ritchie, Joachim von Elbe, wrote that one of his classmates was Gaetan, prince of Bourbon-Parma, the younger brother of the last empress of Austria (Elbe, *Witness to History*, p. 262).

68. Elbe, *Witness to History*, p. 261.

69. Korf memoir, p. 62.

70. Elbe, *Witness to History*, p. 261.

71. Korf memoir, p. 62.

72. Ibid., p. 63.

73. Kurt Korf to Hilde Kallmann, 2 October 1944, Korf Collection.

74. Finnegan, *Military Intelligence*, p. 65.

75. Korf memoir, p. 63.

76. Interview with K. Frank Korf, 8 June 2000.

77. Kurt Korf to Margarete Korf, 8 October 1944 (translated from the original German by the author), Korf Collection.

78. Kurt Korf to Rita Korf, 2 November 1944, Korf Collection.

79. Interview with Rita Korf, 6 January 2001.

80. Kurt Korf to Rita Korf, 7 November 1944, Korf Collection.

81. Korf memoir, p. 64.

82. Ibid.

83. Elbe, *Witness to History*, p. 268.

84. Korf memoir, p. 64.

85. Ibid.

86. Kurt Korf to Rita Korf, 2 November 1944.

87. Kurt Korf to Rita Korf, 7 November 1944.

88. Korf memoir, p. 65.

89. Ibid., p. 66.

90. Ibid.

91. Ibid., p. 67.

92. Ibid.

93. Ibid.

94. Ibid., p. 68.

95. Ibid., p. 67a.

96. Joseph W. Benderesky, *The Jewish Threat: Anti-Semitic Policies of the U.S. Army* (New York: Basic Books, 2000), p. 336.

97. LSTs were landing ships that could "run aground to unload troops and vehicles. . . . The U.S. LSTs were 328 feet long and could carry over a ton of cargo" (Norman Polmar and Thomas B. Allen, *World War II: Encyclopedia of the War Years, 1941–1945* (New York: Random House, 1996), p. 87.

98. Korf memoir, p. 68.

99. Ibid.

100. Kurt Korf to Rita Korf, 14 December 1944, Korf Collection.

101. Korf memoir, p. 69.

102. "LSTs demonstrated a remarkable capacity to absorb damage and survive. Despite the sobriquet 'Large Slow Target' which was bestowed by irreverent crewmembers, the LSTs suffered few losses in proportion to their numbers. Their structural arrangement provided unusual strength and buoyancy. Of the 1,052 American-built LSTs . . . only twenty-six were lost to enemy action" (Polmar and Allen, *World War II*, p. 489).

103. Korf memoir, p. 69.

104. Ibid.

105. Ibid., p. 76a.

106. Kurt Korf to Rita Korf, 20 December 1944, Korf Collection.

107. Ibid.

108. Ibid.

109. Korf memoir, p. 70.

110. Ibid., p. 71.

111. Ibid.

112. Ibid.

113. Ibid., p. 76a.

114. K. Frank Korf to Rita Korf, 24 January 1945, Korf Collection.

115. Korf memoir, p. 73.

116. Ibid., p. 77.

117. Ibid.

118. Ibid., p. 76.

119. K. Frank Korf to Rita Korf, 16 June 1945, Korf Collection.

120. Korf memoir, p. 76.

121. The Supreme Headquarters of the Allied Expeditionary Force was established in 1942 near London as headquarters for General Dwight D. Eisenhower. SHAEF also provided the "command structure for Allied ground forces in Europe." By the time Korf reached Europe in late 1944, SHAEF had moved to Paris (Polmar and Allen, *World War II*, p. 781).

122. Korf memoir, p. 74. German-born soldiers in the American army were not always shot, but they did suffer ill-treatment. John Bitzer, who emigrated from Germany as a small child, became a ball turret gunner in the air force and was shot down in France in 1943. He spent the rest of the war in prison camps in Germany. Though he never divulged any information beyond his name, rank, and serial number, the Germans somehow found out he was born in Germany and singled him out for beatings and sessions in solitary confinement. He recalled that at Luft Stalag IV there was "one guard who singled me out. He hit me on the side of the head and sent me sprawling. After a few more punches he let me know that he was not happy about my fighting against the 'Fatherland'" (interview with Jay Bitzer, December 2003).

123. One German-born soldier, Ulrich Heinicke, voluntarily changed his name. Before he was shipped overseas, he remembered, "I suddenly realized that with my German name . . . if I were caught, I would be considered a traitor, and I would be tortured or killed at once rather than taken prisoner as an ordinary American soldier would. I rushed to the adjutant general's office, and the captain . . . told me to change my name at once." He was given half an hour to do this. Heinicke grabbed a phone book and one hour later emerged with the name Tom Frazier. See Frazier, *Behind the Lines*, p. 131.

Chapter 4   Into the Abyss: 1944–1945

1. On the American side, 20,000 were killed, 20,000 were captured, and 40,000 were wounded. German casualties were more severe: 30,000 were killed, 40,000 were wounded, and 30,000 became prisoners of war (Polmar and Allen, *World War II*, p. 97). Research by the historian Stephen Ambrose has shown that a large number of German soldiers were only fifteen or sixteen years of age (Ambrose, *Citizen Soldiers*, p. 185).

2. Korf memoir, p. 84.

3. Ibid., p. 75. The camaraderie between Jews and gentiles on Korf's team stands in contrast to the historian Joseph Benderesky's contention that although "Jewish soldiers found that their non-Jewish fellow soldiers were equally devoted to the same [democratic] ideals . . . their commitment to such principles did not preclude anti-Semitic attitudes or expressions" (Benderesky, *The Jewish Threat*, p. 298).

4. Historical Section, Military Intelligence Service, comp., "An Evaluation of Military Intelligence Service Specialist Teams, European Theater of Operations, United States Army," July 1945 (original manuscript, Records of Headquarters, European Theater of Operations, U.S. Army [World War II], ETO Historical Division, Program Files, USFET, G-2 Operations Reports, 1945–1946, RG 498, Box 833533, National Archives), p. 24.

5. Records show that over two thousand V-1 missiles fell on England; approximately the same number that fell on Belgium. See Polmar and Allen, *World War II*, p. 860.

6. Rita Korf to K. Frank Korf, 20 February 1945, Korf Collection.

7. Korf memoir, p. 79.

8. Interview with K. Frank Korf, 20 December 1999, Korf Collection.

9. Korf memoir, pp. 79–80.

10. Ibid., pp. 80–81.

11. Interview with K. Frank Korf, 15 June 1999.

12. Ibid.

13. Korf memoir, p. 81.

14. K. Frank Korf to Rita Korf, 12 February 1945, Korf Collection.

15. Rita Korf to K. Frank Korf, 20 February 1945.

16. Korf memoir, p. 76.

17. Ibid., p. 83.

18. Ken Hechler, *The Bridge at Remagen*, 4th ed. (Missoula, Mont.: Pictorial Histories, 1999), p. 113.

19. Stephen Ambrose, *American Heritage New History of World War II* (New York: Viking, 1997), p. 545.

20. Polmar and Allen, *World War II*, p. 513.

21. Korf memoir, p. 85. Several years later, Korf met LeMaitre, whose only complaint about his stint as a POW in the United States was that he hated the food.

22. In theory the business of attaching units was meant to increase the number of trained specialists at the front, but in practice it was fraught with administrative difficulties. One G-2 of the Third Army complained, "Administrative problems were constant. The attachment of teams from MIS to any headquarters, which permits administrative control to be exercised by that distant Headquarters, adds a tremendous burden on an operating staff section which controls the functioning of the team. MIS personnel should be provided as are all other reinforcements. The presumption that only MIS can dispose of these teams to meet operational exigencies is not concurred in" (Historical Section, Military Intelligence Service, comp., "An Evaluation of Military Intelligence Service Specialist Teams, European Theater of Operations").

23. According to the Third Army historian Charles Province, "The G-2 section was responsible for all matters pertaining to the collection, evaluation, interpretation and distribution of information about the enemy. Also, they were responsible for counterintelligence activities. Generally . . . this section is responsible for informing the commander regarding the enemy's situation and capabilities, the weather and terrain." Province, *Patton's Third Army: A Daily Combat Diary* (New York: Hippocrene Books, 1992), pp. 307–308.

24. Korf memoir, p. 87.

25. Ibid., p. 87a. The Maginot Line was a series of defenses that the French had constructed along its border with Germany during the 1920s and 1930s. Although the French thought that the line would protect France in the event of a German invasion, it failed miserably; the Germans were able to invade France by going through Belgium.

26. K. Frank Korf to Rita Korf, 28 March 1945, Korf Collection.

27. K. Frank Korf to Rita Korf, 3 April 1945, Korf Collection.

28. Korf memoir, pp. 89–89a.

29. Ibid., p. 91.

30. K. Frank Korf to Rita Korf, 10 April 1945, Korf Collection; Kennett, *G.I.: The American Soldier in World War II*, p. 214.

31. Korf memoir, p. 90.

32. Historical Section, Military Intelligence Service, comp., "An Evaluation of Military Intelligence Service Specialist Teams, European Theater of Operations," p. 24.

33. Korf memoir, p. 89a.

34. Ibid., p. 89b.

35. Ibid.

36. Ibid., p. 89d.

37. Polmar and Allen, *World War II*, pp. 734–735.

38. Korf memoir, p. 89f.

39. Counterintelligence is a government operation designed to protect the government's own information and to secure the secrecy of its intelligence operations. In January 1944 the U.S. Counterintelligence Corps was restructured. In the European Theater of Operations this "resulted in the creation of a 17-man divisional CIC detachment composed of an administrative team and two operational teams. Larger counterintelligence detachments were attached to higher tactical echelons and to rear area service organizations. Finally, a more realistic allowance of equipment was secured, allocating a jeep to every two counterintelligence agents and giving the CIC the mobility it needed in a combat environment." See www.army.mil/cmh-pg/books/Lineage/mi/ch6.htm.

40. Korf memoir, p. 92.

41. Ibid.

42. K. Frank Korf to Center Manager, National Personnel Records Center, St. Louis, Mo., 23 January 1978, Korf Collection.

43. Korf memoir, p. 98.

44. Ibid.

45. Ibid.

46. Ibid., p. 99.

47. Korf to Center Manager, 23 January 1978.

48. Korf memoir, p. 99a.

49. Ibid., p. 99b.

50. K. Frank Korf to Rita Korf, 28 March 1945.

51. Korf memoir, p. 100.

52. K. Frank Korf to Rita Korf, 20 April 1945, Korf Collection.

53. Korf memoir, p. 100.

54. Ernst Linde to K. Frank Korf, Heidelberg, Germany, 29 June 1945, Korf Collection. This letter was written on stationery of the Nazi Chancellery in Munich.

55. Korf memoir, p. 101.

56. Ibid.

57. Ibid., p. 101b.

58. Ibid.

59. Ibid.

60. K. Frank Korf to Rita Korf, 28 April 1945, Korf Collection.

61. Korf memoir, p. 102. In his memoir Korf states that he entered the camp on 1 May, but the National Archives contains Korf's detailed report on the camp, which summarizes his investigation and states that he was present at the camp from 29 April to 1 May 1945 (Report from K. Frank Korf, 2nd Lt. AUS CIC MII TEAM, to Assistant Chief of Staff, G-2, 97th Infantry Division, 1 May 1945, Records of the Third Army Interrogation Center, Detailed Interrogation Reports, 1944–1945, folder: Concentration Camp Flossenbürg, RG 498, Box 66, National Archives).

62. Interview with K. Frank Korf, 9 August 2000, Korf Collection.

63. K. Frank Korf to United States Holocaust Memorial Council, 20 November 1981, United States Holocaust Memorial Museum, United States Holocaust Memorial Council, International Liberators Conference, Collection: Flossenbürg, Archives—RG-02.005*12.

64. According to Hacker, "Fred Huber, a squad sergeant of the Military Police Platoon of the 97th Infantry Division, was at the camp with three jeeps; six people. . . . Huber and his squad were detailed to the 303rd Infantry Regiment for traffic control and other Military Police duties. . . . Furnare remembers helping to knock off the lock on the camp gate. He also remembers the delousing building. Fred Huber remembers a colonel with a command car. After the gate was opened, some of the prisoners rushed out. . . . The colonel . . . was probably from the 90th Division and was the one who reported the 'liberation' of Flossenbürg. . . . The above anecdotes indicate that the Huber party was probably the first American

Army unit to arrive at the Flossenbürg Concentration Camp. . . . This was a casual encounter and not reported up either chain of command. The significance of the incident was not realized for almost 50 years." See Robert W. Hacker, *Flossenbürg Concentration Camp: A Compilation of Material* (Phoenix: Self-published, 2000), p. 1.

65. Ibid.

66. Korf, memoir, pp. 102–103.

67. See Christopher Robbins, *Test of Courage: The Michael Thomas Story: One Man's Heroic WWII Journey from Survival to Triumph* (New York: Free Press, 1999), pp. 186–187.

68. Korf memoir, p. 102.

69. Ibid., p. 103.

70. Ibid., p. 105.

71. Ibid, p. 104.

72. Interview with K. Frank Korf, 9 August 2000.

73. Interview with Victor Wegard, May 1987, United States Holocaust Memorial Museum, Record Group 50, oral history interviews of the Kean College of New Jersey Holocaust Resource Center, Archives—RG-50.002*0066, Acc.1993A.0088.

74. William G. Cantrell, *Records Relating to the Participation of the 90th US Infantry Division in the Liberation of Flossenbürg*, United States Holocaust Memorial Museum, Washington D.C., Archives—RF-09.021*01, Acc. 1993A.0022.

75. Dwight D. Eisenhower, *Crusade in Europe* (Garden City, N.Y.: Doubleday, 1948), p. 441.

76. Interview with K. Frank Korf, 9 March 2000.

77. Korf memoir, p. 104.

78. Ibid., p. 105.

79. Interview with K. Frank Korf, 24 February 2000.

80. Korf memoir, p. 105.

81. Bob Hacker, a veteran of the 97th, concurs that members of his division helped the inmates quite a bit: "The 97th Division performed many duties at the camp. They treated the sick and dying; buried the dead; interviewed former prisoners and gathered evidence for trials of former camp officers and guards; etc. Brig. General Halsey, the commanding officer of the 97th Division, inspected the camp as did General Hasbrouck, the

commanding officer of the division artillery." Hacker, *Flossenbürg Concentration Camp*, p. 1.

82. Korf memoir, p. 108.

83. Ibid., p. 107.

84. Ibid.

85. Ibid., p. 108.

86. Ibid., p. 110.

87. Report from K. Frank Korf to Assistant Chief of Staff, 1 May 1945.

88. Interview with Victor Wegard, May 1987.

89. Interview with Rita Korf, 20 March 2001. Korf had two cameras, a Rolleiflex with a 2.5 lens and a Weltix Kleinkamera (similar to a Leica) with a 2.9 lens. His pictures are archived in the Korf Collection.

90. Korf memoir, p. 109.

91. Ibid.

92. Ibid., p. 110.

93. A number of these leaflets can be found in the Korf Collection.

94. Korf memoir, p. 110a.

95. Ibid., pp. 112–113.

96. Ibid., p. 114.

97. The historian Arnold Krammer reports that in May 1945 alone, "the U.S. army bagged 116 German generals, and the British captured 127." See Krammer, "American Treatment of German Generals in World War II," *Journal of Military History* 54, 1 (January 1990): 43.

98. Korf memoir, p. 116.

99. Ibid. This account squares soundly with research on the subject of how the Allies treated captured German generals. According to Arnold Krammer, "German generals had substantially different experiences in captivity, based largely on the nationality of the captor. Britain doted on its captives, and handled them with the chivalry traditionally reserved for fellow aristocrats and professional soldiers. . . . [But] to the Americans, these generals . . . represented the very antithesis of the democratic ideals which America was fighting to restore to Central Europe. Perhaps most important, these generals were seen as losers" (Krammer, "American Treatment of German Generals in World War II," p. 46).

100. Headquarters of Military Intelligence to Korf, 6 July 1945, Records of Headquarters, European Theater of Operations, U.S. Army (World War

II), ETO Military Intelligence Service, Specialist Team Personnel Reports, 1944–1945, MII no. 493–546, RG 498, Box 745008, National Archives.

101. Korf memoir, p. 85a. Korf was not the only one who was denied rewards: Halsey's coveted promotion to major general never came through because the 97th Division "came too late to take part in the assault on Japan, and merely served as an occupation force" (Korf memoir, p. 120).

102. Historical Section, Military Intelligence Service, comp., "An Evaluation of Military Intelligence Service Specialist Teams, European Theater of Operations," p. 24.

103. Korf memoir, p. 117.

104. K. Frank Korf to Rita Korf, VE Day (8 May 1945), Korf Collection.

105. K. Frank Korf to Rita Korf, VE Day plus 3 (11 May 1945), Korf Collection.

106. Korf memoir, p. 117.

107. Interview with Rita Korf, 27 June 2001. Korf Collection.

108. Korf memoir, pp. 117–118. He never got the chance to see if his orders were obeyed. After VE Day, Korf and his men received orders to return to Germany. Korf assumed that the woman's collection of jewelry and precious glass was later "swallowed" by the Soviets (Korf memoir, p. 110).

109. Certificate on captured enemy equipment signed by Korf. K. Frank Korf to Rita Korf, 12 May 1945, Korf Collection. Korf also arranged for family heirlooms to be shipped home. On a customs declaration form (in the Korf Collection) he informed authorities that one box of "enclosed articles have been property of my family for generations and were recovered by me from Berlin where they had been hidden from the Nazis. . . . Under Public Law 790 [the articles] are entitled to free entry."

110. K. Frank Korf to Rita Korf, 12 May 1945.

111. K. Frank Korf to Rita Korf, 13 June 1945, Korf Collection.

112. K. Frank Korf to Rita Korf, VE Day plus 5 (13 May 1945), Korf Collection.

113. Ibid.

Chapter 5   The Hunt for War Criminals: 1945–1946

1. Korf memoir, pp. 118–119.

2. Ibid.

3. Ibid., p. 121a.

4. Ibid.

5. K. Frank Korf to Rita Korf, 25 May 1945, Korf Collection.

6. Ibid.

7. Korf memoir, p. 121b.

8. Günter Bischof and Stephen Ambrose, eds., *Eisenhower and the German POWs: Facts against Falsehood* (Baton Rouge: Louisiana State University Press, 1992), p. 5.

9. Leon C. Standifer, *Binding Up the Wounds: An American Soldier in Occupied Germany* (Baton Rouge: Louisiana State University Press, 1997), p. 77.

10. Interview with K. Frank Korf, 13 July 2000; Standifer, *Binding Up the Wounds*, p. 77.

11. Korf memoir, p. 122; interview with K. Frank Korf, 13 July 2000.

12. Interview with K. Frank Korf, 13 July 2000; Kennett, *G.I.: The American Soldier in World War II*, p. 214.

13. Interview with K. Frank Korf, 20 December 1999. Recent work on the history of the American occupation corroborates this view to a certain degree. Petra Goedde's research shows that the positive interaction between American GIs and German civilians helped to reconcile their respective countries even before they allied against the Soviets in the cold war. Her theories, however, challenge those of other historians who argue that the relations on the two sides were not always benevolent. Relations were indeed complicated by issues such as American hostility to German atrocities at the concentration camps on the one hand and Germans' resentment of American economic exploitation of Germany on the other. See Petra Goedde, *GIs and Germans: Culture, Gender, and Foreign Relations, 1945–1949* (New Haven: Yale University Press, 2003); also, Johannes Kleinschmidt, *Do Not Fraternize: Die schwierigen Anfänge deutsch-amerikanischer Freundschaft, 1944–1949* (Trier: Wissenschaftler, 1995), and John Willoughby, *Remaking the Conquering Heroes: The Postwar American Occupation of Germany* (New York: Palgrave, 2000).

14. Korf memoir, p. 123.

15. Ibid.

16. Ibid.

17. Interview with K. Frank Korf, 13 July 2000.

18. The wartime agreements compensated the Soviet Union with territory in eastern Poland. The latter, in turn, received one hundred square miles of territory in eastern Germany. Germans who lived in these eastern territories now belonging to Poland had to leave their homes and move west.

19. Bischof and Ambrose, eds., *Eisenhower and the German POWs*, p. 6.

20. Korf memoir, pp. 123–124.

21. Ibid., p. 124.

22. Ibid., p. 133.

23. Ibid., p. 125.

24. Ibid.

25. Ibid., p. 126.

26. Ibid.

27. Ibid., p. 126a.

28. K. Frank Korf to Rita Korf, 25 May 1945.

29. K. Frank Korf to Rita Korf, 16 June 1945, Korf Collection.

30. K. Frank Korf to Rita Korf, 5 July 1945, Korf Collection.

31. Ibid.; K. Frank Korf to Rita Korf, 25 July 1945, Korf Collection.

32. Interview with K. Frank Korf, 24 February 2000.

33. K. Frank Korf to Rita Korf, 10 July 1945, Korf Collection.

34. K. Frank Korf to Rita Korf, 1 June 1945, Korf Collection.

35. K. Frank Korf to Rita Korf, 11 July 1945, Korf Collection.

36. Korf memoir, p. 127.

37. Ibid.

38. Ibid., pp. 127–128.

39. Ibid., p. 128.

40. Ibid.

41. Ibid., p. 129.

42. Ibid.

43. Ibid., pp. 129–130.

44. K. Frank Korf to Rita Korf, 25 July 1945.

45. K. Frank Korf to Rita Korf, 14 August 1945, Korf Collection.

46. K. Frank Korf to Rita Korf, Auerbach, 24 August 1945, Korf Collection.

47. K. Frank Korf to Rita Korf, 20 August 1945, Korf Collection.

48. Rita Korf to K. Frank Korf, 15 August 1945, Korf Collection.

49. K. Frank Korf to Rita Korf, 30 August 1945, Korf Collection.

50. Korf memoir, p. 130.

51. Ibid.

52. K. Frank Korf to Rita Korf, 9 October 1945, Korf Collection.

53. K. Frank Korf to Rita Korf, 18 September 1945, Korf Collection.

54. K. Frank Korf to Rita Korf, 22 October 1945, Korf Collection.

55. K. Frank Korf to Rita Korf, 9 October 1945, Korf Collection.

56. K. Frank Korf to Rita Korf, 9 November 1945, Korf Collection.

57. Interview with K. Frank Korf, 16 March 2000.

58. Rigg, *Hitler's Jewish Soldiers*, p. 3.

59. Cited in Bischof and Ambrose, *Eisenhower and the German POWs*, Appendix A, p. 236.

60. K. Frank Korf to Rita Korf, 5 November 1945, Korf Collection. He added that it was difficult for him to get permission to go to Lippstadt because "it is English-occupied territory and you have to travel under orders through there. As I belong to USFET things are pretty complicated. It is even more difficult with Berlin which I have not managed yet."

61. K. Frank Korf to Rita Korf, 22 October 1945.

62. K. Frank Korf to Rita Korf, 4 December 1945, Korf Collection.

63. Korf memoir, p. 131.

64. Ibid., pp. 131–132.

65. Ibid., pp. 132a–132b.

66. Ibid., p. 132b.

67. Ibid., p. 132c.

68. Ibid.

69. Ibid., p. 134a.

70. Ibid., p. 134.

71. Ibid., p. 139.

72. Rita Korf to K. Frank Korf, 16 January 1946, Korf Collection.

73. K. Frank Korf to Rita Korf, 8 December 1945, Korf Collection.

74. Ibid. Korf found his services in demand: "There are several other agencies which would like to have me very much. Berlin District HQ already wrote to USFET (US Forces European Theater) for me, but Third Army told me that they do not want to let me go—in spite of the fact that I will be under Corps shortly. The Information Control—which is in charge of all newspapers, etc. also offered me a job. But my condition is that I will

be allowed to go home as soon as I become eligible, and not a minute later, and that I am not interested in taking a civilian job over here" (ibid.).

75. K. Frank Korf to Rita Korf, 22 December 1945, Korf Collection.

76. Rita Korf to K. Frank Korf, 16 January 1946, Korf Collection.

77. K. Frank Korf to Rita Korf, 19 January 1946, Korf Collection.

Chapter 6   From World War to Cold War

1. Korf memoir, p. 135.

2. K. Frank Korf to Rita Korf, 13 March 1946, Korf Collection.

3. Korf memoir, p. 136.

4. Ibid.

5. K. Frank Korf to Rita Korf, 12 March 1946, Korf Collection.

6. K. Frank Korf to Rita Korf, 7 February 1946, Korf Collection.

7. K. Frank Korf to Rita Korf, 12 March 1946.

8. Korf memoir, pp. 136–137.

9. Ibid., p. 138a.

10. Ibid.

11. Ibid. Nonetheless, the Mossner family vetoed the plan to transfer operations out of Berlin.

12. K. Frank Korf to Rita Korf, 1 April 1946, Korf Collection.

13. Interview with Rita Korf, 6 January 2001.

14. Korf memoir, pp. 137–138.

15. Ibid., p. 138.

16. Ibid., p. 137.

17. Ibid. Two letters from prisoners to Korf are housed in the Korf Collection.

18. K. Frank Korf to Rita Korf, 30 March 1946, Korf Collection.

19. Ibid.

20. Korf memoir, p. 138a.

21. K. Frank Korf to Rita Korf, 18 March 1946, Korf Collection.

22. Korf memoir, p. 139.

23. Ibid., p. 139a.

24. Ibid., p. 139b. Korf described them as "victims of the period which followed that was termed 'cessation of open hostilities' rather than peace. Some of the boys had come over recently, just out of high school, with little

training and understanding of the things and the tasks they were to face. . . . The separation from home, the new and strange continent, the combination of undreamed of independence and ironclad army discipline had been enough to break down their flimsy mental structure. They were heading for home now—'homicide maniacs,' as the medical sergeant had introduced them."

25. Korf memoir, p. 140.

26. Ibid., p. 141.

27. Ibid.

28. Ibid.

29. Ibid.

30. Ibid., p. 142.

31. Ibid.

32. Ibid.

33. Ibid., p. 143.

34. Interview with Rita Korf, 6 January 2001.

35. Korf memoir, p. 143.

36. Ibid.

37. Ibid., pp. 143–144.

38. Ibid., p. 144.

39. Ibid.

40. Ibid., p. 145.

41. Ibid.

42. Ibid., p. 146.

43. Ibid.

44. Ibid., p. 147.

45. Ibid., p. 146.

46. Ibid., p. 149a. "The Overseas Mission (later Overseas Branch) was part of the Office of Alien Property of the Department of Justice. [It was] on equal footing with the Civil Division, Criminal Division, Antitrust Division, etc. Its principal area of enforcement was the Trading with the Enemy Act of 1917, which had been amended many times. Its purpose was to prevent an enemy from using economic power against the United States in case of war. From this mandate flowed many responsibilities."

47. Ibid. "Additionally, the U.S. government could now, with access within the former enemy countries and its satellites, vest property considered to be enemy property for court determination in the United States."

48. Ibid., p. 147.

49. GS stands for General Schedule pay grade level. Candidates with graduate law degrees qualify for GS-12. See www.usdoj.gov.

50. Korf memoir, p. 149.

51. Ibid., p. 166.

52. Ibid.

53. Ibid., p. 167.

54. Ibid., p. 168.

55. Ibid., p. 150.

56. K. Frank Korf to Rita Korf, 15 March 1948, Korf Collection.

57. K. Frank Korf to Rita Korf, 20 March 1948, Korf Collection.

58. K. Frank Korf to Rita Korf, 5 April 1948, Korf Collection.

59. Ibid.

60. K. Frank Korf to Rita Korf, 15 March 1948.

61. Ibid.

62. Cited in William G. Hyland, *The Cold War: Fifty Years of Conflict* (New York: Times Books, 1991), p. 48.

63. K. Frank Korf to Rita Korf, 5 April 1948. Korf duly reported this incident to his superior Paul McGraw in a memorandum dated 8 April 1948, Korf Collection.

64. "The Air Force organized the 'bridge' into a steady flow of planes on three levels: planes from Frankfurt to Berlin-Tempelhof cruised at altitudes between 7,000 feet and 9,000 feet. Planes flying from Berlin to Frankfurt cruised at between 11,000 and 13,000 feet. Medical supply planes and special flights to Hamburg or Munich flew at 15,000 feet" (Korf memoir, p. 157).

65. Ibid., p. 155.

66. Frank Korf to Rita Korf, 1 May 1948, Korf Collection.

67. Korf memoir, p. 155.

68. Ibid., p. 156.

69. Ibid., p. 155.

70. K. Frank Korf to Rita Korf, 8 July 1948, Korf Collection.

71. Interview with Rita Korf, 18 September 2001, Korf Collection.

72. Ibid.

73. Korf memoir, p. 162.

74. "There was close to two hundred million dollars involved (the case went to the Supreme Court twice and to the World Court once. It finally

was settled by Bobby Kennedy in 1962 when he was Attorney General)." Ibid., p. 157.

75. Ibid., p. 159.

76. Ibid.

Chapter 7   The Goebbels Diaries

1. Korf's letters to and from the Hoover Institution and the Institute for Contemporary History are in the Korf Collection.

2. Reuth used the K. Frank Korf Papers at the Hoover Institution in his discussion of Goebbels's final days. See Ralf Georg Reuth, *Goebbels* (New York: Harcourt Brace, 1993). David Irving also used the Korf papers for his 1996 biography, *Goebbels: Mastermind of the Third Reich* (New York: St. Martin's Press, 1996). Elke Fröhlich, who edited the most recent edition of the Goebbels diaries in 1995, included Korf's findings in her introduction.

3. According to the historian Henry Ashby Turner, "All the victors [of World War II] . . . agreed that the four-power Allied Control Council should minister Germany as one economic entity. The council was, however, not accorded full control over the country, since the victors assigned executive authority in each of the four occupation zones to the American, British, French and Russian commandants, who were responsible solely to their own governments" (Turner, *Germany from Partition to Reunification* [New Haven: Yale University Press, 1992], pp. 11–12).

4. K. Frank Korf, "The Story of Goebbels' Diary," undated draft, Korf Collection, p. 1.

5. K. Frank Korf, "In Search of Nazi Treasure," draft, February 1993, Korf Collection.

6. Cited in Alan Bullock, *Hitler: A Study in Tyranny* (New York: Harper and Row, 1964), p. 789.

7. See Dennis Piszkiewicz, *From Nazi Test Pilot to Hitler's Bunker: The Fantastic Flights of Hanna Reitsch* (Westport, Conn.: Praeger, 1997).

8. Korf, "In Search of Nazi Treasure," p. 7. Hanna Reitsch resumed her career as a pilot after the war and eventually established a glider school in Ghana, Africa. In her later years she is said to have become dismayed with the evils perpetrated by the Nazis. She died in 1979 at the age of sixty-four. See Hanna Reitsch, *The Sky My Kingdom* (Mechanicsburg, Pa.: Stackpole Books, 1997).

9. Interrogation of Hans Fritzsche by K. Frank Korf, 2 February 1948, pp. 2–3 (copy), Korf Collection.

10. Korf, "The Story of Goebbels' Diary," p. 4.

11. Cited in ibid., p. 2.

12. Ibid., p. 4.

13. Article in *Die Welt*, official German newspaper in the British zone, Hamburg, 9 March 1948 (translation by the author), Korf Collection.

14. Hermine Herta Meyer to Daniel McGrath, memorandum, Re: Goebbels Diaries, Berlin, 30 March 1948, p. 4 (copy), Korf Collection.

15. Interrogation of Erwin Richter by Hermine Meyer, K. Frank Korf of the Department of Justice, and George Elkan, investigator, 23 February 1948, p. 4 (copy), Korf Collection.

16. Heimlich was a member of the U.S. Air Force, 1940–1946. In addition to his work in OMGUS and RIAS, he was assistant chief of staff, G-2, U.S. forces in Berlin, in 1945, and a staff member on the U.S. Senate Judiciary and Foreign Relations Committees. He also served as director of Public Affairs of the White House National Security Council. See www.ecommcode2.com/hoover/research/historicalmaterials/oral.html.

17. Statement by Daniel Montenegro, vice consul of the United States at Berlin, 3 March 1948, Korf Collection. Montenegro was one of Heimlich's CIC associates in 1945. According to Montenegro, he and Heimlich had searched Hitler's Reich Chancellery for documents in the fall of 1945; he recalled: "When an excavation was made near Hitler's air raid shelter in an effort to find the bodies [of Hitler and Eva Braun], several items of interest were discovered . . . [including] two bound documents of book format. . . . At least one of the volumes . . . contained handwriting, and I naturally assumed that they might be personal diaries of a person or persons who had been in the air raid shelter during the last days of the battle of Berlin." Because of the difficulty of deciphering the handwriting, these diaries were not published until 1963, under the title *The Early Goebbels Diaries* (K. Frank Korf, "The Goebbels Diary Material: Previously Published and the New Material," memorandum, Korf Collection).

18. Meyer to McGrath, memorandum, p. 8.

19. Ibid., p. 11.

20. George H. Elkan, Department of Justice Mission APO 742 U.S. Army, to Colonel Peter Rodes, Director of Intelligence, Berlin, 18 February

1948, statement (copy in Korf Collection). In 1947 Heimlich complained to Elkan that he was being threatened with termination of his contract with the Military Government (OMGUS) on the ground that he had "included a classified document in a package of clothing [to be] sent to a private address in the United States" (ibid.). When asked in 1990 whether he knew anything about the illegal removal of property from Germany, Heimlich noted that it was Hoover, not Heimlich, who was accused of doing this, but that Hoover had been authorized by both President Truman and General Eisenhower to collect documents. Transcription of interview with Colonel William F. Heimlich at his home in Falls Church, Va., by Dwight W. Miller, 29 March 1990, Hoover Institution, Stanford University, Stanford, Calif.

21. Meyer to McGrath, memorandum, p. 13.

22. Korf, "In Search of Nazi Treasure," p. 6.

23. Korf, "The Story of Goebbels' Diary," pp. 4–5.

24. Korf memoir, p. 164.

25. Ibid.

26. Interrogation of William Friel Heimlich by Hermine Herta Meyer, K. Frank Korf, and George Elkan, Berlin, 21 February 1948 (copy), Korf Collection.

27. K. Frank Korf to Daniel McGrath, Chief of Department of Justice Mission, Berlin, memorandum, 12 March 1948, p. 6, Korf Collection.

28. Korf, "In Search of Nazi Treasure," p. 7.

29. Korf, "The Story of Goebbels' Diary," p. 6.

30. K. Frank Korf, "Goebbels' Private Life," draft, p. 5, Korf Collection.

31. Korf, "The Story of Goebbels' Diary," p. 2.

32. Korf, "Goebbels' Private Life," p. 3.

33. Ibid. Göring and Goebbels had clashed over control of theaters in the Reich. Göring wanted to control the theater in order to promote the career of his wife, the actress Emma Sonnemann. Goebbels, however, felt that his position as minister of propaganda and culture made his control of the theater a foregone conclusion.

34. Ibid., p. 4.

35. Ibid.

36. Ibid.

37. Hugh Trevor-Roper, ed., *The Goebbels Diaries: The Last Days* (London: Secker and Warburg, 1978), p. xxxviii.

38. K. Frank Korf to files of the Overseas Mission, Berlin, memorandum, 13 April 1948, Korf Collection.

39. Ibid.

40. Ibid. Goebbels wrote his diaries by hand from the 1920s until 1941. Thereafter he dictated his diaries to his stenographer, who transcribed them on a typewriter with a specially large font. See Trevor-Roper, ed., *The Goebbels Diaries*, p. xxxv.

41. Goebbels Diary File, Korf Collection.

42. Korf, "In Search of Nazi Treasure," p. 7; interrogation of Hans Fritzsche by K. Frank Korf, pp. 4–5. Accounts of the deaths of Goebbels and his wife vary. In his 1964 biography of Hitler, the historian Alan Bullock states that Goebbels shot his wife and then himself in the Chancellery garden. But in his classic work *The Rise and Fall of the Third Reich*, the journalist William Shirer states that, after poisoning their children, Goebbels and his wife went to the garden above the bunker, where an SS orderly shot them both in the back of the head. Bullock's 1993 work on the lives of Hitler and Stalin revises his 1964 version of Goebbels's death to conform to Shirer's account. See Bullock, *Hitler: A Study in Tyranny*, p. 801; Bullock, *Hitler and Stalin: Parallel Lives* (New York: Vintage, 1993), p. 887; and Shirer, *The Rise and Fall of the Third Reich* (Greenwich, Conn.: Fawcett Books, 1960), p. 1474.

43. Cited in Reuth, *Goebbels*, p. 357.

44. "Very Dear Diary," *Time* (European ed.), 8 March 1948, p. 38.

45. Notarized agreement between Frank Mason of Fireside Press, Louis P. Lochner, and William F. Heimlich, and J. Howard McGrath, Attorney General, 10 November 1950 (copy), Korf Collection.

46. Interview with Colonel William F. Heimlich, March 29, 1990.

47. Agreement between the Goebbels estate and François Genoud, 15 March 1956 (copy), Korf Collection.

48. Agreement between François Genoud and Doubleday and Company, 20 September 1956, Korf Collection.

49. Korf, "In Search of Nazi Treasure," p. 8.

50. Korf's correspondence to and from the Hoover Institution and the Institute for Contemporary History regarding the donations is housed in the Korf Collection.

51. Korf's correspondence with David Irving is in the Korf Collection.

52. Deborah Lipstadt referred to Irving as a Holocaust denier in her 1993 book, *Denying the Holocaust: The Growing Assault on Truth and Memory* (New York: Free Press, 1993). In response, Irving sued Lipstadt and her British publisher, Penguin Books, for libel in London. Lipstadt and Penguin resoundingly won the case in 2000. The trial also helped publicize the inner workings of Holocaust deniers. Details of the case can be found on the Web site www.holocaustdenialontrial.org/ieindex.html.

53. Interview with K. Frank Korf, 23 March 2000, Korf Collection.

Conclusion

1. Kozloski, *Hitch Your Wagon to a Star,* p. 3.

2. Korf recalled that many years after Hilde's death, the Air and Space Museum wanted to have an exhibit on the women in early space research, but President Reagan vetoed the idea. Interview with Frank Korf, 8 June 1999, Korf Collection.

3. Interview with Rita Korf, 8 December 2000, Korf Collection.

4. Korf, addendum to memoir, p. I.

5. Rigg, *Hitler's Jewish Soldiers,* and Tent, *In the Shadow of the Holocaust.*

6. Interview with K. Frank Korf, 8 June 2000.

7. Goedde, *GIs and Germans.*

8. James J. Sheehan, "The Germans and the Final Solution: Public Opinion under Nazism," *Journal of Interdisciplinary History* 24, 3 (Winter 1994): 550.

9. According to the historian Peter Hoffmann, "Tens of thousands of Germans were killed for one or another form of resistance. Between 1933 and 1945, Special Courts killed 12,000 Germans, courts martial killed 25,000 German soldiers, and 'regular' justice killed 40,000 Germans" (Hoffmann, *The History of the German Resistance, 1933–1945,* 3d ed. (Montreal: McGill-Queen's University Press, 1996), p. xiii.

10. Martin Broszat, "The Sociohistorical Typology of Resisters," in David Clay Large, ed., *Contending with Hitler: Varieties of German Resistance in the Third Reich* (New York: Cambridge University Press, 1991), p. 32.

11. Hans Mommsen, *Alternatives to Hitler: German Resistance under the Third Reich* (Princeton: Princeton University Press, 2003), pp. 9–10.

12. Broszat, "Sociohistorical Typology of Resisters," pp. 32–33.

13. One man responded to Nazism in a mind-bending fashion: he opposed Nazism and fled the country, only to end up becoming a spy for the Gestapo. See James Barnes and Patience Barnes, *Nazi Refugee Turned Gestapo Spy: The Life of Hans Wesemann, 1895–1971* (Westport, Conn.: Praeger, 2001).

14. Prominent émigrés included Hannah Arendt, Thomas Mann, Albert Einstein, Bruno Walter, and Bruno Frank. See Anderson, ed., *Hitler's Exiles*; Peter Gay, *My German Question: Growing Up in Nazi Berlin* (New Haven: Yale University Press, 1998); and Sebastian Haffner, *Defying Hitler: A Memoir* (New York: Farrar, Straus and Giroux, 2000).

15. Korf, addendum to memoir, p. I.

16. According to statistics of the U.S. Military History Institute, over 33,000 men who served in the army were born in Germany. Of that group, over 14,000 were not yet citizens. It is possible that many in this group left Germany after Hitler came to power, and hence had some direct experience with Nazism (Miller, "Foreign Born in the US Army during World War II," Table 1.

Bibliography

Primary Sources

K. Frank and Rita Korf Collection, Florida Atlantic University Library, Boca Raton, Fla.

K. Frank Korf Papers.
K. Frank Korf, unpublished memoir, 1991–1992.
Taped interviews with K. Frank Korf, June 1999–August 2000.
Interviews with Rita Korf, October 2000–September 2001.
Taped interview with Jay Bitzer, Mentor, Ohio, 26 December 2003.

United States Holocaust Memorial Museum Archives, Washington, D.C.

Cantrell, William G. *Records Relating to the Participation of the 90th US Infantry Division in the Liberation of Flossenburg.* Archives—RF-09.021*01, Acc.1993A.0022.
Interview with Victor Wegard, May 1987, Oral History interviews of the Kean College of New Jersey Holocaust Resource Center Archives—RG-50.002*0066, Acc.1993A.0088.
United States Holocaust Memorial Council 1981 International Liberators Conference Collection: Flossenbürg. Archives—RG-02.005*12.

Library of Congress, Washington, D.C.

Max Adler Collection (AFC 2001/001/4589), audio recording. SR 101 c.1 (ref): Veterans History Project, American Folklife Center.
Jay Bitzer Collection (AFC 2001/001/3532), audio recording. SR 101 c.1 (ref): Veterans History Project, American Folklife Center.
Ludwig Fromme Collection (AFC 2001/001/4926), audio recording. SR 101 c.1 (ref): Veterans History Project, American Folklife Center.

National Archives, College Park, Md.

RG 242—Records of SS Officers A3343 SSO-044—Ludwig Baumgartner.

RG 242—Records of SS Officers A3343 SSO-190A—Max Kögel.

Adjutant General's Office, World War II Operations Reports, 1940–1948, Third Army, 103-2.1, March–May 1945. RG 407, Entry 427, Box 735017.

Adjutant General's Office, World War II Operations Reports, 1940–1948, 97th Infantry Division, 397-0.9–397-0.24. RG 407, Entry 427, Box 14058.

Adjutant General's Office, World War II Operations Reports, 1940–1948, 97th Infantry Division. RG 407, Entry 427, Box 14061.

Records of Headquarters, European Theater of Operations, U.S. Army (World War II), ETO Historical Division, Program Files, USFET, G-2 Operations Reports, 1945–1946. RG 498, Box 833533.

Records of Headquarters, European Theater of Operations, U.S. Army (World War II), ETO Military Intelligence Service, Specialist Team Personnel Reports, 1944–1945, MII no. 493–546. RG 498, Box 745008.

Records of Headquarters, European Theater of Operations, U.S. Army (World War II), ETO MIS-USFET Weekly Intelligence Summaries, August 1945–January 1946. RG 498, Box 816543.

Records of the Office of Alien Property, Records of German Organizations: Deutsche-Amerikanische Berufsgemeinschaft, Records of FBI Investigations and Exhibits in Court Cases, 1936–1943, Expert Testimony, Exhibits. RG 131, Box 3.

Records of the Third Army Interrogation Center, Detailed Interrogation Reports, 1944–1945, Folder: Concentration Camp Flossenbürg. RG 498, Box 66.

U.S. Military Institute, Carlisle Barracks, Pa.

Counter Intelligence Corps: History and Mission in World War II. Fort Holabird, Md.: Counter Intelligence Corps School, 1959.

Watson B. Miller, commissioner of Immigration and Naturalization, "Foreign Born in the US Army during World War II, with Special Reference to the Alien" (1948). Table 1. "United States Citizenship Status of Foreign Born Who Enlisted or Were Inducted, United States Army, July 1, 1940, to June 30, 1945." UB323 M55.

Hoover Institution on War, Revolution and Peace, Stanford University,
Stanford, Calif.

Interview with Colonel William F. Heimlich at his home in Falls Church,
Va., by Dwight W. Miller, 29 March 1990. Transcription.

Secondary Sources

Abrams, Alan. *Special Treatment: The Untold Story of Hitler's Third Race.*
Secaucus, N.J.: Lyle Stuart, 1985.

Abshagen, Karl Heinz. *Canaris: Patriot und Weltbürger.* Stuttgart: Union,
1957.

Adam, Uwe. *Judenpolitik im Dritten Reich.* Düsseldorf: Droste, 1972.

Adams, Willi Paul. *The German-Americans: An Ethnic Experience.* Translated by LaVern J. Rippley and Eberhard Reichmann. Indianapolis: Indi-
ana University Press, 1993.

Allen, Peter. *One More River: The Rhine Crossings of 1945.* New York:
Scribner, 1980.

Ambrose, Stephen E. *American Heritage New History of World War II.* New
York: Viking, 1977.

———. *Americans at War.* Jackson: University Press of Mississippi, 1997.

———. *Citizen Soldiers: The U.S. Army from the Normandy Beaches to the
Bulge to the Surrender of Germany.* New York: Simon and Schuster,
1997.

———. *D-Day, June 6, 1944: The Climactic Battle of World War II.* New
York: Simon and Schuster, 1994.

———. *Ike's Spies: Eisenhower and the Espionage Establishment.* Jackson:
University Press of Mississippi, 1999.

———. *The Victors: Eisenhower and His Boys: The Men of World War II.*
New York: Simon and Schuster, 1998.

Anderson, Mark M., ed. *Hitler's Exiles: Personal Stories of the Flight from
Nazi Germany to America.* New York: New Press, 1998.

Annan, Noel. *Changing Enemies: The Defeat and Regeneration of Germany.*
Ithaca: Cornell University Press, 1997.

App, Austin J. *German-American Voice for Truth and Justice.* Takoma Park,
Md.: Boniface Press, 1977.

Arthur, Billy A., and Bruce H. Simon. "The Bridge at Remagen: A German-American Staff Ride to Study Its Capture." *Army Historian* 8 (1985): 1–5.

Austra, Kevin R. "The Battle of the Bulge: The Secret Offensive." *Military Intelligence* 17, 1 (January–March 1991).

Bartov, Omer, ed. *The Holocaust: Origins, Implementations, Aftermath.* New York: Routledge, 2000.

Benderesky, Joseph. *The Jewish Threat: Anti-Semitic Policies of the U.S. Army.* New York: Basic Books, 2000.

Bennett, Rab. *Under the Shadow of the Swastika: The Moral Dilemmas of Resistance and Collaboration in Hitler's Europe.* New York: New York University Press, 1999.

Bischof, Günter, and Stephen Ambrose, eds. *Eisenhower and the German POWs: Facts against Falsehood.* Baton Rouge: Louisiana State University Press, 1992.

Bullock, Alan. *Hitler: A Study in Tyranny.* New York: Harper and Row, 1964.

———. *Hitler and Stalin: Parallel Lives.* New York: Vintage, 1993.

Butler, J. R. M., ed. *History of the Second World War.* Volume 4, *Grand Strategy, October 1944–August 1945,* of United Kingdom Military Series. London: Her Majesty's Stationery Office, 1956.

Canedy, Susan. *America's Nazis: A Democratic Dilemma.* Menlo Park, Calif.: Markgraf, 1990.

Charles, Douglas M. "Informing FDR: FBI Political Surveillance and the Isolationist-Interventionist Foreign Policy Debate, 1939–1945." *Diplomatic History* 24, 2 (Spring 2000): 211–232.

Clarke, Jeffrey J., and Robert Ross Smith. *Riviera to the Rhine.* Washington, D.C.: Center of Military History, United States Army, 1993.

Cole, Hugh M. *The Ardennes: The Battle of the Bulge.* Washington, D.C.: Center of Military History, United States Army, 1993.

Coles, Harry. *Soldiers Become Governors.* Washington, D.C.: Center of Military History, United States Army, 1964.

Courtney, Richard. *Normandy to the Bulge.* Carbondale: Southern Illinois University Press, 1997.

Davis, Franklin M. *Come as a Conqueror: The United States Army's Occupation of Germany, 1945–1949.* New York: Macmillan, 1967.

Diamond, Sander A. *The Nazi Movement in the United States, 1924–1944.* Ithaca: Cornell University Press, 1974.

Doubler, Michael D. *Closing with the Enemy: How GIs Fought the War in Europe, 1944–1945*. Lawrence: University Press of Kansas, 1994.

Dupuy, Trevor N., David L. Bongard, and Richard C. Anderson. *Hitler's Last Gamble: The Battle of the Bulge, December 1944–January 1945*. New York: HarperCollins, 1994.

Eisenhower, Dwight D. *Crusade in Europe*. Garden City, N.Y.: Doubleday, 1948.

Eisenhower, John. *The Bitter Woods: The Battle of the Bulge*. New York: G. P. Putnam's Sons, 1969.

Elbe, Joachim von. *Witness to History: A Refugee from the Third Reich Remembers*. Madison: University of Wisconsin Press, 1988.

Ellis, John. *On the Front Lines: The Experience of War through the Eyes of the Allied Soldiers in World War II*. New York: John Wiley and Sons, 1980.

Farago, Ladislas. *The Game of the Foxes: The Untold Story of German Espionage in the United States and Britain during World War II*. New York: David McKay, 1971.

Finnegan, John Patrick. *Military Intelligence*. Washington, D.C.: Center of Military History, United States Army, 1998.

Foley, Charles. *Commando Extraordinary: Otto Skorzeny*. 1954. Repr., Toronto: Batan, 1979.

Ford, Corey. *Donovan of the OSS*. Boston: Little, Brown, 1970.

Fraiman, Sarah. "The Transformation of Jewish Consciousness in Nazi Germany as Reflected in the German-Jewish Journal *Der Morgen*, 1925–1928." *Modern Judaism* 20, 1 (2000): 41–59.

Frazier, Tom. *Between the Lines*. Oakland, Calif.: Regent Press, 2001.

Fussell, Paul. *Wartime: Understanding and Behavior in the Second World War*. New York: Oxford University Press, 1989.

Gabel, Kurt. *The Making of a Paratrooper: Airborne Training and Combat in World War II*. Lawrence: University Press of Kansas, 1990.

Gantter, Raymond. *Roll Me Over: An Infantryman's World War II* (New York: Ivy Books, 1997).

Gay, Peter. *My German Question: Growing Up in Nazi Berlin*. New Haven: Yale University Press, 1998.

Goebbels, Joseph. *The Goebbels Diaries: The Last Days*. Edited and translated by Louis Lochner. Garden City, N.Y.: Doubleday, 1948.

Goedde, Petra. *GIs and Germans: Culture, Gender, and Foreign Relations, 1945–1949*. New Haven: Yale University Press, 2003.

Goldstein, Donald M., et al. *Nuts! The Battle of the Bulge: The Story and Photographs*. Washington, D.C.: Brassey's, 1994.

Hacker, Robert W. *Flossenbürg Concentration Camp: A Compilation of Material*. Phoenix: Self-published, 2000.

Harrison, A. Cleveland. *Unsung Valor: A GI's Story of World War II*. Jackson: University Press of Mississippi, 2000.

Haydock, Michael D. *City under Siege: The Berlin Blockade and Airlift, 1948–1949*. Washington, D.C.: Brassey's, 1999.

Hechler, Ken. *The Bridge at Remagen*. 4th ed. Missoula, Mont.: Pictorial Histories, 1999.

Hecht, Ingeborg. *Als unsichtbare Mauern wuchsen: Eine deutsche Familie unter den Nürnberger Rassengesetzen*. Hamburg: Hoffmann and Campe, 1984.

Heideking, Jürgen, and Christof Mauch, eds. *American Intelligence and German Resistance to Hitler: A Documentary History*. Boulder, Colo.: Westview Press, 1996.

Higham, Charles. *American Swastika*. Garden City, N.Y.: Doubleday, 1985.

Historical Section, European Theater of Operations Staff, eds. *Utah Beach to Cherbourg*. Nashville, Tenn.: Battery Press, 1984.

Hoffmann, Peter. *The History of the German Resistance, 1933–1945*. 3d ed. Montreal: McGill-Queen's University Press, 1996.

Holian, Timothy J. *The German-Americans and World War II: An Ethnic Experience*. New York: Peter Lang, 1998.

Hyland, William G. *The Cold War: Fifty Years of Conflict*. New York: Times Books, 1991.

Irving, David. *Goebbels: Mastermind of the Third Reich*. New York: St. Martin's Press, 1996.

———. *Hitler's War*. New York: Viking, 1977.

Jarausch, Konrad H. *The Unfree Professions: German Lawyers, Teachers, and Engineers, 1900–1950*. New York: Oxford University Press, 1990.

Kahn, David. *Hitler's Spies: German Military Intelligence in World War II*. New York: Macmillan, 1978.

Keefer, Louis E. *Scholars in Foxholes: The Story of the Army Specialized Training Program in World War II*. Jefferson, N.C.: McFarland, 1988.

Kennett, Lee B. *G.I.: The American Soldier in World War II.* Norman: University of Oklahoma Press, 1997.

Kershaw, Alex. *The Longest Winter: The Battle of the Bulge and the Epic Story of World War II's Most Decorated Platoon.* New York: Da Capo Press, 2004.

Kleinschmidt, Johannes. *Do Not Fraternize: Die schwierigen Anfänge deutsch-amerikanischer Freundschaft, 1944–1949.* Trier: Wissenschaftler, 1995.

Koehn, Ilse. *Mischling, Second Degree: My Childhood in Nazi Germany.* New York: Greenwillow, 1977.

Kotlowitz, Robert. *Before Their Time: A Memoir.* New York: Knopf, 1997.

Krammer, Arnold. "American Treatment of German Generals in World War II." *Journal of Military History* 54, 1 (January 1990): 27–46.

———. *Undue Process: The Untold Story of American's German Alien Internees.* Lanham, Md.: Rowman and Littlefield, 1997.

Krüger, Helmut. *Der halbe Stern: Leben als deutsch-jüdischer "Mischling" im Dritten Reich.* Berlin: Metropol, 1993.

Large, David Clay. *Berlin.* New York: Basic Books, 2000.

———, ed. *Contending with Hitler: Varieties of German Resistance in the Third Reich.* New York: Cambridge University Press, 1991.

Leber, Hannelore. *Conscience in Revolt: Sixty-four Stories of Resistance in Germany, 1933–1945.* Boulder, Colo: Westview Press, 1994.

Lomax, Judy. *Women of the Air.* New York: Dodd, Mead, 1987.

Luebke, Frederick C. *Bonds of Loyalty: German-Americans and World War I.* DeKalb: Northern Illinois University Press, 1974.

MacDonald, Charles B. *The Last Offensive, with Maps: United States Army in World War II: The European Theater of Operations.* Washington, D.C.: Office of the Chief of Military History, United States Army, 1986.

———. *The Mighty Endeavor: American Armed Forces in the European Theater in World War II.* New York: Oxford University Press, 1969.

———. *A Time for Trumpets: The Untold Story of the Battle of the Bulge.* New York: Morrow, 1985.

Mansoor, Peter R. *The GI Offensive in Europe: The Triumph of American Infantry Divisions, 1941–1945.* Lawrence: University Press of Kansas, 1999.

McLean, French. *The Camp Men: The SS Officers Who Ran the Nazi Concentration Camp System.* Atglen, Pa.: Schiffer, 1999.

McManus, John C. *The Deadly Brotherhood: The American Combat Soldier in World War II.* Novato, Calif.: Presidio Press, 1998.

Mendelsohn, John, ed. *The German View of Cover and Deception.* Volume 17 of *Covert Warfare.* New York: Garland Press, 1988.

Meyer, Beate. *"Jüdische Mischlinge": Rassenpolitik und Verfolgungserfahrung, 1933–1945.* Hamburg: Dölling and Galitz, 1999.

Mommsen, Hans. *Alternatives to Hitler: German Resistance under the Third Reich.* Princeton: Princeton University Press, 2003.

Moon, Tom. *This Grim and Savage Game: The OSS and Covert Operations in World War II.* Los Angeles: Burning Gate Press, 1991.

Mulligan, Timothy P., comp. *Guide to Records Relating to U.S. Military Participation in World War II.* Washington, D.C.: National Archives and Records Administration, 1996–1998.

Munch, Paul G. "Patton's Staff and the Battle of the Bulge." *Military Review* 70 (May 1990): 46–94.

National Museum of American Jewish Military History. *Liberating the Concentration Camps: GIs Remember.* Washington, D.C.: Museum of American Jewish Military History, 1994.

Neill, George W. *Holding the Line at the Battle of the Bulge: Infantry Soldier.* Norman: University of Oklahoma Press, 2000.

Noakes, Jeremy. "The Development of Nazi Policy towards the German-Jewish Mischlinge, 1933–1945." *Leo Baeck Institute Yearbook* 43 (1998): 292–354.

Oberndorf, Ludwig. "The German Press in the United States." *American-German Review* 6 (December 1939).

O'Connor, Richard. *The German-Americans: An Informal History.* Boston: Little, Brown, 1968.

O'Neill, William L. *A Democracy at War: America's Fight at Home and Abroad in World War II.* New York: Free Press, 1993.

Pauwels, Jacques R. *Women, Nazis, and Universities: Female University Students in the Third Reich, 1933–1945.* Westport, Conn.: Greenwood, 1984.

Perret, Geoffrey. *There's a War to Be Won: The United States Army in World War II.* New York: Random House, 1991.

Persico, Joseph E. *Nuremberg: Infamy on Trial.* New York: Viking, 1994.

———. *Piercing the Reich: The Penetration of Nazi Germany by American Secret Agents during World War II.* New York: Viking, 1979.

Peukert, Detlev J. K. *Inside Nazi Germany: Conformity, Opposition, and Racism in Everyday Life.* New Haven: Yale University Press, 1987.

Piszkiewicz, Dennis. *From Nazi Test Pilot to Hitler's Bunker: The Fantastic Flights of Hanna Reitsch.* Westport, Conn.: Praeger, 1997.

Polmar, Norman, and Thomas B. Allen. *World War II: Encyclopedia of the War Years, 1941–1945.* New York: Random House, 1996.

Province, Charles M. *Patton's Third Army: A Daily Combat Diary.* New York: Hippocrene Books, 1992.

Reitsch, Hanna. *The Sky My Kingdom* (Mechanicsburg, Pa.: Stackpole Books, 1997).

Reuth, Ralf Georg. *Goebbels.* Translated by Krishna Winston. New York: Harcourt Brace, 1993.

Rigg, Bryan Mark. *Hitler's Jewish Soldiers: The Untold Story of Nazi Racial Laws and Men of Jewish Descent in the German Military.* Lawrence: University Press of Kansas, 2002.

Rippley, LaVern J. *The German-Americans.* Boston: Twayne, 1976.

Robbins, Christopher. *Test of Courage: The Michel Thomas Story. One Man's Heroic WWII Journey from Survival to Triumph.* New York: Free Press, 1999.

Rosengarten, Adolph G., Jr. "The Bulge: A Glimpse of Combat Intelligence." *Military Review* 41 (June 1961): 29–33.

Schelbert, Leo, and Hedwig Rappolt. *Alles ist ganz anders hier: Auswandererschicksale in Briefen aus zwei Jahrhunderten.* Freiburg im Bresgau: Walter, 1977.

Schmitt, Hans. *Lucky Victim: An Ordinary Life in Extraordinary Times, 1933–1946.* Baton Rouge: Louisiana State University Press, 1989.

Selective Service and Victory: The 4th Report of the Director of Selective Service. Washington, D.C.: Government Printing Office, 1948.

Sereny, Gitta. *Into That Darkness: An Examination of Conscience.* 1974. Repr., New York: Vintage, 1983.

Shirer, William. *The Rise and Fall of the Third Reich.* Greenwich, Conn.: Fawcett Books, 1960.

Skorzeny, Otto. "An Interview with Oberstleutnant Otto Skorzeny: Ardennes Offensive" (European Theater Interrogation no. 12, 12 August 1945). In *World War II German Military Studies,* edited by Donald S. Detwiler et al. Vol. 2. New York: Garland, 1979.

Smith, Michael. *Station X: Decoding Nazi Secrets*. New York: TV Books, 1999.

Snyder, Louis L. *Historical Guide to World War II*. Westport, Conn.: Greenwood, 1982.

Standifer, Leon C. *Binding Up the Wounds: An American Soldier in Occupied Germany*. Baton Rouge: Louisiana State University Press, 1997.

Stannard, Richard. *Infantry: An Oral History of a World War II American Infantry Battalion*. New York: Twayne, 1993.

Steele, Richard W. "Franklin D. Roosevelt and His Foreign Policy Critics." *Political Science Quarterly* 94, 1 (Spring 1979): 15–32.

Stern, Fritz. *Einstein's German World*. Princeton: Princeton University Press, 1999.

Stouffer, Samuel A. *The American Soldier*. Princeton: Princeton University Press, 1949.

Taylor, Barbara Woodall, and Charles Taylor. *Miss You: The World War II Letters of Barbara Woodall Taylor and Charles Taylor*. Edited by Judy Barrett Litoff et al. Athens: University of Georgia Press, 1990.

Tent, James F. *In the Shadow of the Holocaust: Nazi Persecution of Jewish-Christian Germans*. Lawrence: University Press of Kansas Press, 2003.

Tolzmann, Don Heinrich, ed. *German-Americans in the World Wars*. 5 vols. Munich: K. G. Saur, 1995–1998. Specifically, vol. 4, part 1, sections 1 and 3; part 2, section 2; and vol. 5.

Trevor-Roper, Hugh, ed. *The Goebbels Diaries: The Last Days*. London: Secker and Warburg, 1977.

Turner, Henry A. *Germany from Partition to Reunification*. New Haven: Yale University Press, 1992.

Vieregg, Hildegarde, et al. *Begegnungen mit Flossenbürg: Beiträge, Dokumente, Texte, Interviews, Zeugnisse Uberlebender: Spintler Druck und Verlag*, Weiden: Midenhaus, 1998.

Weinberg, Gerhard L. *Germany, Hitler, and World War II*. New York: Cambridge University Press, 1995.

Whiting, Charles. *Skorzeny*. New York: Ballantine Books, 1972.

Willoughby, John. *Remaking the Conquering Heroes: The Postwar American Occupation of Germany*. New York: Palgrave, 2000.

Wilson, George. *If You Survive*. New York: Ballantine Books, 1987.

Index